African Literature and US Empire

African Literature and US Empire

Postcolonial Optimism in Nigerian and South African Writing

Katherine Hallemeier

EDINBURGH
University Press

Edinburgh University Press is one of the leading university presses in the UK. We publish academic books and journals in our selected subject areas across the humanities and social sciences, combining cutting-edge scholarship with high editorial and production values to produce academic works of lasting importance. For more information visit our website: edinburghuniversitypress.com

© Katherine Hallemeier 2024, 2025

Edinburgh University Press Ltd
13 Infirmary Street
Edinburgh EH1 1LT

First published in hardback by Edinburgh University Press 2024

Typeset in 10.5/13 Adobe Sabon by
IDSUK (DataConnection) Ltd

A CIP record for this book is available from the British Library

ISBN 978 1 3995 1616 7 (hardback)
ISBN 978 1 3995 1617 4 (paperback)
ISBN 978 1 3995 1618 1 (webready PDF)
ISBN 978 1 3995 1619 8 (epub)

The right of Katherine Hallemeier to be identified as the author of this work has been asserted in accordance with the Copyright, Designs and Patents Act 1988, and the Copyright and Related Rights Regulations 2003 (SI No. 2498).

Contents

Acknowledgments — vi

Introduction: Postcolonial Optimism — 1

PART I: NIGERIAN LITERATURE AND PAN-AFRICAN OPTIMISM

1. Pan-African American Dreams of the First Republic — 25
2. The United States of 'Emelika' and Literature of the Second Republic — 43
3. The Pursuit of Happiness After the Third Republic — 61

PART II: COMPOUNDING OPTIMISM IN SOUTH AFRICAN FICTION

4. A Tiny Ripple of Hope *Between Two Worlds* — 83
5. The American Dreams in *The Heart of Redness* — 103
6. The Last Best Hope of *White Wahala* — 123

Coda: The Dream of the Postcolonial Future — 140

Notes — 147
Works Cited — 176
Index — 190

Acknowledgments

I am grateful to those who read or listened to material that became this book. My deep gratitude to members of my writing group at Oklahoma State University, who generously read many drafts of many chapters and offered insights and encouragement that kept me challenged and dissatisfied: Andrew R. Belton, Rafael Hernandez, Lisa Hollenbach, Alyssa Hunziker, Jeff Menne, Graig Uhlin, and Lindsay Wilhelm. Other colleagues who asked sharp questions about the project and provided wonderful mentorship include Linda Austin, William Decker, Elizabeth Grubgeld, Edward Jones, Tim Murphy, Lindsey Claire Smith, and Martin Wallen. Rose Casey gave incisive feedback on the book at all stages, along with great friendship, and Lewis Freedman reminded me again and again of what writing could be. My thanks to Moradewun Adejunmobi, Stephanie Bosch Santana, Jeanne-Marie Jackson, and Tsitsi Ella Jaji, who each provided encouragement that was more significant than they know during times of doubt. I am thankful to members of my graduate seminars in postcolonial literature and affect for their patience, curiosity, and discernment: Daniel Andrade Amaral, Siddharth Arora, Breanna Beaty, Allyn Bernkopf, Hayden Bilbrey, Rebecca Brings, Mark DiFruscio, Brianne Grothe, Dane Howard, Kyu Jeoung Lee, Kevin Kourakos, Douglas Koziol, Kaila Lancaster, Forest Lebaron, Holly Mayfield, Komal Nazir, Chimene Remedi, and Matthew Williams. This project is indebted to Adam Frank, who introduced me to affect studies, and to Sneja Gunew, who asked me what it would mean to decolonize that field.

I am fortunate to have had institutional funding that supported uninterrupted writing time and the presentation of my work. I gratefully acknowledge financial support provided by the College of Arts and Sciences and the Department of English at Oklahoma State University, as well as the Oklahoma Humanities Council. I am thankful to have had the opportunity to present ideas related to this book at the African

Literature Association Conference, the Annual Meeting of the African Studies Association, the Annual Meeting of the American Comparative Literature Association, the Conference of the Association for Commonwealth Literature and Language Studies, and the Modern Language Association Annual Convention. I am especially thankful to attendees of the 2021 MLA Convention who participated in a panel on Postcolonial Optimism I co-organized with Jeremy De Chavez. Subsequently working with Jeremy to co-edit a special issue on Postcolonial Affect for *ariel* was a joy. I'm grateful to the contributors to that issue, whose work prompted me to think more deeply about the relation between postcolonial studies and affect while revising my manuscript: Frances Hemsley, Neetu Khanna, Anwesha Kundu, Eunice Lim, Rebecca Oh, Hannah Pardey, Bede Scott, and Andrew van der Vlies.

I am grateful to Edinburgh University Press for publishing this book, as well as to Knowledge Unlatched Select Humanities and Social Sciences 2024 for providing the opportunity for Open Access publication. My thanks to editors Michelle Houston and Emily Sharp for their support, clarity, and transparency. My gratitude to Susannah Butler and Elizabeth Fraser for their fantastic administrative support. I am greatly indebted to the Press's three anonymous readers. Their thoughtful comments, on everything from general arguments to individual sentences, were invaluable, and this book is more than it was thanks to them. I am honored by their attentive reading.

My endless thanks, my endless love, always, to my parents. Their great-spiritedness amazes me daily. How to express my gratitude to Akhi for his listening and care. I cannot imagine the shape of my life, much less a writing life, without the friendship and love of Nermeen, Sarah, and Azim. As for JG, who startles with his thoughts, our life with A is "even more."

Introduction: Postcolonial Optimism

In studies of anglophone African literature, the oft-told narrative of the postcolonial nation is one of progressive disillusionment. Exemplified by E.N. Obiechina's 1978 account, this history suggests that literature of the 1950s and early 1960s "was dominated by nationalist assertiveness."[1] It reflected a hopeful political context in which ideas proliferated on the character of a postcolonial global order. "In the wake of the euphoria that came with independence," Obiechina observes, "better and better prospects were held out to the masses."[2] By the late 1960s, however, African writers such as Chinua Achebe and Ayi Kwei Armah had published works that expressed disappointment not only with specific postcolonial national governments but also with the postcolonial nation as such.[3] "The stage at which we find ourselves," asserted Wole Soyinka of "The Writer in a Modern African State," "is a stage of disillusionment."[4] Writers channeled a broader social milieu in which "hopes had collapsed" following the entrenchment and exacerbation of inequality under postcolonial governments that were themselves marked by political instability.[5] Per Frantz Fanon, nationalism, "that magnificent song that made the people rise against their oppressors, stops short, falters, and dies away on the day that independence is proclaimed."[6] When Kwame Anthony Appiah declared in 1991 that the postcolonial is postoptimistic, as well as postnational, he offered a concise synthesis of a critical commonplace.[7] That consensus was somewhat disrupted by South African democratic elections in 1994. Having voted Nelson Mandela to the presidency and adopted the most liberal constitution in the world, the "new" South Africa was conceived, as Jennifer Wenzel puts it, as "a second chance to redeem the failures of African decolonization."[8] Yet, this sense of exceptionalism waned as euphoria was once more followed by disillusionment; what is sometimes called post-transition South African fiction has been markedly "disenchanted."[9] Writing in 2021, Keguro Macharia, tracing how "pessimism has transferred and morphed across different African generations," suggests that those generations of African writers subsequent to independence and structural adjustment have "absorbed cynicism and treat it as wisdom."[10]

Anglophone African literary studies have reflected the national disillusionment associated with postcolonial African literature, including in accounts of the gendered exclusions of postcolonial nationhood.[11] At the same time, the field has seen the productive methodological decentering of the nation in its engagements with globalization. Scholars have highlighted the multifocal, Afropolitan, and vernacular address of texts, while charting how their production and circulation are imbricated in a system of global capital.[12] In a 2016 article that considers the futures of this trajectory, Tejumola Olaniyan declared African literature to be "post-global." For Olaniyan, "the global assumed and did not question much the certainty of the nation-state and territorial sovereignty."[13] The "post-global" of African literature "is a query, in part, of this certainty," as "probably no one can tell a more moving story about the emptying out of the nation-state and territorial sovereignty than the African of the last thirty years or so."[14] The evacuation of national sovereignty, Olaniyan argued, is a primary reason for "the extreme corporeal, locational, linguistic, formal, and thematic dispersion of contemporary African literature and literary theorizing."[15] In African literary studies, the nation has become an increasingly problematized framework for understanding African literatures.

Concomitantly, twenty-first-century analyses of hope and optimism in African literature rarely highlight the nation, and instead attend to how aspiration has been both individualized and globalized in the decades following political independence and structural adjustment. In his literary anthropology of twenty-first-century Accra, for example, Ato Quayson described how the city's "gymmers" commit to intensive daily exercise in the hopes of one day finding employment in Hollywood, whether as celebrity bodyguards or otherwise. Quayson contended that the phenomenon of gymming demonstrates how widespread unemployment has created a "burden of enforced free time" that generates "epic dreaming of an economic kind."[16] Such dreaming is of a piece with a broader "discourse of enchantment" that Quayson argued emerged in Ghana in the mid-1980s as an effect of neoliberal policies and that materialized in texts ranging from tro-tro slogans to cellphone ads to the literature of prosperity churches.[17] As the editors noted in *Hard Work, Hard Times* (2010), "African subjects, despite the crises produced by austerity and privatization, continue to produce, to aspire, and to fantasize while laboring under incredible hardships."[18] Scholarship such as Quayson's suggested, however, that these fantasies have been targeted less toward national futures than individual achievement. James Ferguson described this process in *Global Shadows* (2006) as the "de-developmentalization of historical time," whereby the very "hope and dream" of overcoming colonial inequality in postcolonial Africa declined and was replaced by experiences of "*nonprogressive* temporalizations" centered not on "societal becoming" but on individuals negotiating spatial boundaries and borders.[19]

My study brushes against the grain of this scholarship on hope and the African nation by selecting out anglophone African literature in which, to adapt Olaniyan, even the non-sovereign, hollowed-out nation persists as an object of optimistic attachment. What I call literature of postcolonial optimism asks why dreams of the postcolonial nation die hard, despite decades of disillusionment with national governments beholden to a global system characterized by imperial hierarchy and oppression. I argue that literature of postcolonial optimism answers this question by illuminating, on the one hand, how postcolonial national dreams have been integral to the expansion of US empire, and, on the other, how they function to maintain hope for a world after empire in which anticolonial politics are fully realized. Literature of postcolonial optimism thus describes an ambivalent relation between postcolonial national dreams and US empire, suggesting how these dreams at once entrench and exceed imperial control. Neither embracing nor condemning attachment to the postcolonial nation, this study explores the affective power of nationalisms that reflect both US efforts to globalize the so-called American dream and anti-imperial efforts to disengage, reform, or transcend that dream.

Insofar as postcolonial optimism describes an attachment to postcolonial nationhood under conditions of US empire, it offers an interpretative lens that could apply to a range of African and postcolonial literatures. For two reasons, I will turn to Nigerian and South African anglophone writing from the 1960s to the 2010s to develop and concretize my claims. First, this writing responds to robustly articulated dreams of exceptional postcolonial nationhood, encapsulated in formulations such as the "pan-African nation" (Nigeria) and the "new" or "rainbow" nation (South Africa), that to some degree have exemplified the expression of US empire through the globalization of the American dream. As the biggest US export markets in Africa, both Nigeria and South Africa have been targets of US economic, military, cultural, and diplomatic power that has, in turn, significantly affected anglophone cultural production.[20] This project examines creative nonfiction and novels that engage this international relation, especially as it pertains to US influence on Nigerian education and South African economic policy. I chart how the prioritization of higher education as a key to decolonization in Nigeria in the mid-twentieth century corresponded with US investment in the same to entrench influence during the Cold War.

Considering South African state support for the expansion of credit on a US neoliberal model reflects a shift in US imperial strategic emphasis by the late twentieth century. Comparative study of Nigerian and South African literature of postcolonial optimism thus offers the opportunity to analyze distinct mechanisms of US imperialism since the mid-twentieth century. Taken together, Nigerian and South African literature of postcolonial optimism critically responds to dreams of exceptional postcolonial nationhood whose celebrations of education and entrepreneurship have reproduced the racialized, gendered, and classed inequalities endemic to US empire. This literature's critiques of the university and credit redound across Nigeria, South Africa, and the US.

The second reason for focusing on Nigerian and South African anglophone literature pertains to the ways stubbornly affecting Nigerian and South African dreams of exceptional nationhood exceed the American dream and engage pan-African imaginaries. Achebe wrote in 1984 that the "vast human and material wealth with which she [Nigeria] is endowed bestows on her a role in Africa and the world which no one else can assume or fulfill."[21] These resources have been a recurrent source of what Andrew Apter called "unbridled optimism" for Nigeria to emerge as a "pan-African" model for nationhood that fulfills the promises of decolonization.[22] Visions of an exceptional "new" South Africa have similarly emphasized its perceived exceptional potential for realizing decolonization and modeling Black liberation. The years surrounding the transition to democracy in South Africa, as Mahmoud Mamdani observed in 1996, were rife with accounts of South African exceptionalism, as South Africa's historical development was conceived apart from that of the rest of the continent.[23] As in the Nigerian instance, hopes for national becoming included the realization of pan-African aspirations for political and economic justice for Black people. In tandem with African-American reworkings of the American dream,[24] these articulations of exceptional postcolonial nationhood maintain the hope that the nation may yet facilitate Black liberation.

The project's comparison of Nigerian and South African anglophone literature permits a transatlantic study of how experiences of national optimism under US empire are enforced, embraced, and contested. Deeply felt national dreams, as they are represented by these African writers, are not necessarily naïve or symptomatic of ideological hoodwinking. Rather, in literatures of postcolonial optimism, they are opportunities for reflecting on pan-African aspirations that are not always liberatory in their effects, as well as opportunities to imagine structures of feeling alternate to those propagated by empire and the nationalisms that support it.[25]

As this overview of postcolonial optimism intimates, two key methodologies inform this study. First, the book's approach to postcolonial African literature foregrounds the nation, albeit with attention to its imperial and pan-African dimensions. Second, a focus on optimism brings affect studies—a field that in anglophone literary studies of the past thirty years has predominately engaged European and US works—into conversation with Nigerian and South African literatures. How I conceive of these methods deserves additional explanation.

The Postcolonial Nation

This project's commitment to examining scenes of national affect places it in a subset of postcolonial studies that, working besides the turns to the world, global, and cosmopolitan, has maintained the significance of the nation for conceptualizing postcoloniality and its literatures. As early as 1997 Arif Dirlik warned that postcolonial studies risked underplaying the appeal of nationalism to many postcolonial subjects, whose livelihoods had come to depend upon the incorporation of the nation into the global economy.[26] Soon after, Timothy Brennan argued that the postcolonial nation remained, however imperfectly, a crucial institutional defense against the operations of global empire and global capitalism.[27] Pheng Cheah's *Spectral Nationality* (2003) likewise emphasized how the postcolonial nation stands as a potentially resistant force to domination by global capitalism, although, for Cheah, the postcolonial nation remains a potent horizon for imagining freedom precisely because it is haunted by this domination.[28] More recently, Weihsin Gui has argued against conceptualizing postcolonial national consciousness as homogenizing and exclusionary.[29] As a literary study, this book makes no claims that its fictions reveal anthropological truths about the affective investments of living postcolonial subjects. Nor does it seek to defend or recoup resistant potential in postcolonial nationalisms. Its bid, rather, is that examining literary works that address ongoing attachments to the postcolonial nation reveals something about how those attachments simultaneously maintain both US empire and imagined pan-African communities that makes it reductive to designate them either oppressive or liberatory. By focusing on the postcolonial nation but declining to read its literature as strictly national, this book aligns with the scholarship outlined here. Yet, by thinking the nation in relation to US empire and pan-Africanism, specifically, it offers a distinctive approach to conceptualizing how the nation intersects with the transnational in anglophone African literary spaces.

Thinking about the relation of the postcolonial nation to US empire necessitates considering the ways US imperialism has been addressed (and not addressed) in postcolonial literary studies. Scholarship on the relation between US empire and postcolonial literature during the Cold War has tended to favor continental and global frameworks over national ones and to focus on disciplinary and cultural histories.[30] US empire figures prominently in accounts of how US institutions, such as the CIA, the Congress for Cultural Freedom, and the Ford Foundation, sought to foster international cultural production in line with US Cold War agendas across Africa and the global South.[31] Monica Popescu's field-defining work situates this activity in relation to Soviet imperialism and institutions of Afro-Asian solidarity to better understand how African writers were shaped by and gave form to the "development of a global Cold War culture."[32] While drawing on this scholarship and inspired by its model of thinking about African cultural production vis-à-vis imperialism, my work diverges from the paradigm of postcolonial Cold War literary studies by foregrounding African literature's engagement not only with US cultural imperialism but also with US influence at the level of national policy. I further build on these foundations in postcolonial Cold War studies by charting these influences into the twenty-first century.

In postcolonial literary studies focused on the decades after the Cold War, US empire has tended to be subsumed by broader discussions of globalization. The approach makes sense insofar as the center of global capitalism is not unitary or clear.[33] "Empire," as Michael Hardt and Antonio Negri described sovereignty in the late twentieth century, "establishes no territorial center of power and does not rely on fixed boundaries and barriers": "The distinct national colors of the imperialist map of the world have merged and blended in the imperial global rainbow."[34] Yet, as Neil Lazarus argued in *The Postcolonial Unconscious* (2011), postcolonial studies risks the mystification of the postcolonial world if it does not reckon directly with not only the enduring representative power of nationalism, but also the emergence of the US as the "postwar hegemon."[35] The "urgent" task of postcolonial studies in the twenty-first century, Lazarus maintained, "is to take central cognizance of the unremitting actuality and indeed the intensification of imperialist social relations in the times and spaces of the postcolonial world."[36] Lazarus called for "a new reading, above all of the second half of the twentieth century" that emphasizes, among other concepts, US capitalist imperialism.[37]

This project contributes to Lazarus's "new reading" insofar as it traces literature's reckoning with histories of US imperial intervention within specific African national contexts. Eschewing debates as to the degree to which globalization expresses or delimits US power,[38] this book's two case studies chart distinct US imperial ideologies and practices, respectively dominant when Nigeria claimed political independence in 1960 and South Africa instituted democratic elections in 1994, as they echo through literary engagements with national becoming. Part I, titled "Nigerian Literature and Pan-African Optimism," focuses on the historical and literary legacies of US Cold War policies that prioritized educational aid in order to secure US political and cultural influence in newly-postcolonial nations. Chapters on literature of the First Republic (1963–66), the Second Republic (1979–83), and the Third Republic (1993) engage respectively with US–Nigeria relations during the Kennedy (1961–63), Carter (1977–81), and Bush (1989–93) administrations. These chapters demonstrate that a postcolonial national imaginary in which universities were central to decolonization efforts both endured across decades and overlapped with instantiations of US imperial power, whether exercised through educational aid and the promotion of technical training in the 1960s and 1970s or through the global dominance of US MFA and MBA programs in the 1990s.[39] Part II, "Compounding Optimism in South African Fiction," moves from education to finance, as it shows how the expansion of credit was key to both the South African postcolonial national imaginary and to US imperial power in the 1990s. South Africa, that is, became "postcolonial" in a moment when neoliberal ideologies proffering so-called market solutions had usurped Cold War commitments to education as a keystone in both US and postcolonial developmentalist discourse. The three chapters in this section construct a literary history of US–South African relations centered on credit by examining fiction of the apartheid era (1948–94), the postapartheid Mandela presidency (1994–99), and the post-transition Zuma presidency (2009–18) that correspond respectively to the Johnson (1963–69), Clinton (1993–2001), and Obama (2009–17) administrations. By examining the lead-up to and aftermath of the globalized celebration of microloans and market competition that shaped the policies of the "new" South Africa, these chapters chart how US empire has been enfolded in national dreams of the postcolonial, postapartheid nation.

Bringing these literary histories of US imperialism together highlights that dominant US ideologies and policies of development have shaped postcolonial nationhood in ways that have both impeded decolonization and proven remarkably enduring. The aim here is not to claim that US power has operated or continues to operate exclusively or discretely through educational or financial institutions in either Nigeria or South

Africa. As individual chapters demonstrate, debt has been crucial to the pursuit of higher education in Nigeria (chapter 2), and the pursuit of higher education has in some cases redoubled commitments in South Africa to the expansion of credit (chapter 5).[40] Instead, this comparative study of African literatures that emphasize different dominant modes of US empire intends to throw into sharp relief a shared affective trajectory. The chapters in each part parallel each other in their progression from anticolonial or anti-apartheid movements (chapters 1 and 4) through a period often described in terms of progressive disillusionment (chapters 2 and 5) and then on to decades of accelerated financialization and further hollowing of national sovereignty in the twenty-first century (chapters 3 and 6). Yet, both parts also present a narrative of continually-renewed investment in visions of postcolonial nationhood centered on the very educational and financial institutions that have repeatedly compromised it.

It is through examining the stubbornness of optimism under empire that pan-Africanism emerges in this study as constitutive of postcolonial national dreams, which are consequently in an important sense never only national. In Adom Getachew's clear formulation, the "ambitions of anticolonial nationalism" have always been "global" and "world-making."[41] Tsiti Jaji has exemplarily explored this dynamic in a cultural register. Jaji calls on George Shepperson's distinction between small "p" and capital "P" pan-Africanism. Where capital "P" Pan-Africanism designates more formal political organizations and movements of the twentieth century, exemplified by the Pan-African Congresses, small "p" pan-Africanism designates "an eclectic set of ephemeral cultural movements and currents."[42] Jaji's *Africa in Stereo* (2014) showed how "the informal and formal registers of transnational black solidarity have variously reinforced, cross-fertilized, and interfered with each other."[43] Acknowledging that "the language and efficacy of pan-Africanism seem attenuated, and even dated," Jaji traces histories of pan-Africanism in order to "uncover and renew" the "latent political energies" of these forms of solidarity.[44] If pan-Africanism, like the nation, is to some degree a belated concept, Jaji's work on African-American, Ghanaian, Senegalese, and South African cultural production demonstrated how critically and politically enlivening it can be to consider pan-Africanism as "a continuum" of exchange that generates and regenerates practices of solidarity, including across national movements.[45] As literature of postcolonial optimism considers national histories informed by pan-African solidarities, it contributes to the critical project of examining postcolonial national movements that have stood in continuum with nonnational and often transnational visions of a decolonized Africa.[46]

This project charts dreams of Nigerian and South African nationhood shaped by pan-African exchange, particularly with Black Americans. Nigerian literature of postcolonial optimism suggests how hopeful attachments to US universities as a means to national development are not only symptomatic of US imperialism. They also evoke a history in which institutions of higher education, and particularly Historically Black Colleges and Universities (HBCUs), have been centers for dreaming international Black decolonization and have played an important role in Nigerian anticolonial imaginaries (chapters 1 and 2). Even as the potency of political Pan-Africanism declined over the second half of the twentieth century, this literature suggests that the US university remains an imagined site for cultural pan-African exchange and for Black people to reckon with the shared and divergent challenges of life under US empire both at home and abroad (chapter 3). The university, to cite Stefano Harney and Fred Moten, is figured as a place to "steal what one can" to further the radical collective hopes that undercut official developmentalist policies.[47] South African literature of postcolonial optimism likewise posits a pan-African dimension to national dreams produced under conditions of US empire. Dreams of democratized credit are bound to early and mid-century histories in which South Africans associated African Americans with an aspirational modernity that encompassed the free exercise of economic rights (chapter 4). The expansion of credit after apartheid not only follows the neoliberal ideologies espoused by US international policy makers: it also follows from resonant struggles in the US and South Africa to secure Black people's access to capital (chapters 5 and 6).

My interest in imagined—which is to say cultural and literary—pan-African connections between Nigeria and the US and South Africa and the US builds on contemporary scholarship on pan-African and Black Atlantic literary histories.[48] Following Black feminist critics who chart the lines of mutual influence between Black American women writers and African women writers,[49] I deploy a similar biographical approach when, for example, discussing the significance of Buchi Emecheta's identification with writers such as Toni Morrison (chapter 2), or the expansion of Chimamanda Ngozi Adichie's writing workshop to include Black American participants (chapter 3). Further, as scholars such as Stéphane Robolin have charted connections between US and South African writers and contextualized them in relation to liberation movements,[50] I too am interested in how, say, Miriam Tlali sought aid in publishing her first novel from a seemingly sympathetic African-American bishop during apartheid, or how Hugh Masekela understood the contribution of Black South African mobility to the development of solidarity with African

Americans (chapter 4). While the project emphasizes Black Americans' influence on Africans insofar as it centers African writers and their influences, pan-African exchanges were mutual, and chapters emphasize that the African literature under discussion speaks to Black American histories and aspirations. This literature extends its own invitations to pan-African solidarity.

Relating the nation to US imperialism and pan-African exchange produces readings of African literature that reorient its relation to empire, as well as the disciplinary deployment of categories such as "postcolonial" and "global anglophone" literature.[51] Anglophone postcolonial literary studies have often centered the relation between former colonies and metropoles, emphasizing that literature "writes back" to British empire. Literature of postcolonial optimism, however, highlights that this "writing back" has often been simultaneous with a "writing back" to US imperialism and a writing for pan-Africanism; postcolonial writers as canonical as J.P. Clark-Bekederemo, Emecheta, and Tlali reckon with how US empire's rhetoric of democracy and equality appeals to pan-African anticolonial and anti-apartheid sentiment. Concomitantly, the turn to global anglophone and world literature accentuates that writers negotiate a set of contemporary political and economic circumstances described in terms of globalization, late capitalism, or neoliberalism. Read through the framework of postcolonial optimism, however, exemplars of global anglophone literature such as Chimamanda Adichie and Zakes Mda prove engaged with how US empire produces neocolonial relations.

A limit of this study is that it does not substantially account for the ways in which US empire has increasingly defined itself against Chinese global power, which has rapidly extended its sphere of influence across the African continent.[52] That said, this project is in conversation with approaches to the postcolonial nation that have emerged from the burgeoning movement to address China in African literature. For example, Duncan M. Yoon builds on postcolonial Cold War studies to think about Chinese investment from the perspective of "southern globalization" and to identify the critical possibilities in conceiving of contemporary African fiction as the "global South novel."[53] Yoon's reading of Koli Jean Bofane's *Congo Inc.* (2014) demonstrates how this approach cracks open new understandings of postcolonial nationhood: "The novel reimagines the [Democratic Republic of Congo] not simply as a catachresis of the Western nation-state, but as a series of temporalities compressed together by the collision between the Internet Age and Chinese investment in the Congo."[54] While delimited by a continued focus on Western empire for framing discussion of African literature, this project likewise seeks to understand the postcolonial nation as other than catachrestic by focusing not on temporality but on affect.

Postcolonial Affect

In describing postcolonial optimism, I mobilize the analytic possibilities of affect studies, while also running up against some of its limitations. To look for affect in a text is often to describe textures, moods, and atmospheres—to undertake what Eve Kosofsky Sedgwick described as reparative, as opposed to paranoid, reading. It is to sketch relationality as it is expressed through feeling.[55] To be sure, this descriptive project is not necessarily divorced from structural critique in the paranoid style: feelings and emotions, the field has proven again and again, are always public and political.[56] But affect studies explores how and why intimate iterations of power can be alternately vulnerable and impervious to ideological critique. Sara Ahmed has shown that the study of emotion can help us understand how we become attached "to the very conditions of our subordination."[57] This project contributes to this claim by examining, in postcolonial optimism, how subjects come to desire conditions that both subjugate and liberate, and by considering how the desire for conditions of subjugation can persist even when it is consciously known that those conditions and the opportunities they offer for individual or national freedom are collectively oppressive. Focusing on affect can seem to delay the project of imagining worlds after structural critique. Why study attachments to visions of the democratic nation when thinking beyond the nation is already a rich field of inquiry in postcolonial and Black studies? Why dwell with the powerful attraction of expanding lines of credit when arguments to abolish racial capitalism are well-established? Though a study like this one might seem to lag behind the vanguard of disciplinary critical thought, I would posit that the precondition for acting for or even wanting a world that is radically otherwise is understanding how relations of domination intimately shape agential potential, a shaping that is affectively structured all the way down.

The coming chapters find no easy answers to the contradictions marked by postcolonial optimism. Literature of postcolonial optimism does not propose a singular, clear alternative to postcolonial optimism, such as, say, "postcolonial happiness," which Ananya Jahanara Kabir theorizes as a positive, future-oriented affect that resists neoliberal regimes.[58] Instead, each part of the book looks at a collection of works that scrutinize an exhausting and exhausted optimism. These works do so not by encouraging disillusionment or despair (which inevitably calls for the renewal of optimism) but by considering and, indeed, exemplifying how pan-African creative and intellectual exchanges have yet been possible under an imperial affective regime. Literature of postcolonial optimism, by dwelling with the nation and its key educational and financial institutions, implicates itself in both the perpetuation and dissolution of the affects that maintain nation and empire. In this fundamental political ambivalence, postcolonial optimism, despite its "positive" valence, is like the "ugly feelings" attached to experiences of suspended agency that Sianne Ngai found resist being reduced to either oppressive or liberatory.[59] It is thus unlike the more redemptive "educated hope" described by Ernst Bloch, which, as Andrew van der Vlies highlights, is informed by past disappointments and imagines an always contingent futurity.[60] Postcolonial optimism often remains uneducated by the past as it conjures a certain future. Literature of postcolonial optimism exposes the critical necessity of understanding this seemingly uncritical orientation.

In its analyses of optimism, this project is beholden to scholarship within postcolonial and Black studies that challenges the assumed universality of the subject within institutionalized affect theory. Neetu Khanna, for example, has looked to writing from the Progressive Writers Movement, a Marxist group active in India in the mid-twentieth century, to theorize how specifically "colonial traumas and their structures of feeling [are] inherited," which requires in turn thinking through "the transformative potentialities of various visceral states that motivate 'progressive' feeling."[61] Sneja Gunew has similarly demonstrated the critical productivity of attending to "the affective grammars arising out of specific languages and belief systems," arguing that "affects and emotions are useful tools for registering distinctive forms of embodiment or the somatic."[62] Working from within Black Studies, Tyrone S. Palmer shows how affect studies has not fully reckoned with blackness in its articulation of what it means to affect or be affected by others.[63] The ontological meditations on blackness that have been undertaken under rubrics such as Afropessimism and Black optimism, Palmer contends, suggest how blackness precedes and defines the feeling subject, both by producing racialized affective experiences and by rendering Black feelings illegible within global anti-Black epistemological regimes.[64] While this project does not intervene in the metaphysics of Black being, it does attend to the capacity for literature to expose optimism as a relentlessly racialized feeling that is differentially bound to other feelings, including despair and disillusionment.

To theorize postcolonial optimism within specific, racialized geographies of the postcolony and its diasporas, I draw on critical writing grounded in African literary and cultural studies that, while trenchant in its analyses of affective conditions, is not often included under the rubric of affect studies per se. For example, I discuss Appiah's description of postcolonial postoptimism (chapter 2) and Andrew van der Vlies's recent descriptions of postcolonial disillusionment (chapter 4). Throughout the book, however, literary works provide the main criterion for thinking about feeling. The concept of postcolonial optimism is given dimension through discussions of, say, J.P. Clark-Bekederemo's cautious optimism, Chimamanda Ngozi Adichie's uncertain futurity, and Miriam Tlali's retrospective hopefulness.

Because the maintenance of postcolonial optimism is a function of US empire, I also draw on analyses of affect in the context of the US. Lauren Berlant's *Cruel Optimism* (2011) is a touchstone for several chapters in part I, while Martjin Konings's *The Emotional Logic of Capitalism* (2015) informs part II. In drawing on this work, I do not assume its easy application to African contexts. Postcolonial optimism, I show, is like and unlike Lauren Berlant's account of cruel optimism. A relation of cruel optimism, as Berlant describes it, "exists when something you desire is actually an obstacle to your flourishing."[65] To be sure, anglophone African literature often anticipates Berlant in making clear the cruel optimism of Nigerian attachments to US universities and South African attachments to US-style financialization as a means to securing individual and national thriving. Yet, a diagnosis of cruel optimism is also inadequate to such scenes of aspiration. For one, such optimism is rarely only cruel, as its continuance produces hoped-for and unexpected effects, including opportunities for forging and reflecting on relations of anticolonial Black solidarity. For another, whereas Berlant tracks how cruel optimism elicits postoptimistic responses characterized by a moving-past-optimism, postcolonial optimism's positioning within the crucible of empire means that optimism is often redoubled: frayed fantasies produce not postoptimistic forms of (im)passivity but an ever-amplified performance of optimistic attachment. The deeper the despair, the more pronounced the euphoria, as the very possibility of continuing to exist in the world as it is requires the performance of ongoing investment in, say, the educational and financial institutions that are known to delimit aspirations as much as realize them. Postcolonial optimism is thus both more promising and crueler than the relations Berlant locates in US and European affective scenarios of the early twenty-first century. While affirming that the postcolonial nation and the attachments it engenders are tools of empire, literature of postcolonial optimism recalibrates the affective force of such attachments by amplifying their entwinement with intimately felt desires for transnational Black thriving.

Similarly, Konings's analysis of hope and disappointment in the US capitalist economy, driven by the historical widening of credit and grounded in salvific Protestantism, is useful but insufficient for understanding the cycles of euphoria and despair engaged by South African writers. Part II qualifies and builds on this account of the imbrication of capitalism and sociality by reading it in connection to racialized histories of credit apartheid and the distinctive postapartheid economic regime that Deborah James has called "redistributive neoliberalism."[66] The cycles of hope and disappointment that Konings describes are amplified in the South African context, where writers have long anticipated Konings's insight that credit and debt are central affective mechanisms of state control, especially for regimes characterized by widespread poverty and extreme inequality.[67] Literature of postcolonial optimism centers the peculiar hopefulness of nations formed after mid-century anticolonial movements. It also, however, speaks to the US settler colonial nation, where imperial modes of domination continue to structure domestic governance.

Postcolonial optimism does not finally index a unified, homogenous experience. Nigerian and South African literatures register how distinct constellations of national history and imperial intervention produce different forms of postcolonial optimism. Nigerian literature scrutinizes a persistent, self-consciously performative optimism that maintains that US educational institutions may yet facilitate national democratic becoming. As the betrayals of US empire accrue, writers mark how optimistic attachments to US universities become increasingly untenable but are nevertheless sustained as a means of pursuing individual and national thriving. Writers of the First Republic (chapter 1), reflecting on the role of HBCUs and land-grant institutions to Nnamdi Azikiwe's anticolonial project, express hope that they might yet steal from the Cold War US university opportunities and resources that promote Black liberation. In writing of the Second Republic (chapter 2), this optimism gives way to what I describe as postoptimism, in which the "post" signals not just an aftermath but a continuance. In writing of the Third Republic (chapter 3) that engages histories of the new Nigerian diaspora in the US and of educational strikes and decline at home, I find a postoptimistic optimism; the recursive absurdity of the term signals how an exhausted optimism is nonetheless performed in order to maintain the fictions of individual upward mobility and so-called national development. As Nigerian writers grapple with the stubborn persistence of an optimism that has never fulfilled the future it promises, they both diagnose and short-circuit the affective workings of empire vis-à-vis the ideals of democracy and education.

In contrast to an ever-attenuated optimism that is performed despite disappointments, South African fiction delineates a boom-and-bust, cyclical optimism that associates US-style financialization with equality. In this form of postcolonial optimism, optimism gives way to disillusionment but is ever-renewed in hopes that the extension of credit will yield an equitable nation. Apartheid (chapter 4), postapartheid (chapter 5) and post-transition (chapter 6) writing scrutinizes why hopes for national transformation have recurrently prioritized Black people's access to credit, even as these hopes unfailingly have yielded the miseries of debt. Nigerian and South African authors present forms of postcolonial optimism that are linked to distinct histories of US imperial power (in education, in finance); they are comparable but nonequivalent constellations of feeling.

Nigerian and South African Dreams

African Literature and US Empire offers the first book-length study of how postcolonial national feeling has been imagined in relation to US imperialism. While offering a sustained critique of the affective dimensions of US empire, the project is original for emphasizing how Nigerian and South African writers imagine opportunities for pan-African solidarity within the context of US-enforced national initiatives for "development" and austerity. Examining the interplay of imperial and national affect, the book shows how subjectification and resistance to US empire shapes expressions of futurity in different literatures that must be conceived as simultaneously national and pan-African in their imaginative scope.

Part I, titled "Nigerian Literature and Pan-African Optimism," includes three chapters that offer a cumulative argument about the place of the US university in visions of Nigeria as a democratic, pan-African nation. Chapter 1, "Pan-African American Dreams of the First Republic," examines postcolonial optimistic attachments bound to US universities in writing by Chinua Achebe and J.P. Clark-Bekederemo. There is a through-line, I show, between Achebe's late twentieth-century lectures and his mid-twentieth-century education and fellowships, as his nonfiction highlights how the global Cold War aspirations of US universities unintentionally facilitated opportunities for honing pan-African critiques of US power. Achebe's mid-century relation to the US university was, he emphasizes, mediated by the writing and career of Nigeria's first president, Nnamdi Azikiwe, who cultivated connections with both HBCUs and land-grant universities in the US as part of a national anticolonial project that dreamed of securing pan-African sovereignty. Achebe's optimism, I argue, was enabled by his historical proximity to an inter-war pan-African Nigerian imaginary cultivated, at least in part, within institutions of US higher education. As this chapter goes on to trace a legacy of this optimism, it turns to J.P. Clark-Bekederemo's 1964 travelogue *America, Their America*, which excoriates the appropriation of this imaginary by predominately white educational institutions during the early decades of the Cold War. At the same time, Clark-Bekederemo's writing shares with Achebe a marked optimism regarding the possibilities of stealing, in terms resonant with Harney and Moten's work on the undercommons, Black solidarity from the jaws of US Cold War imperial institutions, not least because his fellowship to Princeton allowed Clark-Bekederemo to sustain relationships with Black US writers such as Langston Hughes. Black artists, these writers optimistically suggest, might yet secure Nigerian authority from predominately white US campuses.

Chapter 2, "The United States of 'Emelika' and Literature of the Second Republic," interprets the renewal of a national optimism oriented to the US, including the US university, in the years leading up to the Second Republic. Buchi Emecheta's 1979 novel *The Joys of Motherhood* has long been read as an exemplar of postcolonial literature of disillusionment insofar as it critiques the gendered and classed inequalities of postcolonial Nigeria. Its representation of the cusp of national independence promises that US neocolonialism will supersede British dominance.[68] I argue, however, that the novel is as much about the Second Republic as it is about the First, especially as it meditates on how optimistic attachment to US education and aid is sustained and renewed despite its clearly devastating effects, not least following the thawing of US–Nigerian relations abetted by the US civil rights leader Andrew Young in the late 1970s. Emecheta's novel anticipates Berlant by describing an amplified, overlapping set of cruelly optimistic attachments that entrench US empire and perpetuate gendered oppression and immiseration. Nigerian dreams under empire are not so much illusions with which one may become disillusioned: they are compelled and maintained as a function of the inequalities and circumscribed opportunities that British and US empires simultaneously produce in the postcolonial nation. They worsen lives as they make lives possible. Considering Berlant's discussion of postoptimism alongside Kwame Anthony Appiah's highlights how postcolonial postoptimism productively registers the *ongoingness* of an optimistic attachment that persists despite its attenuation and exhaustion—despite the lived experience and knowledge that this optimism is and never will be curative or transformative. In the chapter's conclusion, I turn to Chris Abani's 2004 *GraceLand* to suggest that a key question for writers of the Second Republic, as for writers of the First, is whether and how the Nigerian writer might steal from US institutions means to effectively and affectively challenge US empire.

Chapter 3, "The Pursuit of Happiness After the Third Republic," argues that the postoptimistic literature of the Second Republic gives way to performative optimism in literature of the Third. Ike Oguine's *A Squatter's Tale* is understudied in the US academy but especially suited for this project insofar as it explicitly links the proliferation of Nigerian immigrant literature of the US in the 1990s to the experiences and aspirations of an earlier generation in the 1970s. For the novel's immigrant protagonist, the American dream is self-evidently a cruelly optimistic story; it is obviously productive of deadlock and despair. Yet it is also a story that is nonetheless intensively rehearsed as a determined performance of optimism, particularly in relation to Obi's aspiration to enter a US MBA program. This performance of a self-sustaining illusion, I contend, is expressed as a kind of madness, as Oguine's representation of what I call postoptimistic optimism exposes anew the limitations of a dreamed Nigerian nationhood that centers US education. Chimamanda Ngozi Adichie's 2013 *Americanah* likewise represents postoptimistic optimism centered on the US university as characteristic of a decade that proclaimed America as the end of history. It explores how affectively compelling dreams of an exceptional nation that transcends global racialized inequality and demands unrelenting optimistic investment can be. The novel finally, however, offers a dream of a Nigerian national identity that recognizes the impossibility of such transcendence, and proposes instead a Nigerian nationhood premised on a shared sense of precarity as it is generated by the imperial operations of US, UK, and Chinese capital.

Part II, titled "Compounding Optimism in South African Fiction," highlights the history and legacies of apartheid lending practices. Chapter 4, "A Tiny Ripple of Hope *Between Two Worlds*," identifies a recurrent form of postcolonial optimism in South African literature that associates national anticolonial and anti-apartheid hopes with Black access to credit and property rights. Miriam Tlali's *Between Two Worlds* scrutinizes apartheid-era aspirations for Black liberation that center financial instruments by drawing a connection between the disappointments of Sophiatown and the US civil rights movement. Unpacking the history of Black South African and Black American cultural and religious exchange in Sophiatown—a site where the narrator mourns the loss of a past home of her own—allows me to situate Tlali's novel in relation to longer twentieth-century histories in which the perceived relative mobility and prosperity of Black Americans informed Black South African movements for economic rights. I go on to consider how the novel takes up this entwined history in the context of the five years of its writing, 1964–69, which correspond roughly to the years of its setting. The hope and despair attached to Sophiatown and its destruction echoes in the hope and disappointment that coheres around the US civil rights movement and its aftermath, marked in the text's evocation of Robert F. Kennedy's 1966 "Day of Affirmation Address" at the University of Cape Town. Transnational cycles of hope and despair—from Sophiatown to Washington D.C.—work to reaffirm in *Between Two Worlds* that Black economic rights are crucial to the undoing of the white supremacist nation. At the same time, the novel evinces a distinct unease that the pursuit of these rights may be too easily co-opted to extend the status quo. The novel engages hopes for the democratization of equity and credit, without daring to hope that such democratization will necessarily lead to the thriving of Black people. The novel marks how optimism attached to credit that produces conditions for disillusionment is a transnational, racialized affect integral to life in the white supremacist, financialized nation-state. I argue in subsequent chapters that this feeling's intensification as euphoria and despair finds renewed expression in postapartheid South African literature of credit and debt.

Chapter 5 charts the endurance of a South African dream of a redeemed economy in the postapartheid moment. Zakes Mda's *The Heart of Redness* shows how the South African and US neoliberal states deploy microloans and other forms of credit to maintain optimism that belies the despair of indebtedness. Within Mda's amaXhosa community, there are multiple visions of what the future ought to be, including those that alternately embrace or decry US imperialism. Yet, these dreams are similar in that they idealize an economy in which credit and real estate accrue to meritorious, self-denying entrepreneurs who work hard. In Mda's fiction, such dreams continuously explode into a South African nightmare of debt and despair, yet they are maintained in part because of the ongoing economic exigency they promise to transcend. The nation thus proliferates forms of euphoria attached to imagined individual potential rather than state action. Even as Mda's novel represents the ubiquity of this affective register, which cycles between euphoria and despair, it also writes against its recurrence. The dream-like aesthetic of *The Heart of Redness*, after all, seems far from instantiating a redemptive work ethic: it celebrates indulgence and dependency rather than austerity and autonomy. Mda's novel dreams of having collective time for dreaming, and for the renewal of creative energies and expansion of aspirations that such a luxury would afford.

Chapter 6 reads Ekow Duker's *White Wahala* as a non-developmental, picaresque fiction that reflects the exhausting stasis of national imaginaries in which residents are perpetually owed their futures. Set in Johannesburg in 2014, the year in which a contraction in the housing market made the insufficiencies of the National Credit Act of 2005 painfully obvious, the novel centers on the massively exploitative credit kiosk known as the "Last Best Hope Financial Service." Thus hope, along with the desperation implied by "last best" hope, is tied both to never-ending debt and to historic speeches by US presidents, from Lincoln to Obama, that affirmed America as the "last, best hope" for freedom. As *White Wahala* charts the triumphs and tribulations of the kiosk's owner, Cash Tshabalala, it shows how US imperial markets, like South African credit markets, promise progressive equality by reproducing an unequal status quo. The novel thus doubles down on the exhaustion produced by a sense of temporariness and enforced optimism within a financialized economy: not just because precarious debt has usurped regular wages but also because ongoing indebtedness is presented as the mechanism for redeeming national dreams. From this exhaustion, the novel finds respite by dreaming of an end to credit apartheid, not through the expansion of credit, but through the desegregation of debt.

The centrality of Nigerian and South African governments and US presidential administrations to the book's periodization reflects how I read literature against political speeches that articulate dreams of national exceptionality and alongside educational and economic policies designed to realize them. The chosen anglophone works are by no means representative of historical eras or national cultures; indeed, this project does not aim to contribute to crucial critical efforts to attend to the diversity of African literatures as they exist across languages, centuries, genres, and media. Each part does conclude with a chapter that addresses a comparatively less studied novel in African literary studies, namely Ike Oguine's *A Squatter's Tale* and Ekow Duker's *White Wahala*. The inclusion of these novels is illustrative of how works have been selected because they are attuned to the imperial effects of US universities and US-style lending institutions. Oguine's treatment of the falsely salvific promises of US university degrees, as well as Duker's send-up of the exploitative South African credit industry, offer probing accounts of why these institutions nonetheless sustain feelings of optimism across generations and despite repeated disappointments. These fictions demand attention to the affective workings of US empire in such explicit terms that they inspire new ways of reading more canonical works.

The fact that the chapters on Nigerian literature are comparative while the chapters on South African literature focus on single novels reflects how the identification of literature of postcolonial optimism has, in these cases, potentially been affected by engagement with and the pressures of the global literary marketplace. Contributing to the robust critical scholarship that demonstrates institutions and audiences in the global North have disproportionately shaped the definition and circulation of "African literature,"[69] the chapters on Nigeria illuminate the ways African literature shaped by the US university critiques the material conditions of its own production and circulation. The US university has proven relatively ubiquitous in late twentieth- and early twenty-first-century Nigerian literature, in other words, in part because it has been central to the material support of African writers (including some of the South African writers in this study). The connection between lending institutions and the South African literary scene are, by comparison, less direct, and so, perhaps, less widely available for authorial scrutiny. That both Tlali and Duker, say, write novels about financial services perhaps has more to do with biographical accident—Tlali worked as an office clerk and Duker in a bank—than with systemic market conditions. The claim is not that literature of postcolonial optimism is necessarily or equally represented across postcolonial national literatures. Those literatures can, however, be generatively read through the lens of postcolonial optimism, producing literary groupings that clarify how US empire variously permeates postcolonial national imaginaries.

The groupings presented here highlight that different national histories of postcolonial optimism are expressed through different kinds of narrative structures. The predominant genre of the Nigerian chapters is historical fiction, broadly defined: Emecheta, for example, reflects slantwise on the Second Republic by writing about the First, Chris Abani reflects on the Third Republic by writing about the Second, and Ike Oguine and Adichie reflect on Nigeria at and after the new millennium by writing about the Third. Writing the histories of Nigeria's Republics, I contend, allows writers to reflect on continuities across "failed" democracies and to expose how ongoing optimistic orientations maintain empire. By evoking past years when democracy seemed imminent and the Nigerian dream realizable, writers are better able to sketch the limitations of contemporary hopes and aspirations. At the same time, this retrospective structure does not prescribe disillusionment, as writers explore fully why and how hope persists when the reasons for disaffection—including the non-sovereign, neocolonial status of the Nigerian nation—are manifest. By contextualizing optimism as part of a longer national history, Nigerian literature of postcolonial optimism historicizes the reasons for its endurance, which include both negotiating the affective demands of empire and deploying them to mobilize pan-African exchanges oriented toward different futures.

South African literature of postcolonial optimism, in contrast, is notable for its episodic quality. To be sure, episodic is a capacious term, and here it describes diverse styles, from Tlali's short, interlinked realist scenes to Mda's magic realism and Duker's postcolonial picaresque. What the term tries to capture, however, is that all these works undercut notions of progressive time. Present hopes become frantically amplified as they are haunted by the past and anticipate their own betrayal. Episodic narratives thus express the compounding dynamic whereby the euphoria of increased access to credit, and the mobility and solidarities credit enables, periodically collapses into the despair of debt. The recurrent narrative that the extension of credit (re)creates is marked at the formal level as exhausting repetition, much like the labor of managing debt itself. As South African literature of postcolonial optimism seeks out an alternative to ever-renewed hopes in the face of despair, it counters exhaustion with a commitment to rest, dreaming, and retirement that is informed by histories of pan-African struggle. The temporal space opened in the affective state of respite offers the opportunity to envision futures other than those cyclical experiences of hope and despair produced through the entrenchment of credit and debt.

The postcolonial, David Scott has argued, defines a "sense of the present as ruined time";[70] it is a temporality haunted by "the trace of futures past."[71] Postcolonial optimism describes a response to the obvious insufficiency of postcolonial nationhood and its development, to the stricken "aftermaths" of anticolonial revolutionary hopes, that lies somewhere between cruel investment and liberatory disinvestment in dreams of their renewal.[72] It describes a feeling where attachments to the nation and its promise of democracy and equality are sustained even though one recognizes their precarity, and, indeed, their cruelty. Education will mean more alienation and debt, not the development of the individual or nation. The expansion of consumer and property rights will further entrench the inequities of empire. Postcolonial optimism is an unsettled and unsettling feeling that anticipates the betrayal of its own desires. It does not proliferate worlds but points us toward the hard and necessary work of unmaking the world of nations under empire.

PART I
NIGERIAN LITERATURE AND PAN-AFRICAN OPTIMISM

Chapter 1

Pan-African American Dreams of the First Republic

Home and Exile collects three talks by Chinua Achebe that were delivered at Harvard University in 1998 during the author's longest period of living in the United States as a faculty member. Having held a post at the University of Massachusetts Amherst from 1972 to 1976 and from 1987 to 1988, Achebe returned to the US in 1990 following a car accident, taking up posts at Bard College and Brown University. In the third talk of the book, "Today, the Balance of Stories," Achebe argues for the Nigerian writer's potential to make use of institutions that have exemplified the inequities of empires. A young aspiring writer in Nigeria, he contends, does not need to move to London or New York: "Write it where you are, take it down that little dusty road to the village post office and send it!"[1] The post office, once a symbol of British empire for Achebe and his friends, who called the mail truck "ogbuakwu-ugwo (killer-that-doesn't-pay-back)" is now, for Achebe, a potential means of self-explication and restitution.[2] Postcolonial national independence, he argues, has created conditions that allow for "an incredible metaphoric transformation of the humble postman from the killer we called him to the healer."[3] Even though the writer at home must implicitly post her manuscript abroad to seek publication, Achebe maintains near the turn of the millennium the possibility of cultivating a restorative Nigerian literary culture.

As for the Nigerian writer abroad, Achebe is similarly hopeful that imperial institutions may be negotiated in a way that enables, rather than inhibits, national self-expression. Though he makes the claim to a US audience at a US university, Achebe asserts that his time in the US has not affected his writing: "People have sometimes asked me if I have thought of writing a novel about America since I have now been living here some years. My answer has always been 'No, I don't think so.'"[4] His reason is a matter of numbers and justice: "America has enough novelists writing about her, and Nigeria too few. And so it is, again, ultimately, a question of balance. You cannot balance one thing; you balance a diversity of things."[5] In Achebe's case, committing to such a balance means navigating how the material conditions of his talk stand in tension with his critique of US hegemony. As Kalyan Nadiminti argues in a provocative analysis of how US universities and creative writing programs have shaped postcolonial and global anglophone fiction, writers such as Achebe secured academic positions in US institutions in part because of "a cold war consensus shaping the global South as a space of regenerative potential for American geopolitical power."[6] On the one hand, Nadiminti contends, "international writers at the American university" were perceived as "a testament to the reach of American knowledge supremacy" that enabled the American university "writ large" to perform "a form of global ventriloquism."[7] On the other, postcolonial writers such as Achebe were remarkable insofar as they publicly resisted this (post-)Cold War ideology, such that "moments of professional harmony between American universities and international writing communities were . . . punctuated by ideological discomfort": "Achebe was hardly a pliant professor," Nadiminti notes, particularly in his critique of Western conceptions of Africa.[8] Achebe's resistance to US cultural hegemony is addressed to a US audience because of the imperial reach of the US university.

Achebe's confidence that a greater balance of stories may be achieved, though the Nigerian writer at home must publish abroad and the Nigerian writer abroad does not always speak to home, qualifies contemporary scholarship on the production and reception of anglophone African literature. Critical lenses such as the "anthropological exotic" and the "extraverted novel," coined by Graham Huggan and Eileen Julien, respectively, describe a postcolonial literary field shaped by privileging works, marketed as "African," that appeal to US and UK readers.[9] While scholarship by Madhu Krishnan, among others, has cracked open this critical framework by highlighting the "multifocality" of African writing, the power of global North and especially of US readerships to define a circumscribed cannon of African literature continues to haunt literary criticism that engages African diasporic fiction that is variously described as "new," "immigrant," and "Afropolitan."[10] Read in relation to this critical discourse, Achebe's hope for the development of Nigerian national culture under conditions of US empire, particularly, stands as an instance of remarkable postcolonial optimism. This optimism plausibly marks Achebe's exceptional status in the anglophone world as the exemplary "African" author of *Things Fall Apart* (1958); by the late 1990s and early 2000s, he enjoyed the relative autonomy he imagines for the young Nigerian writer. Yet, as his essays and criticism from this period suggest, Achebe's optimism can also be understood as extending mid-century visions of Nigerian national becoming that sought to take from US institutions the means for achieving postcolonial ends. The US university, in these visions, is not only a site where US Cold War hegemony is enforced or denounced, but also a place where Nigerian national dreams are pursued.

This chapter situates Achebe's postcolonial optimism in the context of a longer twentieth-century history that sees Nigerian political leadership turn to US institutions of higher education as a means of promoting postcolonial national development. Achebe's mid-century relation to the US university was, he emphasizes in his nonfiction, mediated by the career of Nigeria's first president, Nnamdi Azikiwe, who cultivated connections with Historically Black Campuses and Universities in the US, as well as US land-grant institutions, as part of an anticolonial national project. Achebe's postcolonial optimism registers his historical proximity to an inter-war pan-African Nigerian imaginary cultivated within US universities. As this chapter goes on to trace a legacy of this optimism borne of anticolonial struggle, it turns to J.P. Clark-Bekederemo's 1964 travelogue *America, Their America*. Clark-Bekederemo's writing shares with Achebe's a marked optimism regarding the power of its anti-imperial critique, not least because Clark-Bekederemo's fellowship to Princeton allowed him to sustain relationships with Black US writers such as Langston Hughes. Nigerian artists, both Achebe and Clark-Bekederemo suggest, might yet steal Black solidarity from Cold War US campuses. Such theft promises a greater balance of stories in the service of a pan-African Nigerian national culture resistant to US hegemony.

By reading Achebe's nonfiction in relation to that of Azikiwe and Clark-Bekederemo, this chapter begins to sketch a Nigerian dream of postcolonial nationhood that is distinctly pan-African, embroiled in US empire, bound to the university, and, as subsequent chapters will show, resonant through contemporary fiction. Against discourses of the American dream trumpeted by the US state to proclaim American exceptionalism, this postcolonial national dream is yet to be realized. In the famous phrase of Langston Hughes, it is a "dream deferred," or a dream of "the land that never has been yet."[11] This Nigerian dream is co-constituted with an African-American dream of securing political sovereignty for Black people within the US, and it limns how African-American dreams have shaped and been shaped by Black anticolonial aspirations beyond the US.[12] It is a dream of postcolonial nationality that reveals itself to be remarkably resilient, an object of optimism that endures even as the debts and dependencies incurred by US universities and US imperial investment become ever more manifest.

Nigerian Optimism and Black Universities

As Chinua Achebe told it, he decided to use part of his UNESCO grant to travel to the United States in 1963 because colonial educators had warned him against it:

> I was curious about America, because the British colonial education I had received took pains to put America down. One of my teachers in high school was fond of reading out editorials written by Nigeria's leading nationalist, who, apparently, wrote very bad English. And my teacher linked this deficiency of the Nigerian to his American education, which was, of course, totally inferior to the British brand, and featured such subjects as dishwashing.[13]

In a 1994 essay originally delivered at Lincoln University, Achebe specifies that the "leading nationalist" was indeed Nigeria's first president, Nnamdi Azikiwe, whose anticolonial newspapers unleashed "a sweeping educational project . . . on the streets and pathways of Nigeria's towns and villages."[14] Achebe describes a particular teacher who would attempt to show "how badly written the articles were" by attributing to them a "bombastic" style supposedly consistent with "the low standard of American education."[15] As Achebe's trip attests, the criticisms of Azikiwe only enlivened the writer's desire to follow in the national leader's footsteps.

Achebe's optimistic orientation to Nigerian national independence, then, is part of a longer history of Nigerian national becoming that is tied to the US university. Azikiwe famously spent nine years at US universities from 1925 to 1934 and would be followed in the 1930s—not least because of his own efforts to encourage African students to attend his alma mater, Lincoln University—by nationalists including Nwafor Orizu, Mbonu Ojike, and K.O. Mbadiwe, as well as the Ghanaian leader Kwame Nkrumah.[16] For Azikiwe, the draw of US universities, and especially Historically Black Universities and Colleges, was both financial and ideological. US university fees were cheaper and the curriculum more flexible than in Europe, and African students had the option in the US to work as they studied, which Azikiwe did.[17] While British and French campuses "were expected to stamp colonials with an 'imperial' identity rather than a radical one," Black campuses as different as Howard and Lincoln were similar, as Jason C. Parker notes, insofar as they offered a distinctive forum "to debate the black future."[18] For Nigerians such as Azikiwe and Orizu, this meant renewing and re-envisioning Pan-African politics articulated by thinkers as different as

W.E.B. DuBois and Marcus Garvey by working first for a "United States of Africa," and then for a Nigerian nation that would keep alive pan-African aspirations.[19] "What was imaginable in 1946 but not in 1966," Frederick Cooper notes, "was that there were multiple alternatives to empire that did not presume that the end point was the nation-state," such that "the success of [national] political movements in Africa after World War II was both a liberation and a narrowing of political imagination and political possibilities."[20] The significance of US universities to anticolonial movements was such that Okechukwu Ikejani, a protégé of Azikiwe and fellow alumnus of Lincoln, suggested in a 1946 essay titled "Nigeria's Made-in-America Revolution" that "the first skirmishes in the struggle for the political freedom of the twenty-one million people of Nigeria are being fought today in the colleges of the United States."[21]

Achebe's UNESCO visit extended into the Cold War era a Nigerian national history in which aspirations for pan-African sovereignty were nurtured through Nigerian and Black American political and cultural exchange.[22] Within this history, the optimistic nationalism encapsulated by the so-called American dream was internationalized and rerouted through African and diasporic contexts. Nnamdi Azikiwe was in the US the year James Truslow Adams's 1931 *The Epic of America* was published. The book is often credited with popularizing the notion of an American dream, defined by Adams as "that dream of a land in which life should be better and richer and fuller for every man, with opportunity for each according to his ability or achievement."[23] Adams contrasts the American dream to European class hierarchies and imagines it to be fundamentally individualist and implicitly restricted to white men. Yet, the Nigerian nationalist history that inspired Achebe's first trip to the US highlights that the American dream was also thought in relation to anticolonial and Black radical movements that simultaneously invoked the US as a model of resistance to British colonialism and excoriated the US's anti-Black and therefore anti-democratic political order. Azikiwe's 1937 theory of African history in *Renascent Africa*, for example, firmly associates the US with democracy and freedom, but does so by declaring that the 1847 Liberian Declaration of Independence enshrined ideals of US governance in a state that promised sovereignty to Black people. In his paean to this political "literary masterpiece," Azikiwe lauds the document and assumed nation as that which promises "to the fullest, the right to life, liberty, and the pursuit of happiness."[24] The language of dreaming and unfettered optimism is reserved for the vision of nationhood that seems to extend the possibility of national and global Black sovereignty, albeit by glossing over the history of settler colonialism foundational to the nation: "Who would live in Liberia [on National Independence Day] and not dream dreams and see visions of a more glorious destiny! Beautiful! Wonderful!"[25] Azikiwe establishes a genealogy that routes the American dream through Africa to find its fullest expression, even if, as he acknowledges, the dream of Liberia has been "blasted by the artifices and chicaneries of European diplomacy" and is also yet to be realized.[26] In his 1970 autobiography *My Odyssey*, Azikiwe reiterated the interweaving of Nigerian pan-African dreams with Black American histories, citing as the main inspirations for his decision to seek an education in the US a letter by Garvey in *The Negro World*, a sermon by James Aggrey, and a biography of James A. Garfield (W.M. Thayer's *From Log Cabin to the White House*): "I said to myself that if Garvey could dream of 'One God, One Aim, and One Destiny' in America . . . and if Aggrey could also dream that nothing but the best was good enough for Africa, then not even death would stop me from reaching America in order to make my dreams come true."[27] Those dreams position the achievement of Nigerian national democracy and pan-African federation to come as the fulfillment of Black American dreams yet to be realized, whether in the US or Liberia. This is the American dream collectivized as internationalized Black sovereignty.

As Achebe traveled to the US for the first time in 1963, then, he did so in a culminating moment of decades of rhetorical entwinement of American and Nigerian dreams to promote democracies that were predicated on Black suffrage and sovereignty. In 1959, Azikiwe celebrated a shared history of looking toward a democratic future in his address to the National Association for the Advancement of Colored People in New York on its fiftieth anniversary: "the NAACP has been an inspiration to me and to my colleagues who have struggled in these past years in order to strengthen the cause of democracy and revive the stature of man in my country."[28] This inspiration redounded, in turn, within the US civil rights movement. Martin Luther King Jr., who attended Azikiwe's inauguration, cited the event in an Emancipation Day address delivered in Savannah, Georgia in 1961 titled "The Negro and the American Dream." Newly-independent African nations, King argued, "are looking over here . . . They want to know what we are doing about democracy, and they are making it clear that racism and colonialism must go."[29] He called on his audience to respond by making "a determined effort to achieve the ballot" so as "to help America realize its dream." Pan-African Nigerian dreams were inspired by Black Americans, while American dreams were redefined as necessarily pan-African.

The university remained, for Azikiwe particularly, a lynchpin in these dreams and a locus of national and pan-African optimistic attachment. As Tim Livsey shows in his 2017 study of *Nigeria's University Age*, there was a "striking transnational consensus, from the 1940s to the early 1960s" that universities were "crucial institutions in decolonizing nations."[30] Even so, the mid-century "optimism around Nigerian universities tended to overshadow the practical difficulties of development through higher education."[31] After being elected premier of the Eastern Region in 1954, Azikiwe initiated discussions with the US in 1955 regarding the establishment of the University of Nigeria, Nsukka. Since the 1930s, per Livsey, the establishment of an African university that "would be an agent of social, economic, and spiritual renewal" had been a "long-cherished dream" of Azikiwe's.[32] Facing pressure from the British and fellow Nigerians for the new university to have a special relation to London, like University College Ibadan (established in 1948), Azikiwe compromised on his radical anticolonial vision to work for a university founded with the aid of both the British and the Americans: his new university would be a place where "the philosophy of the [US] land-grant college system can be blended perfectly with our British traditions."[33] While the main US institutional collaborator in the project was Michigan State University, the "philosophy" invoked by Azikiwe was a democratizing one that included legislation against racial discrimination in admissions in the Second Morrill Act and the establishment of seventeen Historically Black Colleges and Universities. The aim of establishing Black institutions that exceeded vocational training resonated with the missions of Storer, Howard, and Lincoln.[34] As Achebe noted near the end of a 1994 conference honoring Azikiwe at Lincoln University, "when Azikiwe founded the University of Nigeria, Nsukka, in 1960, he named schools and colleges and departments after the distinguished African Americans Leo Hansberry, Paul Robeson, and Washington Carver."[35] As Maik Nwosu has detailed, a number of distinguished faculty in the Department of English who taught alongside literary luminaries such as Achebe in the early 1980s had US degrees, including Emeka Nwabueze (Bowling Green State University), Chimalum Nwankwo (University of Texas at Austin), and Ossie Enekwe (Columbia University).[36] The US university was central to plans for the new Nigerian nation, and Nigerian universities evidence how this new nation was conceived as pan-African.[37]

For his part, Achebe, who was a member of the first cohort of students at University College, Ibadan, embarked on his trip to the US eager to encounter African-American literature beyond Booker T. Washington's school-approved *Up From Slavery*; he relished the opportunity to read James Baldwin and to meet with "Langston Hughes, Paule Marshall, Amiri Baraka, then called LeRoi Jones, and others."[38] Achebe noted, in a 1988 tribute to James Baldwin, that his decision to go to the US was also informed by "the strong impression made on me by Langston Hughes—his deus ex machina appearance at that critical moment in the intellectual and literary history of modern Africa, and that unspoken message of support and solidarity after three hundred years of brutal expatriation."[39] A turn to the US was not only a turn to an emergent world power; it was a turn to African-American articulations of resonant dreams of freedom.

Situating Achebe in relation to Azikiwe and the US university as a site of pan-African exchange productively reframes foundational debates around anglophone African literature in the mid-twentieth century. Take, for example, Achebe's famous 1965 defense of English as an African language, which has been a key text in both postcolonial scholarship and classrooms considering the politics of language.[40] As Mukoma wa Ngugi highlighted in *The Rise of the African Novel* (2018), Makerere and post-Makerere writers such as Achebe, though they were part of a small, educated elite, used English to forge "a larger Pan-African identity," insofar as "Africans were getting a sense of larger Africa" by reading "African writers [who had] become national writers in nations outside their own."[41] The emphasis in this analysis is on a continental pan-Africanism ("one where a Zambian in a Kenyan airport is pleasantly shocked by running into Achebe").[42] To be sure, Achebe's defense of English highlighted continental politics: "the only reason why we can even talk about African unity is that when we get together we can have a manageable number of languages to talk in," including English.[43] It is significant, however, that "English and the African Writer," which responded to questions raised at the 1962 conference for anglophone African writers at Makarere University, concludes with a quotation from an African-American writer:

> Writing in the London Observer recently, James Baldwin said:
>   My quarrel with English language has been that the language reflected none of my experience. But now I began to see the matter in quite another way . . . Perhaps the language was not my own because I had never attempted to use it, had only learned to imitate it. If this were so, then it might be made to bear the burden of my experience if I could find the stamina to challenge it, and me, to such a test.
> I recognise, of course, that Baldwin's problem is not exactly mine, but I feel that the English language will be able to carry the weight of my African experience.[44]

Nigerian and African-American negotiations of the English language are here complementary and divergent, negotiated through Achebe's quotation of Baldwin and open to ongoing influence. English is a language of colonialism and slavery, but also a language for articulating global Black solidarity, including through the expression of distinctive experiences. The invocation of Baldwin highlights the importance of pan-African American exchange to the formation of an anglophone Nigerian national literature. Put more broadly, while twentieth-century anglophone postcolonial literature has long been understood as "writing back" to the language of British empire, it has also been simultaneously shaped by US empire and pan-African-American forms of resistance to it.[45]

Similarly, the coalescence of Nigerian national and literary histories around the US university, and especially HBCUs, augments discussions of postcolonial literary resistance to Cold War US imperialism. Achebe and his contemporaries were certainly aware of US attempts to shape emergent postcolonial national cultures. Obiajunwa Wali, for example, argued in *Transition* in 1963 that African literature, "as now understood and practiced [at Makarere]," merely parrots the "current cliches of the English and American new critics."[46] He decried the production and reception of African literature that, for example, proclaimed the playwright and poet J.P. Clark-Bekederemo the "Tennessee Williams of the Tropics."[47] Wali did not know at the time of writing that *Transition*, as well as the 1962 Makarere conference itself, was funded by the CIA working through the Paris-based Congress for Cultural Freedom (CCF), purportedly to combat Soviet influence on the continent.[48] Yet, these facts do not necessarily amplify Wali's denunciation of the anglophone literary scene. Cold War scholars have emphasized that US interventions in emergent postcolonial African national literary cultures did not make African writers "puppets of the United States and its Cold War allies."[49] Peter Kalliney argues that the CIA's "form of indirect patronage afforded a generation of African writers more rather than less autonomy, both politically and aesthetically, largely because the CIA was so concerned about secrecy that it could not make any transparent demands on the intellectuals it supported."[50] African writers, Kalliney contends, were able to "express a version of Cold War neutrality" that took its political tone from "the Bandung Conference of 1955, the nonaligned movement, and the Organisation for African Unity."[51] Taiwo Adetunji Osinubi's reading of Achebe's evasion of binary Cold War rhetoric in *Man of the People* offers an earlier elucidation and concretization of this point.[52] The Nigerian political and cultural turn to HBCUs highlights that African writers' resistance to US hegemony was informed not only by global South solidarities, but also by solidarity with African Americans, whose "dismal civil rights situation," Monica

Popescu notes, the US hoped "to address and dispel" through imperial rhetoric that promised to impart to former colonies "the democratic values and institutions it achieved."[53] Optimistic attachments to US universities could be maintained alongside critiques of US imperialism through pan-African aspirations to both national development and the development of pan-African national literary cultures.

"Don't let them get you!": Postcolonial Optimism and US Empire

In the early 1960s, the US was, for Nigerian intellectuals such as Achebe, an expanding empire and an established site of shared anticolonial and anti-racist struggle. Per Gary Wilder, "decolonization was an epochal process of global restructuring that unfolded on a vast political terrain inhabited by diverse actors and agencies," such that "colonized peoples and European policymakers were not always the primary actors in this drama."[54] There is no drama without conflict, however, and as the poet and playwright J.P. Clark-Bekederemo describes Achebe's arrival in the US in his 1964 memoir *America, Their America*, there was good reason for tempering optimism, albeit without fully ceding it. Clark-Bekederemo begins the first chapter of his account of the academic year he spent at Princeton University with a sentence about the conditions of his departure: "At midnight one Wednesday night in May I fled the United States of America."[55] As he boards the plane, he issues a warning to Achebe, recently arrived "on some ticket to America, unlike mine just ended, a right and proper one from UNESCO" (15). "Countryman," Clark-Bekederemo admonishes, "come home soon; don't let them get you!" (16). The "them," of course, are Americans, and Clark-Bekederemo's warning, like *America, Their America* as a whole, acknowledges and resists the appeal of the US as a potential intellectual home for Nigeria's writers and as a model for Nigeria as nation. For Clark-Bekederemo, the United States is a destination that compels attention but also a nation to escape.[56]

Clark-Bekederemo, notably, was not leaving the US in haste strictly of his own accord. Rather, his "ticket" to America had been abruptly cut short by Princeton administrators who judged him to be in violation of the terms of his fellowship. The Parvin Fellowship Program, announced in 1961 as a partnership between the Albert Parvin Foundation and the Woodrow Wilson School of Public and International Affairs, was "designed to assist in preparing young men and women from the emerging nations for leadership in their own countries while also giving them an opportunity to see at first hand and explore the democratic traditions of the western world."[57] Clark-Bekederemo was one of a handful of "special students" who hailed from what Princeton president Robert F. Goheen described as "new nations" that "greatly need the aid, experience, and educational resources that the more advanced societies can afford them."[58] As a fellow, Clark-Bekederemo was expected to "share fully in the life of the university," take "courses as seemed best suited to [his] individual needs," and once a week attend "an informal seminar" meant to impart a "deeper understanding" of "what the United States is, its place in history, its humane aspirations, and its awareness of its own domestic and international problems."[59] Clark-Bekederemo, in contrast, took every opportunity to hang out with friends in New York City (101); he signed up for a course on the Development of American Literature that he rarely attended (205); and he reported himself to look "perennially sullen" in the seminar that insisted the US was "the nation that today is the mightiest, the richest, and the freest man has ever set eyes on since the sun rose first on the chaos that was then the universe" (121, 123). The university withdrew its support because Clark-Bekederemo refused to learn what Princeton, "the proud custodian of all that is America, beautiful and perfect," was teaching (29).

Clark-Bekederemo's memoir reads in some respects as an exemplar of postcolonial literature of disillusionment of the 1960s and 1970s that emerged in the wake of national liberation movements, although its pessimism is oriented less toward Nigeria than toward the nation that offers itself as a model for Nigerian nationhood. Clark-Bekederemo's caution to Achebe, like his book, points to US Cold War policies that, by the early 1960s, had co-opted anticolonial and postcolonial rhetoric of national liberation to further US imperialism. Clark-Bekederemo's account of his time as a Parvin Fellow at Princeton is defined by continuous opposition to an institutional and national culture suffused by developmental logics that posited the US as a model of freedom and democracy rather than, as per Azikiwe and King, a nation where these ideals had yet to be made "a living reality in American society."[60] Contra Azikiwe, Clark-Bekederemo accordingly denounces US universities, whether predominately white or historically Black, as drivers of imperial oppression. At the same time, Clark-Bekederemo's relation to the university is not only oppositional; as his involuntary departure from the US denotes, the writer was ready to commit to the full term of his Princeton fellowship. For Clark-Bekederemo, as for Achebe, the US university is not defined solely in terms of its Cold War imperial agenda. Rather, the institution's resources can be repurposed by the Nigerian intellectual who pursues pan-African exchanges that further liberatory dreams. America may be "theirs," but optimism persists in the hope that something that is "ours" might yet be stolen away from time on the US campus.

Clark-Bekederemo's refusal of the American "gospel" (120), as it is called in a chapter titled "The American Dream," recurs throughout *America, Their America*, which offers differently scaled structural analyses of US imperialism, including one that targets the writer's host university, specifically. Against the celebration of Princeton's supposed beneficence in "invest[ing] the President of Liberia with several honours and gifts," Clark-Bekederemo notes that the university is in a position to make such gifts in part because it enjoys the patronage of Harvey Firestone, who made "one huge rubber plantation" of Liberia after the jailing of Garvey (33). The few tokens offered to the Liberian president do not compare to the resources enjoyed by those with access to Princeton's Harvey S. Firestone Memorial Library. Concomitantly, the cost of the Parvin Fellow's access to American "democratic traditions" and "American resources" has been the suppression of pan-African movements for sovereignty and the development of extractive plantation economies. In his critiques of Princeton, Clark-Bekederemo was part of a broader cohort of writers, including from Latin America, who participated in what Nadiminti terms the "internationalization of the research university" in the Cold War US, while ensuring that it "was not merely a conduit to professionalism but also a contentious political arena."[61]

Notably, Clark-Bekederemo's critique of and disillusionment with US higher education is not limited to the predominately white institution but extends to those Black universities that were, in many ways, at the vanguard of the US university's internationalization. Noting that the American African Institute, which "in Nigeria alone . . . now airlifts on the average every year a hundred or so students straight into the dormitories and classes in the US" (155–56), the writer contends that the program shows "little awareness" of either the problem of brain drain or of the fact that "Harvard and Howard" alike regularly refused African students the opportunity to pursue graduate degrees (157–58). If, as Jason C. Parker argues, "the black campus quietly represented for black peoples the lodestar of freedom that American cold warriors asserted for the United States as a whole," it was not, as Parker himself demonstrates, unaffected by a Cold War milieu in which American assertions of freedom and beneficence were invoked as realities, thereby effecting the real expansion of US imperialism.[62] In 1960, for example, newly inaugurated Howard president James Nabrit argued that the Historically Black University was especially well-positioned to contribute to the US government's aid and development programs:

We aim to serve our country in making our . . . special attributes freely available to it as our government strives to gain the confidence of the uncommitted colored races of the world. In the deadly contest between democracy and communism the dynamic experience in democracy in action at Howard University may well be among the decisive factors.[63]

Throughout the late 1950s and early 1960s, Howard had "the highest percentage of foreign students enrolled among American [institutions]."[64] It was in practice what other universities aspired to be in theory, and it was able to leverage this act for funding by positioning itself as "an asset to the United States in waging the Cold War."[65] This positioning was particularly important following *Brown v. Board of Education* (1954), as concerns about enrollment and funding were exacerbated after desegregation raised the prospect of HBCUs having to compete for Black students.[66]

While institutions such as Howard thus strategically adopted Cold War rhetoric at least in part to ensure survival, Clark-Bekederemo's criticisms register how difficult it had become by the early 1960s to disentangle the erstwhile radical political and cultural practices nurtured within Black US colleges and universities from US imperial ventures bolstered by Cold War rhetoric. When Azikiwe called on NAACP members in 1959 to "help us" by "opening the doors of your seats of learning to students from Africa" and "giving us the desired technical, technological, and managerial co-operation in the development of our natural resources,"[67] he was in harmony with the administration of John F. Kennedy, which paid out tens of millions of dollars of economic and military "assistance" in the five years following a May 1961 study of Nigeria's six-year development plan.[68] The Kennedy administration, Livsey notes, "allocated more development funding to Nigeria than any other African nation, and overall the United States government supported more educational projects in Nigeria during the 1950s and 1960s than any other nation on earth, including Vietnam."[69] This investment would help to consolidate the US as a major investor in and consumer of Nigerian crude oil over the next fifty years; the maintenance of an extractive economy, in turn, would delimit Nigerian democracy at home and influence abroad.[70]

Clark-Bekederemo's warning to Achebe expresses apprehension about a Cold War context in which the American university proclaims the US as a model of freedom and democracy achieved. "It is difficult," Clark-Bekederemo concludes, "to tell where cold calculating Greek gifts begin with the American people and when warm, altruistic Christian charity is at work with them" (155). Such is Nelson Mandela's view in the 1958 article "American Imperialism: A New Menace in Africa," which describes an "elaborately disguised" form of domination that "maintains that the huge sums of dollars invested in Africa are not for the exploitation of the people of Africa but for the purpose of developing their countries and in order to raise their living standards."[71] The dilemma, Mandela argues, is that "the new self-governing territories in Africa require capital to develop their countries ... but the idea of making quick and high profits, which underlies all the developmental plans launched in Africa by the USA, completely effaces the value of such plans in so far as the masses of the people are concerned."[72] Aimé Césaire, in *Discours sur le colonialisme* (1955), concurred in a style resonant with Clark-Bekederemo's warning to Achebe:

> '*Aid to the disinherited countries*,' says Truman. 'The time of the old colonialism has passed.' That's also Truman.
> Which means that American high finance considers that the time has come to raid every colony in the world. So, dear friends, here you have to be careful!
> I know that some of you, disgusted with Europe, with all that hideous mess which you did not witness by choice, are turning—oh! in no great numbers—toward America and getting used to looking upon that country as a possible liberator.
> 'What a godsend' you think.
> 'The bulldozers! The massive investments of capital! The roads! The ports!'
> 'But American racism!'
> 'So what? European racism in the colonies has inured us to it!'
> And there we are, ready to run the great Yankee risk.
> So, once again, be careful!
> American domination—the only domination from which one never recovers. I mean from which one never recovers unscarred.[73]

The refusal to see "aid" as exploitation and imperialism is exactly the American fantasy Clark-Bekeredemo repeatedly identifies and condemns. "The testimonial and dream" of "the ordinary American citizen," he suggests, is one that erroneously equates freedom with "the right to private property and of the inherent ability and right of man to exploit an existing opportunity for wealth": "so accommodating is the heaven of property and free private enterprise, everybody within enjoys absolute happiness even though one capacity may be no bigger than a jug's and another as large as the Atlantic" (129–30). For Clark-Bekederemo, America is the "limit, both of the dream and of the actuality" of the supposed "achievement" of "western and white civilization" that is "crying pride and power everywhere": it proclaims the dream loudly, but its actuality is "achieved as likely as not at the expense of the dark" (11). European imperialism, Ngũgĩ wa Thiong'o noted, creates the "wasteland" that it then purports to "cure."[74] A US variation lays waste and offers cure in the form of investment in educational institutions that promote the securitization of US empire.[75]

Clark-Bekederemo's treatment of the US and its universities stands as a critical counterpoint to Azikiwe's more optimistic writings that inspired Achebe's travels. The disillusionment Clark-Bekederemo expresses in relation to the US is incomplete, however, and the writer remains disappointed that his fellowship is cut short. There is a remainder of optimism, in other words, in Clark-Bekederemo's writing, and this remainder registers an anticolonial, pan-African valence. While on fellowship Clark-Bekederemo, like Achebe, actively nurtured relationships with African-American artists during his visit to the US, reuniting for example with Langston Hughes, whom he had met at the 1962 African Writers Conference at Makerere University. Hughes in turn introduced him to writers such as the playwright Vinnette Carroll (102). Universities mediated other critically productive relationships. Clark-Bekederemo, for example, gives a detailed account of his time with his friend Gloria, "a girl from Columbia [University] who had only then recently returned home from doing research work in Nigeria" (65). Their conversations—about hair, slavery, and food—open the way for broader reflections about the possibilities and pitfalls of pan-African solidarity. Clark-Bekederemo lauds the "genuine historical stand of Negritude," the "Pan-African Movement of Marcus Garvey and Dr. Dubois," and "writers of real worth" such as James Baldwin, Ralph Ellison, Paul Vessey, and "Papa Langston Hughes himself" (79–81).[76] Clark-Bekederemo's relation to Princeton, finally, is one that Stefano Harney and Fred Moten ascribe to "the subversive intellectual in the modern university," who must "abuse its hospitality" and "spite its mission": "one can only sneak into the university and steal what one can."[77] What Clark-Bekederemo steals from Princeton includes the opportunity to engage off-campus with Black American people, culture, and politics.

Princeton, in other words, is not just an institution to be critiqued for its collusions in imperial developmentalism but also an institution from within which one might pursue other collective visions of futurity. Clark-Bekederemo's refusal of professionalism manifests what Harney and Moten describe as "that criminal impulse to steal from professions, from the university, with neither apologies nor malice, to steal the enlightenment for others, to steal oneself with a certain blue music, a certain tragic optimism, to steal away with mass intellectuality" (40). The optimism secreted in Clark-Bekederemo's exploitation of his fellowship to pursue relationships and passions unrecognized by the university counters the officious forms of hope proffered in Cold War developmentalist policy. Harney and Moten, analyzing US politics after

Reagan, distinguish between hope that appears as "a matter of policy" and an "exuberantly metacritical hope [that] has always exceeded every immediate circumstance in its incalculably varied everyday enactments in the fugitive art of social life" (73). *America, Their America*, analyzing mid-century US politics from the perspective of the recently postcolonial subject, enacts such a distinction in Clark-Bekederemo's persistent optimistic attachment to the university.

The hope borne of Black sociality in Clark-Bekederemo's book diverges sharply from the lessons and futures offered in the Princeton classroom. Against the stultifying teaching of policy, Harney and Moten posit the "beyond of teaching" that "is really about ... not finishing oneself, not passing, not completing; it's about allowing subjectivity to be unlawfully overcome by others, a radical passion and passivity such that one becomes unfit for subjection" (28). More instructive and transformative than any time in a seminar are the pan-African encounters that thus overwhelm. News coverage of the harassment of James Meredith, the first Black student to attend the University of Mississippi, manifests in the writer's consciousness in a dream that also incorporates his concern for his family: "one nightmare featuring my brother and James Meredith all mixed up in one terrible role and struggle for identity and survival, a nightmare short but self-repeating and more live than anything I remember on screen or stage" (64).[78] The nightmare belies the myth of the American dream. It also signals a disordering of self, a profound solidarity that Harney and Moten might describe as "the prophetic organization of the undercommons" (28). Princeton remains a site of optimism to the degree that one might steal from it the opportunity to give focused attention to "the case for action," as presented for example at the "first ever united front Negro meeting at Harlem's 125th Street," where Malcolm X, Martin Luther King, Jr., and Roy Wilkins "spoke in different tongues" of a nation to come (84). Postcolonial optimism persists in the face of US empire, as pan-African interchange looks forward to national futures whose imagining exceeds national bounds.

Pan-African Nigerian Literature

As both Achebe and Clark-Bekederemo travelled into the heart of an expanding imperial power, they were optimistic about the pan-African solidarities they might build and the opportunities for dreaming the postcolonial nation that might be stolen away. Achebe, for one, continually expressed that US educational institutions could be redeployed to anticolonial ends. In the 1993 lecture that was the basis for the title essay of *The Education of a British-Protected Child*, he agrees with Henry Kissinger's account of US interventions in Africa: "even if it is unintentional, we must be doing something right."[79] Achebe was able to take what he needed from a British colonial education; the British empire did something "right," however unintentionally. The invocation of Kissinger and US empire implies that contemporary writers might likewise take what they need from the institutions of US imperialism to further pan-African national imaginaries.

From within the histories that shaped the sojourns of two Nigerian writers to the US in the years following political independence, a series of related questions emerge: to what liberatory uses can English be put? What emancipatory futures can be imagined and pursued within and despite institutions of higher learning committed by their administrations to US imperial interests? How often can a visiting Black writer from Nigeria get away with visiting Harlem when he is technically a Princeton Fellow? To adapt the language of Moradewun Adejunmobi in her incisive meditation on postcolonial cultural production, unequal power relations, and contingent agency: how can "self-expression and a scope of action" be forged from "within the constraints of postcolonial subjectification," notwithstanding "the authority and reach of locally and globally dominant institutions"?[80] Achebe and Clark-Bekederemo answer this question with optimism, in part because of their proximity to a pan-African anticolonial and civil rights history that made use of US universities.

To the degree that this optimism attaches itself to a nation—even a nation to come—it is necessarily fraught. Pheng Cheah has demonstrated that postcolonial nationhood puts paid to the ideology that the nation can be self-actualized outside of global capitalism or the US imperial institutions that maintain it. The postcolonial nation, Cheah argued, is nonetheless "the most apposite figure for freedom today" precisely because in always accounting for its own limits it must imagine the decolonized nation to come outside of ideologies that conceptualize freedom as the transcendence of material conditions.[81] The postcolonial optimism of writers of the First Republic encapsulates this tension: the decolonized nation of the future requires ongoing negotiation with the imperial realities of the present. Insofar as postcolonial optimism registers how this politics of postcolonial nationality are manifest within the feeling subject, it also points toward the subjective comforts and pressures that inhere to living within this contradiction, which Cheah terms "spectral nationality." Achebe and Clark-Bekederemo register these pleasures and pressures when, for example, they express the urgency of writing home and nation from a position of exile, or of wishing to extend a sojourn in a nation that is manifestly not "theirs." The pleasures of taking from US institutions and aid the opportunity to pursue an optimistic anti-imperial national politics are, to borrow Cheah's terminology, tempered by the felt knowledge that these pleasures depend on and maintain the structures and institutions one hopes to dismantle. Thinking the postcolonial nation and the dream of decolonized nationhood through the lens of postcolonial optimism opens the door for considering more fully the entwinement of the affective operations of empire with the affective orientations that oppose it. The next chapters consider how this entwinement helps to account for the renewal of postcolonial optimism after periods of widespread national disillusionment. They also, however, consider the profound psychic costs that accrue to the postcolonial feeling subject when renewed commitments to postcolonial national futurity threaten to overwhelm pan-African dreams of decolonized nationhood.

Chapter 2

The United States of 'Emelika' and Literature of the Second Republic

Chinua Achebe's and J.P. Clark-Bekederemo's first sojourns to the United States in the early 1960s occurred in the afterglow of political and cultural pan-African exchanges that nurtured both Nigeria's "made-in-America" revolution and the US civil rights movement (chapter 1). By the late 1960s, a national milieu amenable to Nnamdi Azikiwe's enthusiasm for the promises of US education and investment was supplanted by one that was more critical of both US imperialism and postcolonial nationhood. Official US neutrality during the war of 1967–70 that followed the secession of Biafra, along with US support for white supremacist regimes in Rhodesia and South Africa, were among the key factors that meant US-Nigeria relations were strained from 1966 until the second half of 1977.[1] In 1976, Nigerian university students attacked the US Embassy and consulate, demanding the nationalization of the American Gulf Oil Company.[2] Disillusionment attached to both the postcolonial nation and the imperial power whose oil markets significantly shaped its economy.[3]

Disillusionment likewise characterized national politics in the US. As the Democratic politician Averell Harriman put it in 1976, Americans became "disillusioned with their own illusions."[4] By the mid-1970s, optimism seemed inadequate for describing conditions at home or influence abroad. The lingering scandal of Watergate, the war in Vietnam, high oil prices, and economic recession contributed to a widespread sense of crisis regarding the perceived legitimacy of US power. This was exacerbated by the evident failure of détente with the Soviet Union to maintain peace, as well as a heightened sense of the contradictions of US Cold War policies.[5] At the same time, prominent and linked African and African-American discourses of the US de-emphasized the nation's democratic potential and critiqued its imperial reality. Stokely Carmichael's June 1966 Black Power declaration, for example, renounced US imperialism within its own national borders and declared Black communities to be "internal colonies."[6]

The Nigerian literature of postcolonial optimism that I take up in this chapter grapples with the tenuous, state-centered renewal of optimistic orientations toward Nigerian nationhood and US institutions following widespread disillusionment with both. In 1991, Kwame Anthony Appiah described the postcolonial as equivalent to "a kind of postoptimism."[7] Studies of postcoloniality have tended to emphasize a valence of this term that equates it with what Appiah calls "a condition of pessimism."[8] Postcolonial literature attentive to the affective workings of US empire, however, suggests that the "post" in postoptimism is resonant with the "post" in postcolonial, insofar as it designates continuance as well as a break. In the Nigerian context, fiction that engages the renewal of optimism around Nigerian–US relations following the election of US president Jimmy Carter in 1976 and the start of the Second Republic (1979–82) scrutinizes how this renewal is possible given the disappointments and human suffering following the collapse of the First. It asks why national disillusionment—and its concomitant demand for a different societal order—can be so difficult to sustain. The problematic of literature of postcolonial optimism is not only how literature can help to imagine a decolonized nation or polity but also why optimism oriented toward an imperial order of nations persists in the wake of disillusionment and despite critique.

My argument unfolds from a close reading of Buchi Emecheta's 1979 novel *The Joys of Motherhood*.[9] The canonical fiction has long been read as an exemplar of postcolonial literature of disillusionment insofar as it critiques the gendered and classed inequalities of postcolonial Nigeria. Its representation of the cusp of national independence promises that US neocolonialism will supersede British dominance. I argue, however, that the novel is as much about the Second Republic as it is about the First, especially as it meditates on how optimistic attachment to a vision of postcolonial nationhood that hinges on US education and aid is sustained and renewed despite its clearly devastating effects. I suggest that Emecheta's novel anticipates Lauren Berlant's theorization of cruel optimism by describing an amplified, overlapping set of cruelly optimistic attachments that entrench US empire and perpetuate gendered oppression and immiseration. In so doing, the novel makes clear that this postcolonial form of cruel optimism, like those Berlant describes, is inadequately conceptualized as ideological hoodwinking or naivete. Critical awareness of the high costs of postcolonial optimism does not inoculate against the material conditions that render it compelling. Although the novel critiques the patriarchal neocolonial conditions under which Nigerian nationhood was imagined in the decades surrounding political independence and again in the years leading up to the establishment of the Second Republic, it makes clear that such critique is insufficient for transforming the affective relations that empire generates. Nigerian national optimism in the context of US empire is not so much an illusion with which one may become disillusioned: it is compelled and maintained as a function of the inequalities and circumscribed opportunities that empire produces. Achebe and Clark, writing in and about the First Republic, hope that Nigerian national culture and pan-African solidarity might be stolen away from institutions of US empire. Emecheta's novel suggests such optimism is both differentially gendered and integral to the workings of empire.

As Emecheta's novel ends with a Nigerian dream of full national sovereignty being optimistically pursued via men's enrollment in the US university, it diagnoses how postcolonial optimism creates an impasse for securing individual and communal thriving in Nigeria. A similar diagnosis of impasse is found within another novel of the Second Republic, Chris Abani's 2004 *GraceLand*.[10] While Emecheta writes during the Second Republic looking back on the First, and Abani writes in the aftermath of the Third Republic looking back on the Second, Abani's novel ends, like Emecheta's, with protagonists desiring a better Nigeria and looking to the US, despite the felt insufficiency of this response to ongoing immiseration. Both Abani and Emecheta, like writers of the First Republic (chapter 1), ask how the Nigerian writer might steal from US institutions the means to challenge US empire. The question remains urgent given the ongoing significance of US universities to the production and circulation of anglophone Nigerian literature from the 1970s through the start of the new millennium. I argue that *The Joys of Motherhood* and *GraceLand* offer an answer through the instantiation of a literary pan-Africanism in a postoptimistic key. This postoptimistic pan-Africanism disinvests from optimistic visions of national futurity that are imagined to nonetheless continue. As Emecheta and Abani situate their writing in traditions of African-American literature by women and queer men, respectively, they suggest that what might be stolen from nationalist Nigerian dreams of American investment, education, and democracy are postoptimistic, transatlantic dreams of anti-imperial Black solidarity.

Cruel Optimism and Nigerian Nationhood

Emecheta's *The Joys of Motherhood* relates Nnu Ego's struggle to live a good life amid a transforming society in early and mid-twentieth-century Nigeria. An optimistic orientation to the US is introduced only near the end of the fiction, at the same time as its characters begin to hopefully anticipate the formal end of colonialism and the establishment of a new nation. This late introduction, however, is precisely the point: as I argue elsewhere, in Emecheta's troping, the US, and especially US education, is integral to the dream of Nigerian political independence.[11] The relation is made clear through the close association of Oshia, Nnu Ego's oldest son, with approaching nationhood. Oshia, as a young adult, desires to go to university in the US to be in a better financial situation to support his family: "Education is a life-long project. If I stop now, I shall only help them half the way" (192). At the same time, Oshia's desire for securing his own and his family's prosperity through a US education is synecdochically in relationship with a more general desire to secure national prosperity in the wake of anticipated political independence. At a party to celebrate Oshia's "grade one in his Cambridge School-leaving Certificate," conversation centers on the form of coming national sovereignty: "in the not-too-distant future we shall be ruling ourselves, making our own laws" (199). Nnu Ego clarifies that this means "we'll have a black District Officer in a place like Ibuza," as well as Nigerian Reverend Fathers, doctors, and politicians (199). Oshia's education promises to forward not only the interests of his family, but also those of the emergent nation. As Nnu Ego hopes that Oshia might "rub shoulders one day with the great men of Nigeria" (202), and indeed become a "great man" himself (193), her son's education is implicitly aligned with the US educations of leaders of the independence movement, such as Nnamdi Azikiwe, who, as we have seen (chapter 1), helped to popularize the idea of US universities as anticolonial alternatives to their British counterparts. Oshia's optimism, like Azikiwe's, does more than promise success in America—it promises that success in the US will lead to thriving in and for Nigeria.

Emecheta's novel exemplifies postcolonial literature of disillusionment insofar as it critiques these dreams of national becoming as both patriarchal and vulnerable to neocolonialism. The differently gendered costs of Oshia's dreams become clear as Nnu Ego suffers marginalization and Oshia faces increasing debt. The novel pointedly highlights that there is no chance of Nnu Ego or her daughters travelling to the US or becoming leading figures of the nation. Rather, after Nnu Ego's younger son, Adim, also leaves home (in his case for Canada), Nnu Ego's "joys as a mother" finally consist of standing in "the sandy square" and telling people that "her son was in 'Emelika'" and that she had another one also in the land of the white men—she could never manage the name Canada" (224). Nnu Ego's pride in her sons' emigration stands in sharp contrast to the reality of her isolation ("her daughters sent help once in a while" (224)). This isolation persists until she dies quietly "by the roadside . . . with no child to hold her hand and no friend to talk to her": "what actually broke her was, month after month, expecting to hear from her son in America, and from [her son] Adim too who later went to Canada, and failing to do so" (224). US empire has rendered even the potential joys of motherhood, such as pride in one's children, all but joyless, and the acerbic tragedy of the novel's final pages inflect its title with famous irony. In Emecheta's account, the pan-African nationalism that Oshia's optimism promises to nurture structurally takes on the attributes of what Nanjala Nyabola, following Nduko o'Matigere, has described as Man-Africanism, a "network that exists solely to protect rich, powerful men."[12] The critique of Azikiwe's nationalism extends through the novel's depiction of what Oshia in fact brings back to Nigeria from the US. When Oshia returns to Nigeria following Nnu Ego's death, he does so to ensure that his mother has "the noisiest and most costly second burial Ibuza had ever seen"; it will, however, take Oshia "three years to pay off the money he had borrowed to show the world what a good son he was" (224). As Robin Goodman argues, Nnu Ego's loss of her sons parallels the loss of her husband when he is forcibly conscripted into the British army earlier in the novel, indicating continuity between colonial and neocolonial eras: "Though Oshia, indeed, consents to go abroad and learn to work for the implementation of colonialist law whereas Nnaife is coerced, Oshia's education to be a technician for the new global economy—in Nigeria, most likely in the service of the oil companies or the military or both—appears here as repeating the colonialist practice of exploitation, violence, and forced conscription for foreign interests."[13] The novel diagnoses the cost of Nigerian dreams within US empire as the entrenchment of patriarchal neocolonialism in both the new nation and in the attitudes of its citizens.

And yet, as much as the novel exemplifies postcolonial disillusionment, it is also strikingly attuned to the remarkable persistence of postcolonial optimism. Both Oshia and Nnu Ego remain hopeful despite ongoing disappointment and the continuous deferral of the good life. "Things *will be* all right," Oshia reassures his mother, as he denies his family the small pleasure of a whisky party to celebrate passing exams so that he can save for university in the States (193, italics mine). Elsewhere, he explicitly acknowledges that "though he would like to help his parents, that help was going to be a very long time in coming" (191). Nnu Ego continues to invest in her sons and their education and sing their praises in the sandy square, even as she acknowledges that "she would have been better off had she had time to cultivate those women who had offered her hands of friendship" (219). Oshia knows that his plans burden his parents, whom he wishes to support; Nnu Ego knows that, by committing her energies to her sons rather than friends, she will continue to be relatively unsupported.

One way to make sense of these paradoxes is to read the novel as critically revealing the hypocrisies of its characters. Stéphane Robolin aligns himself with other readers who have argued that Nnu Ego's "unique personality" renders her stubbornly unable to challenge oppressive patriarchal norms and that Oshia and Adim exploit her willful ignorance to make "manipulative demands."[14] The novel, in these accounts, deploys Nnu Ego as a negative example whose life warns of the urgency of prioritizing traditional forms of women's solidarity and agency.[15]

Yet, I think, the novel parochializes those conceptions of the subject that would deem the characters irrational, passive, or uncritical by foregrounding the material circumstances that make their optimism in the face of ongoing self-denial so compelling. Oshia's anxiety to achieve the job security and income promised by a university degree is not, in the end, irrational. In post-World War II Lagos, Nnu Ego stands agog at the "new exorbitant rents" levied by landlords eager to take a cut of the "fatter pay packets" enjoyed by discharged soldiers (188). The influx of capital—which will be exponentially compounded by the development of the oil industry—means that individuals need more capital to sustain a standard of living. Chances of achieving this are greatly enhanced by a foreign degree and consequent access to government posts. Likewise, Nnu Ego's commitments are shaped by immediate need:

> She had never had the time. What with worrying over this child, this pregnancy, and the lack of money, coupled with the fact that she never had adequate outfits to wear to visit her friends, she had shied away from friendship, telling herself she did not need any friends, she had enough in family. But had she been right? (219).

Nnu Ego, in other words, did not have the resources—the time and the money—to pursue the desires that would have enhanced her long-term well-being. Oshia is eager to adapt to a changing world by taking up new opportunities that promise that he, a poor Igbo youth, might one day become a "great man" (193). Nnu Ego tries to live according to the values with which she was raised: "she had been brought up to believe that children made a woman" (219). Neither approach ensures hoped-for thriving. Given these double binds, the continuance of an optimistic orientation toward US education and postcolonial nationhood is not a simple matter of naivete or self-interest. To adapt Pheng Cheah's phrasing, "psychical coercion or ideological mystification" is beside the point.[16] The dream that Oshia's education in the US will benefit Nigerians and Nigeria is relentlessly aspirational: happiness is promised, but always deferred. Postcolonial optimism under US empire produces isolation rather than desired mutual support; yet, it remains sustaining because material circumstances delimit alternatives.

Emecheta illustrates how gendered Nigerian dreams of postcolonial nationhood are cruel because they are at once desired and oppressive. Optimism is cruel, argues Lauren Berlant, "when the object [or] scene that ignites a sense of possibility actually makes it impossible to attain the expansive transformation for which a person or a people risks striving."[17] The pursuit of the American dream of opportunity and economic and social mobility in the US, Berlant shows, is often cruelly optimistic in racialized ways.[18] Emecheta describes the particular cruelty of optimism in the postcolonial nation. Nigerian dreams are doubly cruel, Emecheta suggests, because they aspire not only to individual prosperity but also to postcolonial national thriving. They are especially cruel because they insist that individual achievement is not, and will never be, enough to ensure national greatness. In other words, it is not enough for Oshia to earn degrees (as a US citizen might be imagined to embody US exceptionalism by virtue of their educational success). He must also seek to impossibly deploy his education to secure the ever-deferred well-being of the polity that has been subjected to neocolonial rule. The 2007 recession led Berlant to assert that, in the US and Europe, "the promise of the good life no longer masks the living precarity of this historical present."[19] Thirty years earlier, Emecheta vividly displays the living precarity that is generated and reinforced by the pursuit of the good life promised by postcolonial nationhood under US empire. As Emecheta makes clear, precarity has characterized Nigerians' negotiation of fantasies of "the good life" before and since the nation's inception in the context of (neo) colonialism's historical disruptions.

The Joys of Motherhood, then, is not only a novel of postcolonial disillusionment but also a novel grappling with the endurance of postcolonial optimism that is especially cruel. It is here that thinking of the novel as being of the Second Republic becomes useful. Emecheta reports in her 1986 autobiography *Head Above Water* that *The Joys of Motherhood* was written in London over the last few weeks of 1976 and the entirety of January 1977.[20] The two biographical events that inspired the novel were both related to the cruel effects of educational aspiration. First, Emecheta's daughter Chiedu left home (then in London) after Emecheta, who had been struggling to afford tuition as she worked toward her own PhD in Sociology, refused to pay for Chiedu to attend a fee-paying school to complete her A-levels.[21] Emecheta explains that

The Joys of Motherhood was initially dedicated to Chiedu because her daughter's departure made her "accept my lot," which is to say, "the worst that could happen to me was to die by the wayside with everybody saying, 'To think she gave all her life for her children.'"[22] Second, at around the same time as Chiedu's departure, a man with whom Emecheta would continue to enjoy a "very, very long friendship" but whom she refused to marry announced that he "was packing in his job and leaving for America to do a PhD in Mineral Economics": "It looked as if he could stand my popularity, he could stand my writing, but the Igbo man still thinks that taking on a serious project like a PhD should be for men only."[23] The diagnosis resonates with the novel's depiction of gendered injustice regarding who is expected to seek an education and for what ends.

The fact that Emecheta's friend left to pursue doctoral work in the US also, however, importantly registers that by the late 1970s the US was enjoying something of a renewal in the Nigerian imaginary as a site for pursuing educational and investment goals closely bound to dreams of national becoming. The energy industry was a significant factor in this resurgence. Following the 1973 oil crisis, US reliance on Nigerian oil grew such that by 1977, the total trade between the US and Nigeria was over $7 billion, more than three times the trade total between the US and South Africa.[24] US domestic politics were another. Following Jimmy Carter's inauguration in January, 1977 marked a "new turn" in US–Nigerian relations, "giving Washington and Lagos an opportunity for a fresh start," in part because of Carter's willingness to identify full democracy as a desirable end in South Africa.[25] Renewed optimism in the US as an ally for democracy and development in the Nigerian postcolonial nation would find multiple forms of state-sponsored expression over the course of the next four years.

For example, the Second World Black and African Festival of Arts and Culture in Lagos and Kaduna, commonly known as FESTAC '77, Wendy Griswold suggests, was designed as a celebration of a "Nigeran dream" of a "fully developed and politically powerful black nation" that was "much like the American dream" of exceptional prosperity and global influence.[26] It was also, however, an event where the US diplomatically reasserted its imagined role as a facilitator of that dream. The event, held from 15 January through 12 February, was attended by civil rights leader Andrew Young, newly appointed to the position of the US ambassador to the United Nations by Carter. Oye Ogunbadejo summarized the effects of Young's diplomacy in a 1979 article for *The World Today*: "[He] tried to allay any suspicions that some African states might have harboured towards the US by visiting most of them . . . He emphasized that the motivating force in US policy was no longer a fear of Communism ... but concern for the welfare of the continent."[27] When Young returned to Lagos in August of 1977, he celebrated the global "idealism" that promoted "progressive democracies": "It is not naïve to believe in the future when one is also committed to work for the fulfillment of one's dreams."[28] His words were cited by Carter less than a year later during the president's visit to Nigeria in April 1978: "I also believe that progress can be made. As Andrew Young said here in Lagos last August, a belief in dreams for the future is not naive if we are ready to work to realize those dreams."[29] Throughout his visit, and at the same speech at the National Arts Theatre, Carter emphasized parallels in African-American and Nigerian struggles for full democracy, and he admired the "energy, the wisdom, the hard work, the sense of optimism" shared by Americans and Nigerians.[30] As in the mid-1960s, the history of pan-African association was self-consciously appropriated by the US administration in an attempt to further US interests.[31] At a speech at a White House reception for Black business executives, Carter celebrated his audience members for demonstrating that "there is an upward mobility possible if one has confidence in the American dream" and exhorted them to use that mobility to exert influence, especially in Africa, where "you're trusted just because you happen to be black."[32]

The diplomatic rhetoric that once again bound optimistic visions of Nigerian and American nationhood was reflected in a renewed Nigerian openness to US economic and political influence. Carter announced that the US would provide for "the need of Nigeria for technical assistance not only in petroleum, but in other aspects of economic development."[33] "Economic development" would be pursued by "several major companies— Ford, Mack Truck, Bechtel, and others—[that] are now coming into Nigeria to invest."[34] This rise in US investment corresponded with Nigerian state preparations to reinstate national democracy on October 1, 1979. Murtala Mohammed began the process of transitioning to civilian rule by appointing a Constitution Drafting Committee in October 1975; its report, delivered a year later, was then subject to three years of public debate as part of Nigeria's "constitutional rebirth" that was carried on by Olusegun Obasanjo after Mohammed's assassination in 1976.[35] In June 1977, the Federal Capital Authority awarded a US consortium a $2 million contract to design the master plan for Abuja, the new national capital.[36] The design of Abuja's National Mall would be inspired by that in Washington, D.C.[37] By 1979, the *Journal of African Law* professed that the 1979 constitution could "aptly be regarded as a version of 'the Washington model.'"[38] In 1980, US Vice President Walter Mondale hoped that the new Nigerian House of Assembly "would become 'a citadel of democracy' comparable to the US Congress," while several Nigerian leaders "insisted that it was in Nigeria that the American constitution was for the first time being introduced outside its frontiers."[39] That same year, bilateral agreements extended political and legal guarantees to American investors.[40] A 1978 article in *Foreign Policy* noted that the "substantial left-wing component of the country's well-educated elite" with "advanced degrees from American and British universities" warned "of the dangers of close ties with the United States," albeit "mostly in vain, for Nigeria's sudden prosperity seems to have turned the country toward, rather than away from, American examples."[41] The pointed reference to the sites of education highlights how these critics to some degree embodied the hopes they critiqued, insofar as they demonstrated how a commitment to Nigerian interests could not only survive but even be strengthened by access to US resources.

The postcolonial optimism probed in *The Joys of Motherhood* is productively read in relation to this international context of the novel's writing. Oshia, notably, is committed to "reading science" in the US (214). As Jason C. Parker argues, the first cohort of Nigerian and other African students on US campuses in the post-World War II era overwhelmingly aimed to learn technicalities of governance.[42] Oshia's research specialization is more evocative of the Carter administration's drive to promote "middle-level technical training in the United States" and to cultivate expertise in "economic development and petroleum" in the lead-up to the Second Republic.[43] "Universal primary education" and "technical assistance," Carter proposed, would be achieved by "tens of thousands of young Nigerians" following Azikiwe "to America."[44] Oshia suggests that going abroad to pursue his education is "just topping it up" (193), as one might fill up a gas tank, and the idiom glances at the increasing significance of the US oil market by the late 1970s as a source of Nigerian economic prosperity and vulnerability.[45] Despite past and foreseeable disappointment, postcolonial optimism persists, Emecheta's novel implies, because it is a means of surviving the circumscription of sovereignty produced by empire.

Pan-African Postoptimism

In Emecheta's novel, postcolonial optimism becomes so attenuated and strained as to become something that is and is not optimistic; it is a performance of optimism that is known to be untenable. When a lorry driver learns from Nnu Ego that she has a son in America and concludes that she "must be full of joy," and "very rich," Nnu Ego prefers to let the driver "live in his world of dreams rather than face reality" (223). This reality includes the fact that "the so-called son in America had never written to her directly, to say nothing of sending her money" (223). Nnu Ego continues to perform an optimistic world for herself and others by constantly celebrating her sons, even as "her sense started to give way" and "she became vague" (224). She finds herself feeling increasingly "adrift" (161). This sense of being adrift, or of becoming "vague," resonates with Berlant's identification of the experiences of "forced loss" and of "coasting through life" as versions of "postoptimistic response" to the sense of the present as "an impasse."[46] Experiencing the present as an impasse, as Berlant notes, can "be an aspiration" of its own in a world of cruel optimism, especially "as the traditional infrastructures for reproducing life—at work, in intimacy, politically—are crumbling at a threatening pace."[47] It is and is not a break with that world, as it marks an experience of the present as a "space of time lived without a genre," as a "holding station that doesn't hold securely but opens out into anxiety."[48]

Whether and how the novel resolves this impasse—where it takes us after Nnu Ego feels adrift—is a source of critical debate. After Nnu Ego's death, her children "were all sorry she had died before they were in a position to give their mother a good life" (224); residents of Ibuza, however, come to agree that Nnu Ego is a "wicked woman" because, thanks to sons who had given her a "decent burial," her spirit "had it all, yet still did not answer prayers for children" (224). For Robolin, drawing on Gayatri Spivak, there is evidence of resistance in Nnu Ego's "withholding" spirit—in death, she frustrates the patriarchal expectations and desires she shared with others in life.[49] Following this reading, the impasse of Nnu Ego's life gives way to a critical break in her death. Attenuated optimism finally yields to disillusionment with an unjust system; Nnu Ego is wiser in death than in life. A sense of impasse, in other words, is converted into the kind of postoptimism described by Kwame Anthony Appiah as being bound to the postcolonial and equivalent to critique: "postcoloniality has become, I think, a condition of pessimism . . . a kind of postoptimism."[50] Reading Yambo Ouologuem's 1968 *Le Devoir de violence*, Appiah identifies as exemplary the postcolonial novelist's rejection of aspirations that are not grounded in the reality of past and present suffering: "it is true, the soul desires to dream the echo of happiness, an echo that has no past," Ouologuem writes, but the living pasts of colonial exploitation and enslavement cannot be ignored, as they are "forever reborn to history beneath the hot ashes of more than thirty African republics."[51] Against optimistic nationalism and hopeful orientations toward the US stand ongoing histories of dispossession and millions of people for whom "one republic is as good (which is to say as bad) as any other."[52] Against the maintenance of a cruelly optimistic attachment to a future good life Nnu Ego's spirit in this reading places imagined futures in crisis; she disrupts a temporal habit oriented toward a desirable future that obscures present and unequal suffering. Pheng Cheah's insight that postcolonial novels of disillusionment are yet Bildung of the nation applies here; implicitly, critiques of the postcolonial nation "still endorse the idea that a radical national culture of the people contains the seeds for the reappropriation and transformation of the neocolonial state."[53]

A reading of the novel that celebrates Nnu Ego's disillusioned spirit, however, like a reading that critiques her life of dreams, underplays Emecheta's attention to the resilience of postcolonial optimism as it is maintained under conditions of empire. As Robolin notes, his reading of Nnu Ego's postmortem resistance to normative expectations is "bleak indeed" and "leaves little hope or inspiration for the living."[54] All the more so, given that Nnu Ego's community quickly co-opts her death into a narrative that positions her in opposition to the living as an active, spiteful, even vengeful force. The narrative that allows readers to find in Nnu Ego's death acts of refusal and critique also sets the stage for the community's disillusionment with Nnu Ego as a "good" spirit. Nnu Ego's community, that is, is by no means swayed by her life's story of considerable suffering to question present conditions or attachments more than they already chronically have by virtue of their lived experiences of ongoing dispossession. Instead, the community celebrates the fact that Oshia was able to increase his debts to provide his mother with a relatively lavish funeral. *The Joys of Motherhood* does not anticipate a generalized disillusionment with the postcolonial nation and the educational and financial institutions that maintain it. Emecheta's novel denies its reader any salvific pessimism. As the reader reckons with the persistence of optimism oriented to Oshia's future in the US in the face of suffering and death, the affective contours of institutionalized US imperial power on the present and future of the Nigerian nation are thrown into sharp relief.

Rather than resolve the impasse produced by postcolonial optimism by converting it into pessimism, in other words, Emecheta's novel arguably invites readers to dwell with postoptimistic feelings such that the "post" acknowledges optimism's continuance rather than its overcoming. The narrative that attaches the reader to Nnu Ego beyond her death, I think, enables an understanding of Emecheta's work whereby Nnu Ego's postmortem unresponsiveness to prayer—her "impassivity," to invoke Berlant's play on the impasse[55]—does not necessarily signify oppositional refusal. By not responding to prayers, Nnu Ego, perhaps, is coasting through death as she came to coast through life: not doing and not knowing what to do toward securing a desired future for the living that continues to be unattainable, no matter how many children there are or are not and no matter what those children do or do not do. Berlant argues that "the present as impasse opens up different ways that the interruption of norms of the reproduction of life can be adapted to, felt out, and lived."[56] Nnu Ego's unresponsiveness to the prayers of the living potentially signals such difference.

Nnu Ego's own understanding of what her physical death might bring intimates how the novel opens up ways of living through its representation of impasse even in death. When Nnu Ego feels "adrift," she feels as though her life "were on an open sea" (161). The connection to the sea is a connection to a vision of death that exceeds the predominant narratives of duty and revenge that attempt to capture women's spirits. This alternate vision of death is described as she contemplates, in the novel's first chapter, what drowning may mean. For a significant moment, her relationship with her *chi*, "her personal god," exceeds narratives of supplication and blame that otherwise attach to women's spirits: "now she was going to her, to the unforgiving slave princess from a foreign land, to talk it all over with her, not on this earth but in the land of the dead, there deep beneath the waters of the sea" (9). In this image of submergence and conversation, aspirations of the living are left behind in favor of the expressed desire to speak with the living-dead. The oceanic land of the dead ties Nnu Ego's afterlife to the afterlife of the catastrophe of the transatlantic enslavement of Africans. This tie is redoubled, as we learn that Nnu Ego's *chi* "had been dedicated to the river goddess before Agbadi took her away in slavery" (31). The allusion is to Mami Wata, "a general name used for the hybridized river and sea goddesses popularized across Africa and the African diaspora in the nineteenth century."[57] By critical consensus a nineteenth-century invention, Mami Wata also signifies a precolonial pantheon of water goddesses known in Igbo as *Nne Mmiri*.[58] Madhu Krishnan notes that critical readings of *The Joys of Motherhood* have tended to neglect "the trope of the water goddess and precolonial feminine agency," yet "traces of the divine feminine and feminine agency remain," including in "the importance of Nnu Ego's *chi*, or destiny-bestowing personal deity, a riverine following of the water goddess."[59] While Krishnan compellingly reads how the divine feminine is erased and occluded in Emecheta's novel, she also opens a space for attending to Mami Wata's often submerged presence. Insofar as the novel's ending leads back to its beginning via the afterlives of Nnu Ego and her *chi*, Mami Wata becomes a framing presence who reminds readers how lands, including those currently known as Nigeria and the United States, are bound by the call to listen to and be with those who have suffered enslavement and colonialism, and by a divine feminine that is indifferent to the aspirations of, say, patriarchal nationalism. In place of Nigerian and American dreams, the novel proffers a vision of pan-African feminine spiritual communion.

The way postoptimistic experiences of impasse may engulf national dreams recurs in another novel of the Second Republic written some twenty years after its end, Chris Abani's 2004 *GraceLand*. While this fiction, as the next chapter addresses, is often read in relation to the Third Republic of 1993, its action spans the 1970s and early 1980s, as its protagonist, the young Elvis Oke, seeks to establish a career as a dancer while navigating poverty, violence, and revolutionary movements. The prominence of national dreams in the text is foreshadowed from the first time we read the protagonist's name. As Elvis Oke paints his face white and performs Elvis Presley, who himself famously performed in the style and sound of Black artists such as Otis Blackwell and Ike Turner in a career that saw the proverbial movement from rags to riches, the novel points toward the entwinement of Nigerian and US aspirational histories. The US is an object of intense hope in relation to which the future of Nigeria and Nigerians is consistently measured. This hope persists despite the well-known critiques issued by the King of the Beggars, who speaks of "the evils of capitalism that the United States of America practiced" (155). Elvis's friend Redemption, for example, continues to see the US as the promised land: "I can go to United States, act inside film and make millions" (54).

As in Emecheta's novel, however, postcolonial optimism under US empire produces an impasse. After Elvis's ambitions to be a dancer in Nigeria collapse, along with the Republic, the protagonist, having suffered torture and dispossession at the hands of state agents, must decide whether to board a flight to Las Vegas. In the novel's final pages, Elvis's friend Okun urges him to take the over-determinedly-named Redemption's offer of a "dream" in the form of a passport: "It is America, Elvis! Take it. You know how many people are planning for dis and can't get it?" (317–18). Although Elvis accepts the gift, he resists this progressive logic: "But this country is just as good as America" (318). Elvis's concern is less with what opportunities will be available to him in the US—a university education is not even imaginable in this instance—and more with how the present crisis has rendered emigration a rational choice: "'When did we start thinking of America as a life plan?' Elvis asked. 'When things spoil here. Don't blame me. I no spoil am,' Okon said" (318). US empire is here explicitly positioned as symptomatic of the "spoil" of Nigeria, a spoilage that Elvis has witnessed through his work for Redemption: profitable trades in cocaine, human parts, and children are sustained by the US market. US wealth structures the Nigerian economy such that economic, and subsequently political, power accrue to those who accede to American market demands and the risks and violence that fulfilling such demands requires, from ingesting drugs for international transport to kidnapping children.[60] Emigration to the US is, to Elvis, a continuation of rather than a solution to the "spoil" of Nigeria. As such, it becomes not only an object of optimism (a "life plan") and therefore of potential disillusionment ("the evils of capitalism") but a shorthand for a postoptimistic trajectory, for a continuation of life in the impasse. As Matthew Omelsky argued, the "ambivalent portrayal of Elvis's departure gives the impression that his 'empowering escape' will be just as contingent as any attempt at agency in Nigeria."[61]

Whether and how the novel resolves this impasse is again a critical question. As he waits for his flight, Elvis reads the title story in a newly-purchased paperback, James Baldwin's 1965 short story collection *Going to Meet the Man*: "As he read, Elvis began to see a lot of parallels between himself and the description of a dying black man slowly being engulfed by flame" (319). Baldwin's description of torture in the mid-twentieth-century American South resonates with Elvis's experience in Nigeria in the 1980s. It also, however, suggests that while the Nigerian state has persecuted Elvis for his association with the art and politics of the King of the Beggars, the US state has always already incorporated him into its body politic as a Black man, and thereby rendered him particularly marked for persecution and incarceration. As Yogita Goyal notes, "immigration and cultural transnationalism are not presented as alternatives to the violence of the postcolony under military rule. Domestic and global economic systems are thoroughly interpenetrated, and both rely on keeping vulnerable people like Elvis marginalized."[62] Fire, not water, dominates the novel's end, and engulfment by flame joins drowning by water as the elemental means by which the living history of transatlantic enslavement and colonialism surfaces:

> He closed the book and imagined what kind of scar that would leave. It would be a thing alive that reached up to the sky in supplication, descending to root itself in the lowest chakra, our basest nature. Until the dead man became the sky, the tree, the earth and the full immeasurable sorrow of it all. (320)

Reading this story, uncertainty is suspended, and Elvis finds something of himself: "He was that scar . . . He and everyone like him, until the earth was aflame with scarred black men dying in trees of fire" (320). Dreams of individual and national aspiration are rendered nonsensical here. Elvis dreams, instead, "nearly every night" of the ghost of his father, who will soon be an ocean away, "wandering aimlessly, searching for his house" (321). James Baldwin, upon meeting Chinua Achebe, reported that, in Achebe's words, "he recognized everybody" in *Things Fall Apart*, though it was "about people and customs of which he knew nothing."[63] In Achebe's report of Baldwin's words: "That man, Okonkwo, is my father. How he got over, I don't know, but he did."[64] Baldwin, a key figure for Achebe and Abani alike, offers the former inspiration for developing a form of anglophone literary expression appropriate to African experience (chapter 1). In *GraceLand*, Baldwin generates pan-African diasporic identifications and conversations that are more scorching and overwhelming in their invocation of ongoing histories of enslavement and colonization.

Like *The Joys of Motherhood*, Abani's fiction articulates a pan-African postoptimistic experience. It undoes fantasies of nationalism that imagine the US and Nigeria as discrete entities, or their literatures as unconnected, and calls into question the possibility of enacting decolonization at the scale of the nation. Jared Sexton argued in "The Social Life of Social Death" (2011), which staged a significant synthesis of discourses of Afropessimism and Black optimism, that the unflinching Afropessimist acknowledgment of a political ontology that defines blackness in opposition to the human does not so much re-inscribe blackness-as-pathology as it pathologizes the world that is structured by this ontology.[65] Nigerian literature of postcolonial optimism by Emecheta and Abani converges with a Black American literary tradition that attends to the impasses produced by US imperialism and the postcolonial optimism that sustains it. In so doing, this literature contributes to a different kind of Nigerian dream that is perhaps not so cruel: a dream of pan-African conversation across US empire. This is a dream that hinges not on what the US state purports to give—be it a university education or a political model—to an "underdeveloped" country and its citizens, but on Afrodiasporic histories and the futures inherited from them.

By invoking the ambivalent, postoptimistic registers of Nigerian dreams, *The Joys of Motherhood* and *GraceLand* interpret conditions of their own circulation shaped by US audiences and institutions, including US universities. As Emecheta's US publishers noted, "'Your books don't go so fast in the book stores but they go like mad in schools.'"[66] *The Joys of Motherhood* is published just as Emecheta embarks, in the late 1970s and early 1980s, on a tour of predominately white American universities (including Pennsylvania State, Rutgers, UCLA, and Yale) as a visiting professor and lecturer, returning to Nigeria in 1980 as Senior Research Fellow and Visiting Professor of English at the University of Calabar.[67] Her American publisher, as usual, had proved to be more efficient than the British Allison and Busby, despite a "slight argument over the title" on the grounds that "the word 'joy' is overused in the States."[68] Abani published *GraceLand* more than a decade after fleeing Nigeria in 1990, where he had been arrested and imprisoned following the performance of his play *Song of a Broken Flute*. After leaving the UK for the US in 1999, he earned graduate degrees from the University of Southern California before taking up academic posts at Antioch University, the University of California, Riverside, and Northwestern University. *GraceLand* was published by Farrar, Straus and Girroux out of New York. Read in relation to the authors' fictions of being adrift, these instances of voluntary visitation and forced exile and settlement seem, on the one hand, to be shrouded in knowing dismay that America has become a "life plan," as well as recognition that this plan is nonetheless imbricated in a national Nigerian history of optimistic orientation toward the US. On the other hand, they also emerge as opportunities for forging solidarities that, however oriented toward the US, are grounded in a postoptimism that is knowingly shared with African-American writers. In a 1992 interview, Emecheta asserted that she felt "more kinship with . . . black American women writers than with . . . Nigerians": "To me, the great writers who come from ethnic minorities writing in English come from America. I think the deep, the real deep thinkers now writing in the English language are the black women, such as Toni Morrison, Gloria Naylor, Alice Walker, etc."[69] Chris Abani is on record that "James has been my muse for a long time. In my study I have pictures of James Baldwin everywhere. I don't work without a picture of Baldwin around me. I never met him before he passed, but I used to collect stories from people about him."[70] As Tsitsi Jaji has shown, the pan-African solidarities fostered and expressed through "creative collaborations rather than diplomatic bodies" are remarkably potent and "durable";[71] they offer "a renewable energy waiting to be tapped."[72] Such collaboration might be identified in reading practices that inform writing practices, such that it makes sense to read Emecheta alongside Morrison and Abani alongside Baldwin as authors of a postoptimistic pan-Africanism. A move to the US can be a sojourn or flight to the center of capitalist power: it may also be a journey to a place where Black women and queer Black men also listen to the living dead to write in codes before, beyond, and apart from the nation-state and empire in which they live. That said, the diminishment of political Pan-Africanism and the entrenchment of neoliberalism is contemporary with literature of the Second Republic. This context gives pause as to the broader efficacy of a Black creative international. The risk that I have read pan-African postoptimism too optimistically is taken up in the next chapter.

Chapter 3

The Pursuit of Happiness After the Third Republic

Chris Abani's *GraceLand*, chapter 2 argues, is a postoptimistic novel of the Second Republic.[1] The 2004 fiction may also be read, however, in relation to the Third Republic. While the novel's setting is the late 1970s, its consideration of the US as a potential "location of exilic recuperation" is part of a broader trend in Nigerian anglophone fiction of the early 2000s that responded to events of the mid-1990s, as Adéléké Adéèkó has shown in one of the most substantial scholarly interventions to date on Nigerian literature and the US.[2] In his 2008 essay "Power Shift: America in the New Nigerian Imagination," Adéèkó engaged Abani's novel, alongside Helon Habila's *Waiting for an Angel* (2002) and Chimamanda Adichie's *Purple Hibiscus* (2003), to argue that in these new millennium fictions, the US represents the kind of "mature nationhood" that protagonists desire for Nigeria.[3] Adéèkó demonstrated that this notable literary turn to the US emerged from the late twentieth-century "crises of terminal proportions" that continually frustrated attempts to foster "national cohesion."[4] Because efforts in the 1970s to create "a trans-Nigeria affective community were driven by oil revenues," they were rendered more or less moot following the sharp decline of oil prices in the mid-1980s; they were further weakened by the privatization and austerity measures required by the World Bank and IMF and implemented by Ibrahim Babangida's structural adjustment policies in the 1990s.[5] The long-planned Third Republic collapsed when Babangida annulled the 1993 elections; that same year, the interim government of Ernest Shonekan was overthrown in a military coup led by Sani Abacha.[6] Anglophone Nigerian literature of the new millenium, Adéèkó contended, maintains the desire for democracy as a national affective cause, despite its deferred implementation: the Nigerian nation is never repudiated because it has never been experienced.[7] The US represents the "stable nation state" that remains desired by Nigerians because it has never been realized for Nigerians.[8]

By framing the proliferation of the US in Nigerian fiction as a twenty-first-century development, Adéèkó provided a compelling account of how national literature shaped by the political turmoil and economic reforms of the 1980s and 1990s redefines the Nigerian nation and affirms the ongoing affective power of national imaginaries. In this chapter, however, I am interested in situating fiction of the Third Republic and beyond as part of a longer Nigerian literary engagement with postcolonial optimism and US empire. I have argued that Nigerian literature of postcolonial optimism of the First and Second Republics stages how dreams of Black sovereignty might be stolen from conditions of US imperial hegemony. Approaching twenty-first-century Nigerian fiction with this longer literary history in mind highlights that the US is not only, per Adéèkó, a refuge and model in the contemporary anglophone Nigerian literary imagination; it also continues to be both a center of imperial control that affects embodied orientations to futurity and a site of potential pan-African negotiation and struggle.

Accordingly, this chapter takes up two novels of the Third Republic that scrutinize the resilience of postcolonial optimism under US empire, especially as it finds expression on university campuses. The first novel, Ike Oguine's *A Squatter's Tale* (2000), is understudied in the US academy but especially suited for my project insofar as it explicitly links the Nigerian turn to the US in the 1990s to the experiences and aspirations of an earlier generation in the 1970s.[9] In so doing, the novel details how the US is decidedly not a place of refuge for its protagonist, Obi. In the fictions Adéèkó considered, he found a recurrent idealization of the US as a place of relative meritocratic promise that offers "recognition of the individual within the nation state" and that guarantees relative "autonomy for the individual."[10] While there are instances of such idealization in Oguine's novel, the US overall encapsulates a different affective contour than the hopeful desire described by Adéèkó. For Obi, the American dream and the Nigerian dream are both self-evidently fictions, and as such they repeatedly produce impasse and despair. Yet these stories of national exceptionalism are nonetheless intensively rehearsed. Experiences of impasse, in other words, do not produce postoptimistic vagueness or coasting—as in literature of the Second Republic—but the determined performance of optimism focused, in Oguine's novel, on the acquisition of an MBA and an entrepreneurial career. The performance of this self-sustaining illusion engenders a kind of madness that exposes its unsustainability and generates exhaustion. As postoptimistic optimism manifests the intense individualization of aspiration that defines national cultures after privatization and austerity, pan-African dreams dissipate.

My second novel of focus, Chimamanda Ngozi Adichie's 2013 *Americanah*, is quite different from Oguine's in its blockbuster status.[11] Whereas

A Squatter's Tale is "criminally overlooked," *Americanah* has received substantial attention from reviewers and academics alike.[12] It is possible that Oguine's novel was simply ahead of its time. As Christopher N. Okonkwo suggests, the novel can be understood as a "cohort-inaugurating work" that "anticipates the black-Atlantic scope" of novels, including *Americanah*, that comprised the African literary renaissance that peaked in the 2010s.[13] I build on the critical insight that Oguine's work anticipates Adichie by attending to the affective workings of nation and empire after the Third Republic in both fictions. Like *A Squatter's Tale*, I argue, *Americanah* represents the performance of an exhausting and exhausted postoptimistic optimism centered on the US university as an institution whose power might be harnessed for the pursuit of postcolonial national becoming. This relentless optimism is the foil against which the novel searches for an alternative structure of national feeling. As the novel's protagonist, Ifemelu, returns to Nigeria after pursuing education in the US, optimism is provisionally redirected toward an embrace of life in the postcolonial nation as enduringly precarious. *Americanah* suggests Nigerians' ongoing experience of instability and uncertainty in national life may itself paradoxically define the mutual self-recognition of Nigerian nationhood, as well as provide the basis for renewed albeit attenuated pan-African solidarity. This embrace of precarity, however, risks the reinscription of individualized entrepreneurialism and the reconstitution, yet again, of Nigerian postcolonial optimism under conditions of empire.

Unhappiness Does Not Exist in the Greatest Country in the World!

A Squatter's Tale begins with its narrator, Obi, describing his first encounter with stories of "America's dazzle" (5): "The most memorable event of the tenth year of my life," reads the novel's first sentence, "was the arrival of my Uncle Happiness at our house in Yaba, Lagos, Nigeria on a visit from America" (1). The year is 1976, and Uncle Happiness, of the overdetermined name, is making his first visit home. As the previous chapter outlined, 1976 was something of a watershed year for US–Nigeria relations. The growth of US–Nigeria trade during the mid-1970s, driven by oil, culminated in a period of renewed diplomatic friendliness following the election of US president Jimmy Carter in 1976. US influence shaped the process of constitutional reform leading up to the inauguration of the Second Republic in 1979. In Yaba in 1976, Obi's uncle is a herald of all the wonders that "a land blessed by God" might offer (6). Sporting "the widest smile on earth" and a "dark brown cowboy outfit, straight from Hollywood, which included a ten-gallon hat and spurs" (1), Uncle Happiness provides evidence for his wondrous stories with gifts of "fabulous riches you hear about in folk-tales," including a matching cowboy outfit for Obi. Those who would potentially be skeptical of Uncle Happiness's claims as to "America's enormous wealth and its miraculous scientific achievements" (6), such as Obi's father, are silenced by a "radio that was also a cassette player and also a calculator" (7). The only person to draw attention to the possibility that suffering and unemployment may exist in the US, the landlord Adeyemo, has not received any such presents (7). Consumer goods compel professions of belief—or at least quell expressions of disbelief—in Uncle Happiness's "fantastic" stories of great riches and endless opportunity (7).

That these stories are in fact as "fantastic" as the myth of the American cowboy, however, is widely recognized, if not explicitly acknowledged. Uncle Happiness's sustained performance of his own happiness is self-consciously a performance, both to himself and others. He is "larger than life" in his celebration of life, which includes pirouettes and "wild" dancing to his favorite highlife songs (2). Obi retells his uncle's stories to his friends at school with similar flare: "since I was already a habitual liar in my own right, I added spices of my own here and there" (8). "America" is here self-evidently a fiction whose reality is maintained only through persistent retelling. The operative affect here is an optimism that is known to be illusory and valued as illusory.

Obi encounters this performative optimism in other members of the new African diaspora, after he follows his uncle to the US. While working as a security guard in California, for example, he is regaled by the stories of imminent business success and constant sex relayed by his Kenyan coworker Maina, who "told of his alleged escapades with crazy happiness. He seemed intoxicated by his own tales, dependent on them, like an alcoholic" (54). Both teller and listener are very much aware that Maina's vision of success is not, in fact, "just a whisker away" (54), but this does not lessen their satisfaction in the stories. This is an approach to the US resonant with one described by Jean Baudrillard in his 1981 travelogue *America*: "What you have to do is enter the fiction of America, enter America as fiction."[14] Once you have done so, "utopia has already been achieved," so "unhappiness does not exist."[15] It is "on this fictive basis," Baudrillard proposes, that the US "dominates the world."[16] This is the useful fiction, in other words, arguably at its peak moment of global dissemination in the 1990s, that US-style democracy and capitalism assure happiness, stability, and opportunity.

In Oguine's novel, however, entering and sustaining this fiction of the US is hard work, and the performance of optimism at times gives way to a disavowed despair. When Obi joins his uncle in Oakland, eighteen years after wearing matching cowboy outfits in Lagos, he finds him living in a "house that smelt of stale sweat and hopelessness" (16). Maina on occasion reveals his "other side," a fierce mood during which "his bitterness was directed against all forms of ambitions, all variants of the American dream" (57). In this mood, he issues dire warnings to Obi:

> I would find out later, I would suffer, all my dreams would be in vain, it was a trick, I aspired to be only a slave, I was doomed, we were all doomed, all those running after MBAs and the American dollar. Out of him poured fumes, warning of disaster. (57)

Readers of *A Squatter's Tale* have focused on Oguine's representation of the precarity of immigrant life, as it is here condemned by Maina, to highlight the novel's commitment to dreaming of a better Nigerian nation. Kwadwo Osei-Nyame, in an argument that anticipates Adéèkó's, contends that "despite being set largely in the USA," the novel "is still very much structured as an allegorical narrative of the nation": it "insistently figures the failure of Nigeria to provide a sense of stability as *the reason* for the immigrant's absence from home."[17] While "Nigeria is negated, it is also being affirmed as a possibility . . . as a non-existent but possible reality."[18] As Louisa Uchum Egbunike argues by reading Oguine's work as part of a Nigerian tradition of "been-to" novels, when stability proves elusive in the US, it "dispels the myth of America" and breaks "the binary which elevates America above Nigeria," thus extending the possibility of a permanent return to Nigeria.[19] In these readings, the possibility of renewing hopes for a more stable Nigerian nation (and, implicitly, a more equitable US one) hinges on the sense that both Nigeria and America are, specifically for young Black men, nations of postoptimistic impasse.

Yet, what strikes me about Oguine's fiction is how moments of attenuated optimism are repeatedly dissipated by redoubled performances of postoptimistic optimism. That is, what binds the US and Nigeria in the imaginary of the text isn't just that real stability and prosperity have yet to be achieved in either country. It is also that a significant part of national life involves affirming that stability and prosperity have already been achieved. Carrie Tirado Bramen observes in her cultural history of "American niceness" that the "nation-state as a collective construct requires an affective, interpersonal component of everyday life . . . national abstractions find quotidian forms through patterns of sociality."[20] *A Squatter's Tale* explores how US and Nigerian fantasies of national exceptionalism are maintained through quotidian, even clichéd, assertions of ongoing optimism.

For, although Uncle Happiness's desire to sustain an illusion of prosperity is closely associated with the US, it is also integral to the novel's depiction of Nigeria. Before leaving for California in 1994, Obi is living in Lagos "twenty-five, happy at work, ambitious and hopeful" (70). In 1991, he accepts a position at one of the "new chic banks and finance companies, which were blossoming like water hyacinths all over Lagos as a result of our latest military government's pseudo-free-market economic policies" (67). The passage alludes to the implementation of structural adjustment policies by Ibrahim Badamasi Babangida (IBB), beginning in 1986. As Andrew Apter detailed in *The Pan-African Nation* (2005), the privatization and deregulation of the oil industry, especially, entailed "diverting revenues into private accounts" and "auctioning block allocations to private concessions that in many cases simply lifted and hawked the oil." This led to both the collapse of the public sector and the nurturing of a national culture in which "illusion became the very basis of survival."[21] As the senior treasury officer at Baobab Trust Finance House (BTF), Obi apparently thrives:

> The gentle patter of brand new computer keyboards, the serious-faced, serious-dressing, fast-talking, fast-walking young men and women sweeping in and out of offices like strong winds, filled me with energy. Fashionable words and phrases—'strategizing, 'intermediation,' 'critical success factors (csfs),' 'key performance indicators (kpis)' leapt out of our mouths at the slightest provocation and sometimes without any provocation at all. (70)

Deploying such language, borrowed "from *The Economist* and CNN and from my own imagination" (73), Obi puts on "a virtuoso performance" and sells potential investors on "the image of a dynamic investment octopus with arms in all the major financial centers of the globe" (74). By 1992, his designer clothes and European vacations belie the fact that "there was recession in Nigeria" (88). Early in 1993, Obi himself can no longer ignore the truth he has always talked over: investors' money is not in London and New York but "right there in Lagos, in places with disheartening names like Kilimanjaro Finance" (89). The stories he can tell subsequently change, and "fearsome rumours about the state of BTF's finances" mean there's "virtually nothing to do at work"; Obi, however, decides it is "better not to know, to continue to hope" (91). He leaves for the US, of which "horror stories abounded" (117), only when it is impossible to continue the performance that it will be possible to "resume my interrupted life of upward mobility" in Lagos (107).

Obi chooses to move to California, that is, in the belief that at least it will be possible to resume the performance of upward mobility, no matter the real obstacles to mobility itself: "I'd chosen Oakland because everyone I'd spoken to . . . said California was wonderful for a new immigrant even with Governor Pete Wilson and the imminence of Proposition 187. It had excellent weather and a huge economy that offered many opportunities" (16). The initiative to prohibit "illegal immigrants" from using public services can be glossed over—like the immiseration of Oakland itself—because California is still a place of storied opportunity. Insofar as the illusions of financialized capitalism hold the potential to be maintained and rehearsed anew, the move from Lagos to Oakland is not a break so much as a continuation.

The US and Nigeria, in sum, are bound by the demand that individual class mobility be maintained as the object of relentless optimism. Such autonomy and optimism, Imre Szeman has shown, can be understood as the dominant affect of the entrepreneur, a label that properly describes many of the characters in Oguine's novel, including Obi, and which, per Szeman, became central to visions of citizenship beginning in the mid-1990s, both in the US and across the globe.[22] As the "neoliberal subject *par excellence*,"[23] Szeman contends, the entrepreneurial subject makes "minimal demands on the state while also working tirelessly to ferret out new possibilities within a system whose logics have brought it treacherously close to collapse."[24] For the entrepreneur, "the utopian situation . . . remains always *the present*."[25] Szeman argues, in a formulation that explicitly diverges from Lauren Berlant's description of cruel optimism (see chapter 2):

> The affect attendant to entrepreneurialism is not one that dissipates the energies for change through a faux reconciliation with the present, as mediated by optimistic fantasies of the future. Rather, it affirms the desirability of the present circumstances that enable entrepreneurialism and equates subjects' systems of attachment with an ideal system of belonging and behaving such that, even as entrepreneurs insist on the significance of their contributions in shaping the future, they occupy an ahistorical social landscape in which time stands still.[26]

Oguine's novel highlights how the affirmation of the desirability of the present—of its nascent possibilities for individual upward mobility—is both ideological *and* a crucial part of the entrepreneur's labor. The ability to tell a convincing story about the present and the profits it makes possible is a precondition for securing the social and monetary investments that make profit-making imaginable. Hence, Obi's friend Ezundu introduces Obi to a white Republican politician as "an economic analyst for many Nigerian companies doing business in the States" and as "one of the leaders of the youth movement" of a non-existent "organization of African immigrants resident in California" (133). This story reprises Obi's grand tales of BTF finance's global reach, told while wearing excellently tailored suits.

In *A Squatter's Tale*, an American dream of abundant opportunity emulates a Nigerian dream. Extended back across the Atlantic, Obi's renewed dreams for Nigeria redouble this mirroring. In the end, his ideal Nigerian nation is much like that of his friend who lives in luxury in California but deplores working in a place where she is treated as an outsider: "Ego wanted the nice things but not the stress of transplantation; a perfect world would be one in which she and her husband moved back to Lagos and Nordstrom and Macy's moved with them" (125). Here is a dream of the nation in which stability is measured by the maintenance of the fiction that capital investment and the consumerist culture it promotes are not a volatile business. It is, what is more, a dream that takes US consumer culture to be a sign and promise of stability. Like the gifts from Uncle Happiness's suitcase, this dream of Nigeria narrates the apparent wealth of a few as affirmation of utopia for all. Oguine the author is perhaps especially aware of the irony of associating Nigerian national success with the selective wealth generated by US investment: prior to his appointment at the Nigerian National Petroleum Corporation in 2014, Oguine worked for over twenty years as in-house counsel with the US-based Chevron Corporation, rising in 2008 to General Counsel for Chevron's Nigeria and Mid-Africa Business Unit.[27] Oguine's satirical object is less a discrete myth about US superiority than an international myth that equates national well-being with the perceived surety of (particularly US, but sometimes Nigerian) investments.

Insofar as such surety is produced by the ability to tell a convincing yarn about the wealth of opportunities in the present ("key performance indicators"!), it is notable that Oguine's critique of circumscribed but optimistic national futures foregrounds the MBA. Previous chapters have explored how optimistic orientations to the US campus recur in Nigerian literature of postcolonial optimism and metonymically register hopes for Black sovereignty under conditions of US empire. Unlike the cautiously optimistic or cruelly optimistic attachments to US universities evident in literature of the First and Second Republics, however, the affinity for a US degree in Oguine's novel is not about acquiring knowledge or skills that promise to abet a better national future. Rather, the US MBA is desired because it ostensibly ensures the individual's capacities to enter more securely into the fiction that they already live in a national utopia. After Obi loses his job at BTF, he encounters a job market that sees six hundred people taking an aptitude test as the first stage of an application process for two entry-level positions in a bank (108). He finally secures only one opportunity: "A friend who worked for an American-owned management consulting firm said his firm couldn't hire me because I had a second class lower degree and the minimum they took was a second class upper, but that if I went to the University of Lagos and got an MBA, he would get me into the firm" (108). The job is so low paying, however, that Obi foregoes this chance. He does not regret his decision, noting morosely that the salary he was offered in 1993 would have been "less than two hundred dollars at the time, less than ninety as I write [in 1995]" (108). The decision speaks to the devaluation of Nigerian degrees as structural adjustment brought further disinvestment in Nigeria's universities and fewer job opportunities in the public sector,[28] as well as the radical devaluation of currency that began with the introduction of the Special Foreign Exchange Market (SFEM) in 1987, which pinned the naira to the world market in a two-tier system of exchange rates.[29] Through the 1980s and 1990s, "many Nigerian students who could afford to do so studied at foreign universities."[30] In the US, it was still possible to imagine the MBA as a ticket to utopia in a way that was no longer feasible in Nigeria following the collapse of the financial market. Hence, for Obi, a US degree becomes central to his "own modest American dream (save some money, do a good MBA and then a nice job in a good corporation)" (27). The endeavor will distinguish him from Uncle Happiness, who suspects he has "suffered in America because I did not go to school for long" (24). The US university is thus a locus sustaining hopes in nations where optimism is a necessary fiction.

In this iteration of entwining the US university and Nigerian nationhood, the representation of the US campus seems far removed from the pan-African hopes and dreams, or even the nation-building expertise, I have discussed in relation to earlier Nigerian fiction of postcolonial optimism (see chapters 1 and 2).[31] Instead, as J. Lorand Matory describes universities in *Stigma and Culture* (2015), they are places where "students of the late twentieth and early twenty-first centuries are driven to pursue upward mobility or to rescue themselves from downward mobility."[32] The US university campus in this era is a "world of the stigmatized," where the "hidden curriculum of the university can be understood as guidance in the flight from social stigma."[33] As a hidden curriculum that prioritizes individual achievement over anti-imperial solidarity, this flight, in turn, can involve stereotyping others "as unworthy relative to the standards of the dominant society."[34] The process of "ethnological shadenfreude," as Matory labels it, is such that as "people feel vulnerable to stereotyping, there is a strong impulse for the stigmatized to deflect those stereotypes onto a group that can be constructed as lower."[35] This hierarchizing dynamic characterizes how Nigerian friends and relatives repeatedly instruct Obi to negotiate potential relationships with African Americans, leading him to reflect:

> The African immigrant sometimes exhibits as much bitterness towards his African-American cousins as the worst white racist. Confronted with scenes like those we saw during that drive through West Oakland and the terrible images of inner-city violence and despair on TV, the success-obsessed immigrant wants to get as far away as possible, psychically if not physically, from that horrible pit. He violently rejects any identification with what strikes him as irreversible disaster. (30)

The logic of "At least I am not—", as Christina Sharpe has shown, may be a way to survive conditions of unfreedom, perhaps especially when one's perceived relative freedom to others is felt to be precarious. Stories of nominative freedom are also, Sharpe demonstrated, how scenes of subjection are repeatedly rewritten and transmitted as stories of freedom that extend redemption to the oppressor.[36] For Obi, laying claim to entrepreneurial acumen, as ideally verified by educational credentialing, promises to shore up the proximity to whiteness that has proven integral to entering the fiction of national utopias; a university education, and specifically the MBA, becomes the groundwork for a persuasive performance of relentless optimism that promotes the "ethnicity narrative" of the recent African immigrant as a good investment and investor.[37] The possibility of a valuable university degree is what allows Obi and other Nigerian immigrants to reassure themselves that they have made the right decision by leaving Nigeria to face "the uncertainty of America" (191).

Crucially, however, Oguine's novel also registers the fear of abjection that underlies the insistent performance of optimism after optimism is rendered a fiction—the performance of postoptimistic optimism. This is not to say that the novel exposes that dreams of national utopia deny the nightmarish realities of skyrocketing inequality and imperial racial hierarchies: those realities, in the novel's world, are already known. Rather, it's to highlight the novel's diagnosis of the affective dynamic whereby knowledge of the nightmare's reality redoubles professions of faith in the dream and so reproduces the nightmare. Obi follows his Uncle Happiness in finding in the US a land of opportunity because the alternative—that the US, like Nigeria, offers no certain path to desired success—is terrifying to him. Obi is driven by stories of Nigerian men that suggest the precarity of postcolonial happiness that is often not, in fact, secured through the lotteries of immigration, entrepreneurial endeavor, and proximity to whiteness. As when watching the TV that introduces Obi to American myth, "excitement" can be instantly "replaced by cyclonic terror" (181). Maina tells the story of a Nigeran roommate who became an "all-American immigrant" by marrying "a girl whose father was a big shot" (57): when the "girl" throws him out after two years, "he began to hear voices, started talking to himself" (58). Maina's scorn for the Nigerian is mirrored in Obi's scorn for Maina, whose "poorly acted play" becomes evidence that "he was just not carrying his own very well" (58). Obi begins to have literal "nightmares about Maina's nameless Nigerian room-mate" and of "Maina himself, armed with a machete chasing me down Grand Avenue at night while people passing in cars laughed, thinking that two black men were merely enjoying a wild but harmless joke" (58). Another figure who "walked into my dreams" is that of "Nebraska Man": a man who was a "fixture of a bar" close to Obi's Nigerian university, who would "go on and on in a gently flowing American accent about his adventures in God's Own Country" (195). He would attract the attention of "university students, young office workers and the unemployed, who all had their dreams of America" (195), but by the time Obi left the country, he "walked the streets at all times of day and night, his minds in shreds, waiting for death" (195). These are the men of whom Obi is determined to say, "At least I am not—" (196). To avoid the failure that is "unthinkable," however, he proclaims he must "somehow find the energy to succeed in America" (196). He is thus at increasing risk for becoming his nightmare: the African who proclaims his entrepreneurial potential but is judged to be obviously lying.

A Squatter's Tale ends with a warning of the costliness of finding the energy to affirm present prosperity. As Obi seeks out Uncle Happiness one last time, his relative, who has "aged terribly," urges him to "get up and dance" (201). Uncle Happiness's energy, as always, is seemingly inexhaustible. His preferred dance track, as always, is Prince Nico Mbarga's "Sweet Mother," whose refrain is quoted earlier in the book during another dance session:

Sweet Mother, I no go forget you
for the suffer wey you suffer for me

If a no sleep, my mother no go sleep
If a no chop, my mother no go chop

She no dey tire o! (137)

The popular highlife song celebrates the tireless work and ongoing suffering of the mother who ensures a sense of well-being for the singer. The song is evocative of the labor and suffering that the novel diagnoses as underlying proclamations of happiness, of the endless work that goes into proclaiming an inhospitable present hospitable. As Uncle Happiness urges Obi to join the dance, he asks him to take up again an exhausting performance of present optimism.[38] The dance, like Maina's plans for opening a resort or Nebraska Man's stories about having "just come in from America" (53, 195), is a way of getting by, of embracing the optimism that asserts belonging in an entrepreneurial, utopic nation. Like cruel optimism, postoptimistic optimism is a way of coping, of living through or even surviving an exploitative present. Whereas cruel optimism hinges on the promise that things will get better, this performed, mad optimism emerges from proclamations that things are already great. In incisive conversations on *Black Madness :: Mad Blackness* (2019), Therí Alyce Pickens notes that madness, as it is deployed in mad studies, "carries a lexical range that includes (in)sanity, cognitive disability, anger, and, for anyone who remembers the slang of the 1990s, excess (usually synonymous with too or really)."[39] This range is in evidence in Iguine's scenes of dance and story. Insofar as the happy fiction of the happy nation is in constant and obvious tension with lived reality in an anti-Black imperial order, it extracts a high, cruel psychic cost that exacerbates the untenability of the present.

Americanah Dreams

If, as Adéèkó has shown, the United States at the beginning of the millennium stood in the Nigerian literary imagination as a symbol for a desired "stable nation state," Oguine's novel unsettles that desire by reckoning with how the US mirrors an unstable Nigerian national condition that hinges on the maintenance of precarious fictions regarding its sustainability and security.[40] A stable Nigerian nation remains desired, perhaps, in Oguine's work, but the US is not a desirable model for its achievement; in the US, the fiction emphasizes, the nation's capacity to engineer what Adéèkó calls "affective institutions of mutual self-recognition" are at once extremely limited and structured according to ideologies of race and racial hierarchies.[41] What is more, democracy and universities, insofar as they are idealized as markers of successful nation-building, help to maintain national optimism, until they don't. An MBA from the US seems to Obi to be more of a haven than the University of Lagos, but the novel is at pains to show the contingent value of degrees awarded by both institutions. The Nigerian financial collapse of 1993, the novel intimates, could also happen in the United States, as indeed it did at the end of the tenure of the so-called MBA president, George W. Bush. As US university graduates burdened with staggering student debt entered a job market characterized by relatively high unemployment rates and part-time and contract work, the story that a degree guarantees the American dream was widely discussed as the fiction it has always been for all but the few.[42]

Chimamanda Ngozi Adichie's *Americanah* scrutinizes optimism oriented toward the predominately white US university campus. As in *A Settler's Tale*, the novel marks the psychic and social costs of both performing and being unable to perform a properly entrepreneurial, ethnologically discrete self that is eligible for inclusion in optimistic national fictions of the US. Whereas Oguine's novel is perhaps most despairing in its representation of a relentless, exhausting performance of optimism in both Nigeria and the US, Adichie's novel seeks an alternative affective mode for defining Nigerian national belonging. While *Americanah* suggests that Nigerians' ongoing experience of instability and uncertainty may itself paradoxically and productively define the mutual self-recognition of Nigerian nationhood, this seeming alternative to the relentless performance of optimism is, I suggest, a re-inscription of postcolonial optimism under conditions of empire.

Americanah was published in 2013, some years after the great recession that began in 2007 revealed how much of the US economy was built on stories of sound investments that rendered illusion a way of life. The novel nonetheless begins on a US university campus on which there seems cause for optimism. "Princeton, in the summer, smelled of nothing," goes the first sentence, "and although Ifemelu liked the tranquil greenness of the many trees, the clean streets and stately homes, the delicately overpriced shops, and the quiet, abiding air of earned grace, it was this, the lack of smell, that most appealed to her, perhaps because the other American cities she knew well had all smelled distinctly" (4). The blankness of the place, without smell and so ostensibly without history, produces a pleasing effect: "She liked, most of all, that in this place of affluent ease, she could pretend to be someone else, someone specially admitted into a hallowed American club, someone adorned with certainty" (3). Clark-Bekederemo warns Achebe against mistaking the "gospel" of the American dream for reality (see chapter 1);[43] here, the American dream is an obvious fiction, of place and of self, that can nonetheless be pleasurable to escape into, like a novel. For Ifemelu, the dream of affluence and certainty enabled by Princeton's blankness is concomitant with the American dream: "The best thing about America is that it gives you space. I like that. I like that you buy into the dream, it's a lie but you buy into it and that's all that matters" (536). The dream is a lie because it requires that you ignore all that exists outside the "hallowed American club," including the "other American cities" that do smell and, by extension, the histories that link wealth to exploitation. But enclaves such as Princeton enable Ifemula to imagine, if only briefly, that she is part of a rarified national dream.

The lie is appealing in part because its equivalent has, for Ifemelu, felt impossible to buy into in Nigeria. Ifemelu leaves Lagos for Pennsylvania in the mid-1990s as strikes become more and more common at the University of Nsukka, where she attends school with her boyfriend Obinze. When Aunty Uju suggests that Ifemelu take the SATs and head to the US for graduate school, the uncertainty of the fate of higher education in Nigeria makes the idea sensible (121). On the Wellson campus in Philadelphia, Ifemelu majors in communications; the degree, along with the connections and documented status she secures in part through her relationships with two American men, places her in a strong position for monetizing her blog, "on the Subject of Blackness in America" (366). On the strength of the blog, Ifemelu is awarded the fellowship at Princeton, and thus can imagine "entry into a hallowed American kingdom" (440). In 1995, a degree from Nsukka seems to hold no such potential for achieving similar status in Nigeria.

The novel suggests a parallel split when it comes to national democracy. Barack Obama's election to the presidency in 2007 is a rapturous event for Ifemelu: "there was, at that moment, nothing more beautiful to her than America" (448). The Nigerian democratic elections in 1999 elicit more ambivalence. Obinze's employer Chief is sanguine about his prospects following the election of Olusegun Obasanjo, the erstwhile military dictator whose administration oversaw the transition to the Second Republic: "I was Babangida's friend. I was Abacha's friend. Now that the military has gone, Obasanjo is my friend" (32). Chief looks forward specifically to exploiting the business opportunities made possible by the planned privatization of the National Farm Support Corporation. Ifemelu's father, in turn, avers that though "one could not describe Obasanjo as a good man ... it must be conceded that he has done some good things in the country; there is a flourishing spirit of entrepreneurship" (247). Democratic elections, in other words, self-evidently bring more privatization and austerity, following the "free market" dictates of the International Monetary Fund. As James Ferguson argued in 2006, in these global neoliberal conditions, "however democratic an African government may be in formal terms, its scope for making policy is radically constrained by the *nondemocratic* international financial institutions themselves."[44] The "ideological frothing" about "democracy in Africa" in development circles around the turn of the millennium, Ferguson suggested, ended up "serving a profoundly antidemocratic end—that is, the simulation of popular legitimation for policies" that were in fact "made in the most undemocratic way imaginable."[45] Bill Clinton, citing Jimmy Carter and the Second Republic, proclaimed in remarks to the Joint Assembly in August 2000 that elections meant "once again, people will know Nigeria as a great nation," and promised substantial aid to "Nigeria NGOs and universities" to ensure "all your children have the chance to live their dreams."[46] In *Americanah*, however, "change you can believe in," per Obama's 2007 election campaign slogan, is located firmly in the US.

As in *A Squatter's Tale*, however, just because it is possible to enter a fiction in the US does not make it real, and the psychic costs of maintaining the fiction are steep. Ifemelu "can pretend to be someone else" at Princeton, but the narrator remarks dryly that "she had to go to Trenton to braid her hair" (3). The American dream symbolized by Princeton offers the fantasy of belonging to an enclave of wealth and certainty. The nation remains, however, a space of immiseration and precarity shaped by white supremacy and anti-blackness. If, as Aretha Phiri argues in an incisive article on *Americanah*, Adichie's novel "significantly extends, enriches and renders inclusive, repertoires of blackness" by taking into account "culturally specific and context-responsive configurations of black subjectivity," it also attends to how these repertoires are differently shaped by and responsive to anti-blackness logics of racialization.[47] Ifemelu's blog meditates repeatedly on how her experiences as a "non-American black" differ from those of "American blacks." Other differences are emphasized in the novel itself. Shan, a Black American writer with whom Ifemelu has an uneasy relationship, experiences a "nervous breakdown" (444) after her recently published book is not well-received. Ifemelu's nephew Dike, who has been told by his Nigerian mother "you are not black" (470), attempts suicide. Ifemelu comes to feel a "cement in her soul . . . an early morning disease of fatigue, a bleakness and borderlessness" (7). Entering the optimistic fiction of national dreams only amplifies the alienation and depression produced by an anti-Black racist US reality.

Yet, *Americanah* does not leave readers with the potent mix of mania and despair that closes Oguine's fiction. As in other Nigerian literature of postcolonial optimism, the ending of *Americanah* is crucial for understanding how the US is imaginatively bound to visions of Nigerian futurity. To shake the cement from her soul, Ifemelu returns to Lagos. Refusing her ever-illusory place in the "hallowed American club," she starts a new blog in which a much-commented-on early piece addresses her experience at the Nigerpolitan Club (519). This post refuses the optimism she finds among other "returnees":

> Most of us have come back to make money in Nigeria, to start businesses, to seek government contracts and contacts. Others have come with dreams in their pockets and a hunger to change the country, but we spend all our time complaining about Nigeria, and even though our complaints are legitimate, I imagine myself as an outsider saying: Go back where you came from! (519)

She defies, in other words, a middle-class Nigerian imaginary that aspires to turn Lagos into New York City and that revolves around complaint and change. She writes instead about young women whose lives are "speckled stubbornly with hope: they wanted to open hair salons, to go to university. They believed their turn would come" (585). Observing these aspirations confirms for Ifemelu not a sense of individualized, performed optimism but of collective, widespread precarity: "*We are just one step away from this life in a slum, all of us who live air-conditioned middle-class lives*, she wrote" (585). If in the US one can be, or at least pretend to be, "adorned with certainty," Nigeria does not provide such an opportunity. Nigeria, rather, is where Ifemelu and Obinze leave behind lives of "floating-along contentment" (588) in favor of the "millions of uncertainties" symbolized in their reunification (542).[48] The lived experience of uncertainty in turn becomes the basis for *Americanah*'s affective construction of the Nigerian nation. Nigeria may not offer space to escape into feelings of surety and certainty, but it does offer the opportunity to reckon with the contingency of life under US-dominated capitalism. Instead of a pleasing and perilous fiction, the novel suggests, Nigeria offers its protagonist realism.

A relentlessly optimistic US nationalism, in other words, is the foil against which Adichie articulates what at first seems to be a clear alternative mode of Nigerian national belonging. The affective construct that the nation does or can or could provide an individual with stability and certainty within its borders is usurped by one that questions this very possibility. This is a distinctively post-global articulation of national belonging. The "post-global," as clarified by Tejumola Olaniyan in relation to African literary studies, queries the certainties offered by a conception of the "global" that became dominant in the 1990s and that itself followed from "three worlds theory."[49] Among these assumptions included "the certainty of the nation-state and territorial sovereignty, especially the constitutive function of these as tools of managing inequality on a global scale."[50] Clinton's 2000 remarks celebrating Nigerian democracy exemplify this sense of the global, particularly in the proclamation that "our common future depends on whether Africa's 739 million people gain the chance to live their dreams. And Nigeria is a pivot point on which all Africa's future turns."[51] The nation is the key unit for imagining the terms of what the speech calls "interdependence."[52] At a "time of change and uncertainty," the "chance to build a new Nigeria" promises in turn "the chance to build a lasting network of ties between Africa and the United States."[53] Clinton cited Ben Okri's *The Famished Road* to consolidate this progressive metaphor: "Okri asks us, 'Who can dream a good road and then live to travel on it?' Nigerians, as much as any nation on Earth, have dreamed this road."[54] In the post-global, Olaniyan shows, such rhetoric rings hollow, perhaps especially in an African context where writers and critics have, for at least thirty years, shown how the "global" has "so far meant little more than a world grouping to which [the continent] belongs in holding pens (nation-states) that both objectively and subjectively lack the capacity to realize for Africa what should be the real potentials of that community."[55] To be sure, one answer "to foundationally failed and failing states and unprecedented global inequality" has been a redoubled investment in national borders and policing: "these global anti-global forces are also profound signs of the post-global."[56] Other answers amplify "centrifugal forces" such as cosmopolitan human rights culture and discourses of planetary ecology. Adichie's novel represents and values the experience of Nigerian national belonging that paradoxically captures the uncertainty of this post-global moment, in which the question of what will come after the global remains unresolved.

By imagining Nigeria as a place that offers the opportunity to feel how the nation does not, never has, and never will provide the stability it has systemically denied to Black people, Adichie cracks open a conception of the global in which the nation continues to be invoked as the "unyielding framework."[57] The Nigerian national structure of feeling that ends the novel is implicitly one that is not necessarily delimited by the national borders that have proven inadequate to the task of managing global capitalism and its planetary catastrophes, human and nonhuman. The felt certainties of Americans are clearly fictions, after all. Even Clinton's speech, as it meditated on the "time of change and uncertainty" in Nigeria, briefly imagined how that uncertainty encompasses, or may come to encompass, the US: "you need us today because at this fleeting moment in history, we are the world's richest country. But over the long run of life and over the long run of a nation's life, and over the long run of civilization on this planet, the rich and the poor often change places."[58] While Clinton is "certain that America will walk with you in the years to come," the slippage from country to class glimpses the inadequacy of the former for responding to how global capitalism deepens fissures in and reconfigures the racialized geopolitical mappings of the latter.⁵⁹ *Americanah*'s interest in the precarity of nation-feeling—and in precarity *as* nation-feeling—suggests it is possible to imagine not just the elimination of the nation as the horizon for political desire but also the end of the supposed certainties of the so-called American century that oversaw the construction of the "global" as a network of nations.

And in that imagining, what comes next? As Christopher T. Fan notes, while the national future symbolized by the novel's heterosexual union

> is never explicitly depicted, the contours of that future can be *felt* through the specific features of Ifemelu's and Obinze's characters and their desire for each other: his refusals of the extravagances of wealth (an allegory for a Nigerian capitalism free of cronyism), her rejection of America's racist capitalist futurity, and their infidelity's enactment of individual desire over traditional values.⁶⁰

To the degree that this future depends, however, on Ifemelu coming to represent "the globalization of the Asian American model minority as it converges with flexible citizenship,"⁶¹ as well as on Obinze's explicit disdain for Chinese investment in Nigeria, what Fan calls "Sinological Orientalism" emerges as the "political unconscious" of the novel:⁶² "the dream of a Nigerian capitalism that supposedly offers an alternative future to American capitalism is itself deeply shaped by Chinese capital," even if "the China-oriented future of their chosen lives in Nigeria is still unimaginable."⁶³ Olaniyan sees the post-global moment as an opportunity to imagine "a rearrangement of global governance" that prioritizes "quality of life universally conceived."⁶⁴ The future structured by Sinological Orientalism in Adichie's novel is in these terms "more aligned with than opposed to the aspirations of neoliberal capitalism," including aspirations that maintain the present as a happy time that entrepreneurs (such as Ifemelu) need only shape into an even better future.⁶⁵ In this light, the novel's interest in national precarity hinges on an attachment to capitalism beyond the uncertain fate of a global order of nations. Its investment in the precarity of the nation signals the reconstitution of postcolonial optimism for an imminent post-global age. The disavowal of US optimism in *Americanah*, in other words, culminates in the reconstitution of postcolonial optimism in distilled form in Nigeria, as a hard-working couple, properly credentialed (including by US universities) and haunted by the specter of Chinese capital, embrace the uncertainty of the present as an opportunity for developing the nation. The optimism here is tempered by uncertainty and thus, perhaps, all the better suited for weathering the fluctuations of the capitalist post-global marketplace. The realism proffered by *Americanah*'s Nigerian national feeling foregrounds the uncertainty of life under US-dominated capitalism and thereby provides an affective basis for becoming a more resilient capitalist.

There is a strong argument to be made that Adichie's novel is not, in the end, in any substantive opposition to neoliberal capitalism dominated by the US but is rather symptomatic of the ongoingness of US imperialism. Kalyan Nadiminti cites Adichie as one prominent example of the "global professional writer" who "default[s] to a critique of the middle class" by formulating "a bourgeois subjectivity that turns inward."[66] Such critique marks "a decisive shift from the revolutionary but often compromised postcolonial novel to a professionalized and market-driven global novel," whereby "global audience" is "almost always a synonym for an *Americanized* audience—that is, an audience that is not necessarily American but that identifies with the tenets of American globalism."[67] As Lily Saint has pointed out, *Americanah* has proven immensely appealing to a US audience: "its title, and its engagement with Americans means readers don't have to work very hard" and can avoid "richer, more varied engagements with African writing and publishers."[68] By focusing on "the central tale of a rising middle class" and thus offering "an easily digestible" representation of the global, Nadiminti argues, the global professional writer (such as Adichie) betrays her common association with post-war US MFA programs, which has demanded a particular "framing of bourgeois life coupled with the primacy of the voice for the nonwhite and non-American writer."[69] Adichie, notably, received an MFA in 2003 from Johns Hopkins University and an MA at Yale before securing a fellowship at Harvard. If, as Camille Isaacs has argued, Ifemelu's blogging unknowingly embeds her in "digital imperial and neo-imperial structures of the United States and its far-reaching policies for the control of digital territory," a parallel argument exists for Adichie's writing in and through the US MFA.[70] Because of this neo-imperial educational structure, and despite the fact that Adichie has taken care to publish her novels with Nigerian presses, writer and protagonist alike reach "only a distinct demographic" that "risks replicating the hierarchies of classical imperialism."[71] The international writer with US degrees becomes in the late twentieth and early twenty-first centuries a variation of the entrepreneur who holds an MBA: equipped to market one's self as a good investment and investor, and also institutionalized as "politically agnostic, white-collar workers."[72]

But perhaps this reading does not do full justice to Adichie's writing and career. Yogita Goyal argues that "critiques of the global African novel" that wish "for the return to the pan-African in a kind of Bandung nostalgia" discount that "it demands more complex scales of comparison and analysis sufficient to navigate local, regional, and global formations."[73] Following this provocation, it is possible to consider how *Americanah*'s ending fuses Black diasporic and national experience to ask, rather than proclaim, what might be possible in a world yet circumscribed by global capitalism, where the nation might yet be always reimagined apart from the state. As Imre Szeman remarks in his overview of what is now a globalized form of entrepreneurial subjectivity, "entrepreneurship may be simultaneously the height of neoliberal subject formation *and* its limit—a peak on the other side of which lie subjects with no fidelity or loyalty to governments or states."[74] Szeman asks whether it is not in this "rejection of a neoliberal state apparatus" that one might find a "kernel of political possibility."[75] What, in the end, might Obinze and Ifemelu, drawing on their diasporic experiences and connections, accomplish together as they imagine a Nigeria that exceeds state-imposed borders? For her part, Adichie has worked actively to "to contribute to the growth of the writing community in Nigeria" in ways that have sidestepped the Nigerian government and offered an alternative to US MFA programs for aspiring writers from across anglophone Africa and its diasporas.[76] As the Creative Director of the Farafina Trust Creative Writing Workshop, Adichie supported the annual program since its inception in 2007. After Nigerian Breweries PLC, a subsidiary of the Heineken Group, withdrew their sponsorship "due to a need to streamline their expenditure" in 2017,[77] the workshop re-emerged in 2018 as the Purple Hibiscus Trust Creative Writing Workshop, with financial support from Trace Nigeria, "the multi-platform media and entertainment company with over 200 million viewers and listeners in 160 countries"[78] that is "75% owned by Modern Times Group, a leading Swedish digital entertainment provider."[79] The initiative is widely recognized as "the highest-profile creative workshop on the continent" that instantiates "Adichie's one-time definition of herself as a 'hopelessly sentimental Pan-Africanist."[80] Many of its participants, who hail from across Africa and the US, have gone on to win awards and grants (themselves often backed by institutions in the global North). Its history one of financial uncertainty and dependency on corporations headquartered in Europe, the workshop is a privatized credential and a post-global institution that seeks to create opportunities for pan-African cultural exchange.[81] In this, the workshop continues a Nigerian literary tradition of postcolonial optimism that continuously finds within educational institutions beholden to imperial centers the potential for nurturing Black creative solidarities amidst the entrenchment of debt, dependency, and alienation. Postcolonial optimism thus maintained registers the ongoingness both of empire and of desires to live beyond its imagined political horizons.

PART II
COMPOUNDING OPTIMISM IN SOUTH AFRICAN FICTION

Chapter 4

A Tiny Ripple of Hope *Between Two Worlds*

A prominent narrative of South African postapartheid history charts an affective national trajectory from elation to disillusionment. According to this narrative, anti-apartheid revolutionary hopes, partially realized in the first democratic elections, were betrayed by the African National Congress's (ANC) postapartheid governance. Postapartheid policies that supported privatization have indeed been antithetical to the party's promises, during the liberation struggle, of equality and justice. Sampie Terreblanche describes the "ideological shifts" in the ANC's economic views since 1990 as "breathtaking": commitments to growth through redistribution were shelved, as "the enabling conditions of the new system were molded in such a way that the imperial aspirations of the American-led neoliberal empire would be satisfied."[1] That the postapartheid system has in practice enriched a small elite in South Africa alongside imperial interests is by now a critical commonplace, and not just in sociological work that charts the high rates of inequality since the establishment of democratic elections.[2] Disillusionment with the postapartheid state, for example, is reflected in accounts of periodization in South African fiction. As Rita Barnard argues, the postapartheid literary period, which "not only invited new dreams for South Africa's future, but a radical reimagination of its past," has been followed by the "post-transition" production of "more disenchanted writing."[3] In this literature, Barnard notes, liberation is less "a dream deferred" than "a dream derailed."[4] Barnard here quotes Cyril Ramaphosa, who adapted Langston Hughes's famous poem to describe the government of Thabo Mbeki (1999–2008).[5] The question of how to get back on the rails, of how to redeem a revolutionary dream of South Africa in an era of US-dominated globalization, has been recurrent up to and including Ramaphosa's presidency.

This forceful narrative of government betrayal and disillusionment vis-à-vis US imperialism can be complicated in two ways. First, the implementation by successive ANC governments of what is broadly conceived as neoliberal policy has been incomplete. As Anne-Maria Makhulu has demonstrated, postapartheid South Africa has not been a "clear-cut 'neoliberal' case" along definitions centered on industrialized democracies in the global North.[6] To be sure, South African privatization and deregulation saw the expansion of the financial sector, such that by 2004 this sector comprised 20% of the national economy while employing only 1% of the workforce. Yet, this expansion has been accompanied by the increase of social grants and grant recipients.[7] These grants, the distribution of which has also been "partially conditioned by the legacy of apartheid racial discrimination," have proven crucial to households struggling to get by without steady wage work.[8] While the South African state has championed privatization, it has also promised state welfare; while it has supported "entrepreneurial" solutions to poverty, it has also deployed a rhetoric of rights that guarantees necessities ranging from food to housing.[9] Deborah James usefully calls this distinct intertwining of state and market forces "redistributive neoliberalism."[10] Although the financialization of the South African economy since the 1990s means that people are ever-more enfolded in the vicissitudes of the market, neoliberal policy has been leavened with the explicitly-stated end-goal of redistributing wealth to redress the ongoing material inequalities of apartheid.[11] Residual dreams of radical redistribution have continued to shape South African neoliberal policies, and those policies have often been justified through a rhetoric of redistribution.

This point leads to the second way a narrative of betrayal and disillusionment potentially simplifies the relation between anti-apartheid hopes and postapartheid realities: dreams of redistribution have often been imagined, during and after apartheid, in terms that resonate with neoliberal discourses of private property and a financialized economy. Goals such as the redistribution of property rights, universal housing, and the democratization of credit have stood as affectively compelling alternatives to an apartheid regime that restricted Black people's access to land ownership, home ownership, and lines of credit. While ANC governance has been a locus of disillusionment, the cause of this disillusionment is often experienced and measured not only in terms of revolutionary ideals but also personal financial insecurity. For example, in his analysis of the 2009 general election that saw the presidential candidacy of Jacob Zuma elicit unprecedented support for the ANC in KwaZulu Natal, Hylton White noted how shifting conceptions of Zulu identity followed from the collapse of migrant and wage labor in the early twenty-first century.[12] In a contemporary situation of "extreme insecurity," White argued, Zuma distinguished himself from his predecessor, Mbeki, who was widely perceived to be "not just an elitist in his personal life but also a leader who had [unfairly] shut the door on the distribution of wealth to those who needed it desperately." Zuma, by contrast, offered hope for the state-sanctioned instantiation of what White describes as "deeply normative impulses" tied to patriarchal, capitalist conceptions of Zulu identity.[13] Postapartheid hopes for redistribution and justice have been pinned in this way to the expansion of financial opportunities for specific individuals and ethnic groups.

Rather than fully opposing US imperialism to anti-apartheid visions of South African nationhood, as Terreblanche does, it is useful to think about how anti-apartheid and postapartheid dreams of a "new" South Africa have been shaped by US-dominated capitalism and its discourses. In an argument that unfolds in the following three chapters, I contend that South African literature that interrogates the affective forcefulness of capital and its instruments is particularly appropriate for a study of South African national becoming under conditions of US empire. Dreams of South African futurity, as they are registered in an anglophone national literary imaginary, have addressed not only state-sanctioned redistribution but also the expansion of financial services. The fictions addressed in these chapters attend, more specifically, to how a desire for the expansion of credit has been a continuous response to the persistence of what James terms "credit apartheid."[14] As South African fiction gives form to these dreams and desires, it teases out the stubborn, sticky emotional appeal of a national mythos that imagines the inequalities of colonialism and apartheid can be overcome via more equitable access to credit. In so doing, this literature of postcolonial optimism considers how dreams of South African nationhood are maintained despite continual disillusionment and under conditions of US empire. It self-consciously grapples with how postcolonial optimism is entwined with globalized articulations of an American dream that maintains the nation as the (potential) safeguard of equal economic opportunity.

Whereas my discussion of Nigerian literature of postcolonial optimism registers the tensions of associating the US university with the instantiation of democratic postcolonial nationhood, my analysis of South African literature of postcolonial optimism addresses national imaginaries that are less invested in the political form of the democratic nation-state per se than in the economic opportunities that such a nation might enable. Accordingly, the central affective dynamic I identify in this fiction is distinct. Rather than a persistent, performative, often attenuated (post)optimism that maintains educational institutions may yet facilitate national democratic becoming, South African literature's affective structures evoke the boom-and-bust cycles of the capitalist economy. It intimates how the cyclical recurrence of disillusionment and hope compounds into cycles of despair and euphoria, as South African dreams of national becoming remain entwined with the financial instruments of US empire.

In this chapter, I introduce this affective dynamic by offering a reconsideration of Miriam Tlali's *Between Two Worlds*, which was the first novel in English to be published by a Black South African woman within the country's borders.[15] The fiction, published in 1975 in censored form by Ravan Press as *Muriel at Metropolitan* before an unredacted edition was issued by Longman in 1979, is famous for its excoriation of the South African Republic, which was established by a referendum of white voters in 1961. Begun in 1964 and completed five years later, the semi-autobiographical fiction is narrated by Muriel, who works as a bookkeeper at a furniture and appliance store called Metropolitan Radio and who observes, endures, and resists apartheid's quotidian humiliations and hypocrisies. These daily injustices, critics have noted, include unequal, racialized access to property and credit. Less remarked is how the novel invokes parallel histories of inequality and struggle in the United States. Unpacking the history of Black South African and Black American cultural and religious exchange in Sophiatown—a site where Muriel mourns the loss of a past home of her own—allows me to situate Tlali's novel in relation to longer twentieth-century histories in which the perceived relative mobility and prosperity of Black Americans informed Black South African political movements for property rights. I go on to consider how the novel takes up this entwined history in the context of the five years of its writing, 1964–69, which correspond roughly to the years of its setting. The hope and despair attached to Sophiatown and its destruction echoes in the hope and despair that coheres around the US civil rights movement and its aftermath, marked in the text by explicit references to Robert F. Kennedy's 1966 "Day of Affirmation Address" at the University of Cape Town. In its invocation of Kennedy's speech, the novel self-consciously articulates its political vision within and against the disappointments of the 1964 Civil Rights Act and Kennedy's logic of economic opportunity that subordinates equality and justice to notions of so-called progress. While affirming Kennedy's exhortation to struggle for an ideal, the ideal Muriel commits to is that of Black economic rights, not in the name of national progress but for the benefit of Black life. The novel dreams of a redeemed nation at the end of a decade that saw many dreams of Black liberation, in both the US and South Africa, shatter into nightmare. It does so both through a renewed commitment to histories of collective, pan-African struggle and the uncompromising prioritization of Black economic well-being.

By marking how a novel that has generally been read as exemplarily "South African" attends to the US as a site for pan-African solidarity in the face of anti-Black imperialism, I am better able to engage the fiction's ambivalence toward freedom dreams centered on the expansion of credit and property rights. Transnational cycles of hope and despair—from Sophiatown to Washington, D.C.—work to reaffirm that Black economic rights are crucial to the undoing of the white supremacist nation. At the same time, *Between Two Worlds* evinces a distinct unease in how the pursuit of these rights may be too easily co-opted to extend the status quo. The feeling that the realization of hopes may produce conditions of disillusionment marks in the novel a transnational, racialized affect integral to life in the white supremacist, financialized nation-state. Consideration of this distinct iteration of postcolonial optimism, this mode of investing in postcolonial nationhood, informs the novel's more radical pan-African national dreams. Subsequent chapters reveal that this genre of postcolonial optimism's intensification as euphoria and despair finds renewed expression in postapartheid literature of credit and debt.

Ownership Dreams

Tlali's *Between Two Worlds* is keenly attuned to the unequal access to property and credit enforced by apartheid, as well as to the despair and violence that this inequality produces. Although Metropolitan Radio is a radio and furniture store, most of its profits accrue through debt collection. At the establishment run by Muriel's white Jewish boss, Mr. Bloch, Black customers are arbitrarily granted or denied lines of credit, charged exorbitant rates of interest, and subjected to repossession without due process. As such, Muriel bears witness to and carefully details a furniture industry, which, Deborah James notes, was historically run by ethnically marginalized groups, including Jewish people, and which became the locus of "credit apartheid" in the mid-twentieth century.[16] The mechanisms of credit apartheid proliferate in the novel. When Muriel notifies a customer that he is "entitled to claim back the interest for the last six months," as he had paid off his loan early, she is "accused of 'educating' African customers" (80). When the customer gives Muriel ten cents in gratitude, she is accused of theft and disloyalty to the firm, and Mr. Bloch threatens to fire her. The corruption of the business is displaced onto her, just as the violent work of forcibly repossessing goods is offloaded onto a Black worker named Agrippa. Access to credit entrenches the immiseration of Black people, whereas, for Mr. Bloch, marginalized as he is within white society, it remains the basis for the wealth he accumulates through real estate: Muriel notes that Mr. Bloch personally makes some money from selling goods and more money from selling loans, but the bulk of his wealth is due to "land transactions" that have paid him "more than I worked for in forty years" (160). By contrast, Black land and home ownership in South Africa was, as the novel dramatizes, all but eradicated by the mid-1960s. As Muriel observes: "Furniture manufacturers were doing a booming business. There was keen competition to exploit the African buying power whose potential the manufacturers as well as the retailers were well aware of and could not ignore" (138). In a situation in which access to credit is unequal and exploitative and property ownership is restricted according to apartheid categories of race, Muriel observes it is not only Black people's labor that is exploited, but also Black people's desire to ameliorate or resist the immiserating effects of that exploitation.

Oppression, in other words, does not eliminate aspirational futurity. As James argues, the mid-century flourishing of furniture stores marked the profound disruption that colonial and apartheid legislation had on Black domestic life. As Black property ownership was increasingly restricted as the century wore on, buying furniture came to stand in for purchasing a home and marking milestones such as marriage and starting a family: "Buying furniture became part of the ceremonial gifts and countergifts associated with a wedding."[17] James continues: "The buying of furniture, then, arose in part within in [sic] a customary ritualization of the life course, entailed aspirations to suave urbanism and modernity, and exposed householders to gradually increasing expenditure—and expanding credit access—over time."[18] Muriel says of a Black customer who has succeeded in purchasing a furniture set to call her own:

> I suppose like the people the world over, we want to feel that we possess something. We need something firm to hold on to, even if it is only a piece of wood. It gives life a meaning, just to hurry home and sit and look at the furniture, even if it is ill suited for the brick boxes they built for us. (198)

Possessing property, however tenuously, offers invaluable felt security in a white supremacist state that throws Black people "out of their houses" (198). Barnard has noted that in *Between Two Worlds*, the acquisition of property may be understood as an act of resistance. Asserting ownership defies apartheid codifications of a racialized "standard of living" (289), in Muriel's words, that denied and sought to suppress Black people's consumer desires and drastically limit their property rights.[19] That these acts of resistance further entrench Black people in exploitative institutions via cycles of credit and debt is a central problematic of the novel that connects to mid-century Black struggles within the US, US empire, and the felt insufficiencies of optimism attached to a dreamed-of South African nation.

The resistant Black desire for property, and its imbrication in access to credit, intersects with histories of the US most strikingly during a trip to Sophiatown, as Muriel remembers a space and time in which home ownership was still possible during her lifetime. Surveying a manicured landscape that belies historical violence, Muriel recalls the neighborhood as it had been before the Nationalists enacted "forcible removal" in 1955 and "transformed" it into "a beautiful township for the lower income group whites" that was named Triomf (147). As one of the last remaining areas of Black home-ownership in Johannesburg, Sophiatown was a political and cultural center prior to its razing by the state.[20] The maintenance of freehold tenure rights, secured prior to the passage of the Native Lands Act of 1913 that effectively denied property rights to most South Africans, supported a distinctive sense of community.[21] Es'kia Mphahlele, one of the many great thinkers and artists to be associated with Sophiatown, described the connection between this sense of home and material aspirations beyond apartheid strictures:

> It was a place where people could express themselves more freely than in any other place. Sophiatown had structures, it was never a shanty town. It was a real suburb with front gates which said, 'This is how I want to live.'[22]

Sophiatown was also famously a place in which the association of Black Americans with aspirational modernity found multiple forms of expression in the mid-twentieth century.[23] Due to its heterogenous population, political significance, and cultural vitality, Sophiatown became known as the "Chicago of South Africa";[24] it was also called the "Harlem of South Africa" (even as Harlem was dubbed the "Soweto of America").[25] As Mphahlele notes, "cinema, dancing, American culture and jazz were very important to the cultural life of Sophiatown."[26] Don Mattera reminisces, in "Other Faces of Kofifi," that "even the traditional African herbalists used brightly painted signs to advertise their USA aphrodisiacs, blood mixtures and lucky charms. And if you rejected the American fad, you would quickly be dubbed *moegoe* or greenhorn" (75).[27] The prominence of African-American urban cultures in mid-century Black South African cultures, as Tsitsi Jaji suggests in her analysis of the magazine glossy *Zonk!*, "implied a parallel set of aspirations for South Africans and African Americans."[28]

These parallel aspirations are evoked insofar as Muriel's reverie, which fortifies her later resolve to work for "a people whom I love and am a part of" (221), occurs while standing next to "the partially demolished walls" of her African Methodist Episcopal (AME) church, where the words "'God Our Father, Christ Our Redeemer, Man Our Brother'" are "still legible beneath the painted crucifix" (149). As Robert Trent Vinson detailed in his history of dreams of African-American liberation in early twentieth-century South Africa, the AME was one of multiple institutions that facilitated the merging of "the history of African Americans with the freedom dreams of Africans."[29] African-American missionaries of the early twentieth century, many of whom were associated with the AME, aligned themselves with Booker T. Washington's "up from slavery" narrative by espousing a "gradualist African upward mobility leading to eventual independence."[30] Washington's program of economic self-reliance remained popular in South Africa long after it had waned in the US, and it was renewed in a new form in the subsequent popularity of a Garveyism that promoted "goals of Black economic and educational advancement" in ways that were "middle class in style and in program—entrepreneurial, business-oriented, and committed to free enterprise and the capitalist model."[31] By mid-century, Alfred B. Xuma, who became president of the ANC in 1940, viewed the AME church as a model for Black South Africans fighting for liberation "'because it is an institution that is run by non-whites.'"[32] Muriel's reverie at the church thus evokes a longer history wherein Black South Africans viewed African Americans, per Vinson, as "inspirational models of Black success" who "shared aspirations to be full citizens" and promised to abet "a dream of African liberation that resonated throughout the world."[33] This shared aspiration finds brief instantiation in the publication history of *Between Two Worlds*. As Tlali notes in her introduction to the 2004 Broadview Press edition, when she was having difficulty finding a publisher, her mother took a copy of the manuscript to a "kind African-American Bishop" of the AME church in Lesotho.[34] The priest to whom the Bishop referred her proved untrustworthy, but there was brief hope that he would help to secure a US publisher.[35]

As Muriel stands near a ruin in a white enclave, she remembers a time and place in which a certain kind of aspiration was possible: hope for upward mobility and a dream of Black modernity. She remembers, that is, a "past which had held hopes of redemption" for the South African nation (150). This redemption, importantly, is tied to property rights and ownership. When Muriel's companion, Henry, assumes that in her reverie she is "admiring the beautiful European houses" (151), Muriel assures him he has it wrong: "I never even saw these houses; all

I 'saw' was our own homes—the poor old so-called 'slum structures.' Don't you know the expression 'a poor thing but mine own'?" (152). Muriel does not dream of owning a fancy house, of being part of the neighborhood of Triomf—as Lewis Nkosi paraphrased the work of mid-century African-American intellectuals, "Who wants to be integrated into a *burning* house?" (86). Or, as Henry reflects, who could possibly take "pride" in a home built on oppression: "all those nice gardens of theirs fertilized by the shit of black children who used to run about here naked and neglected while their mothers cared for white kids" (152). Muriel's dream is for a form of property ownership and felt stability that facilitated dreaming the end of white supremacist nationalism.

The present tense of Muriel's recollections of the past emphasizes the immediacy of their significance to her contemporary moment, suggesting how aspirations to ownership remain compelling yet insufficient responses to apartheid. Henry does not romanticize Sophiatown, where, in fact, most residents never did own homes;[36] those middle-class families that did were treated by the state in all other respects like their proletarian neighbors. Muriel, for all she values her vision of "our own homes," also avoids nostalgia. She remembers how what was "mine own" was also never hers:

> As an infant, you are christened in church, brought up in a Christian home and you acquire some education. Later, as you grow older, you are joined in holy matrimony to the man or woman of your choice. Together, you in turn build a home full of hope for the future. But the truth begins to stare you in the face . . . You are not human. Everything is a mockery. (150)

If a thriving, corrupt furniture industry marks the profound disruption of Black domestic life in the era of apartheid, home ownership in the heyday of Sophiatown does the same. "A home full of hope for the future" was possible, but the realization of those hopes were not. It is here that the novel reckons with limits and contradictory effects of past hopes for national redemption that hinged on economic and property rights.

Muriel's own disillusionment with past domestic hopes signals how, sympathetic as Tlali's novel is to the aspiration to "possess something," be it dresser or house, it is aware of how some forms of possession can exacerbate dispossession. Home ownership, like the extension of credit, deepens the potential for disillusionment; both forms of possession maintain the racialized property regimes that produce the inhuman. Better terms of credit and the capital that flows from property are only ambivalently resistant to apartheid, insufficient as they are for securing the possibility of realizing quotidian hopes for the future.

Individual economic advancement, Muriel learns again and again, runs up against the wall of racism that offers a structural impediment to that advancement. As a woman classified by the apartheid regime as "African" working at Metropolitan Radio, "I would have to give my best and receive very little in return. My presence would be felt but never recognized, let alone rewarded" (165). Yet, finding another job proves infeasible: although the Italian owners of Continental Scooters are eager to hire her, they cannot afford to construct the separate bathroom, office, and cloakroom required by apartheid law. Even leaving the country, Muriel comes to realize, isn't really an option. Although her mother urges Muriel to move to the nominally independent Lesotho—her mother believes that "the [South African] Republic was beyond redemption" (164)—Muriel sees "that the destiny of the one million Basotho would always be intermingled with that of the teeming millions of voiceless, helpless races surrounding them, that no protective mote could be built around Lesotho" (164). Within this context, a mortgage or credit line, like a new job, does not materially change an unjust status quo, and the ambivalence of hopes attached to ownership haunt the novel. This ambivalence is briefly glimpsed as transnational in scope: Muriel discusses the exceptional treatment given to a Black customer "with a big American car" that, she deduces, he owns because he "was in fact an informer paid by the police" (100). Access to US luxury goods is proximate here not to an aspirational modernity but to collusion with the white supremacist state, be it American or South African. The novel anticipates, again and again, that an optimism oriented toward the expansion of economic rights in a dreamed-of postcolonial, postapartheid nation may set the stage for disillusionment with the continuation of an oppressive status quo.

The Time to Dream

In Muriel's contemporary moment of the late 1960s, optimism for a redeemed nation often seems most lively, if always qualified, in visions of the past, as resistant aspirations in the present have been constricted to the scale of furniture ownership. Tlali's representation of the present, however, like the representation of earlier hopes and disillusionments, is attuned to intersecting Black histories across South Africa and the US. The transnational affective shape of the present, the novel suggests, is one in which hope and disillusionment continues in cyclical relationship. This cycle is powered both by Black aspirations to economic empowerment and by nations in which the proffered means of cultivating such empowerment replicate racialized economic inequality.

Specifically, the novel's multiple references to the disillusionment following the US civil rights movement bring the affective dynamics of that movement and its aftermath into parallel with the hopes and disappointments of Sophiatown. One such reference comes from Muriel's white co-worker Mrs. Stein, to whom Muriel listens with scorn:

> She [Mrs. Stein] went on to insist that all racial groups [in South Africa] were happy and living with each other in harmony, how for nearly a decade now there had not been any uprisings or strikes unlike other countries such as America where there were killings and riots. I listened, trying very hard to be patient. (207)[37]

Muriel's impatience registers how the relative absence of "uprisings or strikes" in South Africa was symptomatic not of harmony but of the brutal repression of anti-apartheid movements, symbolized by the Rivonia Trial of 1963–64 that sanctioned the imprisonment of Nelson Mandela and other anti-apartheid leaders. The "killings and riots" to which Mrs. Stein alludes are likewise markers not of a distinction between two white supremacist states but of ongoing, globalized anti-Black racism. Following the passage of the 1964 Civil Rights Act and the Voting Rights Act of 1965 in the US, Mehrsa Baradaran notes in *The Color of Money*, "it was apparent that the victory had been a hollow one," particularly in matters of economic justice.[38] Hence, widespread protests by Black people following the passage of civil rights legislation targeted white businesses and "ghetto lenders" especially.[39] As Baradaran shows, in language that echoes James's analysis of South Africa, "Americans lived in two different worlds of credit—*separate and unequal*. But the civil rights laws had not been designed to address the Jim Crow credit market."[40] Martin Luther King, Jr.'s 1965 sermon "The American Dream" averred that the dream he proclaimed in 1963 "has often turned into a nightmare" and been repeatedly "shattered" by racism and poverty.[41] Post-1965, Black banking, Baradaran notes, became a "key weapon" in King's "arsenal of nonviolent resistance."[42] King amplified others' calls for economic structural reform aimed at poverty alleviation;[43] these would be taken up by subsequent Black leaders who prioritized "wealth, property ownership, and community economic strength."[44] Both South Africa and the US are nations with two racialized worlds of economic existence that delimit the possibility of realizing desired Black futures. The central concerns that Muriel holds as an employee of Metropolitan Radio regarding oppressive credit regimes and restricted ownership extend across the Atlantic, where what Mrs. Stein calls "killings and riots" are grounds for Black solidarity and potential harbingers of the protests soon to come in South Africa.

At the same time, Tlali's novel does not uphold the US as only a place where Black protest stands as a potential model for the South African scene, as perceived Black American mobility did earlier in the century. Rather, as it brings discourses of the civil rights movement into relation with a history of disillusionment with property ownership in Sophiatown, it thinks critically about aspects of the movement for Black economic rights in the US. Informed by how hopes centered on Black economic rights have collapsed into disappointment in South Africa, *Between Two Worlds* imagines an alternate, potentially pan-African affective orientation to futurity.

I locate Tlali's affective critique in the novel's remarkable engagement with Robert F. Kennedy's 1966 "Day of Affirmation Address" at the University of Cape Town. Near the end of the novel, Muriel recounts one of the few times her coworker Lennie, "the white mechanic," spoke to her during their years of working together (187). "It was just after the late Robert Kennedy had visited the Republic," Muriel recalls, when Lennie, seeing her reading a pamphlet about the visit, asked her if she were "a Communist" (188). US Senator Kennedy's visit occurred in June 1966, and it is remembered most for the address that Kennedy delivered to members of the anti-apartheid National Union of South African Students (NUSAS). Kennedy was certainly not a communist, but he was a supporter of civil rights legislation in the US, and his speech at the University of Cape Town implicitly challenged some white political privileges in South Africa. "The essential humanity of men," Kennedy declared, "can be protected and preserved only where government must answer—not just to the wealthy, not just to those of a particular religion, or a particular race, but to all its people." In the recording of the speech, Kennedy improvises from the transcript and repeats the last words, to thunderous applause: "I mean all of its people."[45] The limited, somewhat oblique critique of the apartheid regime was typical of the administrations of John F. Kennedy (1961–63) and Lyndon Johnson (1963–69), which offered rhetorical condemnations of human rights violations while being careful not to risk the US's substantial military and economic interests in southern Africa.[46] Kennedy's rhetoric of democracy, however, resonated with an organization that had adopted the 1955 Freedom Charter, which famously proclaims "The People Shall Govern!"[47] Property rights are central to this foundational document of the South African Congress Alliance, which calls for land to be redistributed to all "those who work it" and asserts people's right "to be decently housed, and to bring up their families in comfort and security."[48]

The mention of Kennedy is the only time that we see Muriel the narrator-writer reading something apart from work documents, and it is the only time we are given a hint of Muriel's potential formal political sympathies. And to some degree, Muriel seems to be in alignment with Kennedy's political views. As she departs Metropolitan Radio for an uncertain future, Muriel is explicitly confident that by doing so, her "conscience would be clear" (221). Muriel leaves her job, to quote Kennedy's speech, to "stan[d] up for an ideal" and thereby "sen[d] forth a tiny ripple of hope," her only "sure reward" for doing so—and here Robert cited his brother John F. Kennedy—"a good conscience."[49] *Between Two Worlds* exemplifies Kennedy's exhortation that governments can be recalled "to their duties and obligations" through "the freedom of speech" and the "power to be heard."[50] It is, after all, precisely these capacities that Muriel claims as she composes her formal letter of resignation "in my own handwriting" and without "false starts" (221). Notably, the reader is not informed of the exact contents of this "beautiful" letter, but the novel itself is its ready stand-in.

The novel's politics are also in tension with Kennedy's, however, insofar as the latter represents the US as being on a path toward economic justice. For Muriel, in contrast, a historical sense of optimism's orientation to something of "my own" that is always precarious, and which is liable to become a source of disillusionment makes her a keen critic of this discourse of eminent happiness that upholds the sufficiency of something called economic opportunity. Noting the "wide and tragic gaps between promise and performance, ideal and reality" that he understood as "profoundly repugnant to the theory and command of our [US] Constitution," Kennedy described the US as having "struggled to overcome the self-imposed handicap of prejudice and discrimination."[51] That this struggle is one shared by South Africans is part of the point of Kennedy's opening joke:

> I came here because of my deep interest and affection for a land settled by the Dutch in the mid-seventeenth century, then taken over by the British, and at last independent; a land in which the native inhabitants were at first subdued, but relations with whom remain a problem to this day; a land which defined itself on a hostile frontier; a land which has tamed rich natural resources through the energetic application of modern technology; a land which once imported slaves, and now must struggle to wipe out the last traces of that former bondage. I refer, of course, to the United States of America.[52]

The joke is one instance of the fact that, as Robolin notes, the US and South Africa have generated "constant comparisons across the twentieth century, not only because their patterns of race-based oppression and resistance are at time strikingly resonant, but also because these national histories have long been intertwined with one another."[53] In his account of US and South African history, Kennedy drastically minimizes the scope of white supremacy and Black and Indigenous struggles through the past tense and reference to "last traces." In that minimization, however, lies the heart of the affective economic system he offers: the possibility of "the achievement of equal opportunity in fact." The US and South Africa might yet become nations of "full opportunity" for Black and Indigenous peoples, Kennedy promises, particularly through the realization of a "world of constantly accelerating economic progress—not material welfare as an end in itself, but as a means to liberate the capacity of every human being to pursue his talents and to pursue his hopes."[54] Equal and full opportunity, Kennedy avers, is and ought to be a national and indeed global dream, both because it is "the right thing to do" and because it is "economically advantageous."[55]

In Kennedy's account, racialized exploitation is a glitch in, rather than integral to, the operation of a capitalist economy, and a capitalist economy will thrive when the "self-imposed handicap of prejudice and discrimination" is relinquished. His is a dream that hinges on a logic of exclusion and inclusion: "sons of Italian or Jewish or Polish parents" were long "denied the opportunity to contribute to the nation's progress," but they have been given opportunity, Kennedy suggests, and so the nation has progressed, morally and materially.[56] By this logic, there is a "price"—moral and economic—to continuing to deny "full opportunity to millions of Negro Americans."[57] James Baldwin's words on "The American Dream and the American Negro" at Cambridge in 1965 excoriated Kennedy's politics of liberal gradualism, in which Black aspirations remain subordinate to narratives of (white) national economic progress:

> When the ex-attorney general, Mr. Robert Kennedy, said that it was conceivable that in 40 years in America we might have a Negro president—and that sounded like a very emancipated statement, I suppose, to white people. They were not in Harlem when this statement was first heard and did not hear and possibly will never hear the laughter and the bitterness and the scorn with which this statement was greeted. From the point of view of the men in the Harlem barbershop, Bobby Kennedy only got here yesterday. And now he's already on his way to the presidency. We've been here for 400 years, and now he tells us that maybe, in 40 years, if you're good, we may let you become president.[58]

A national narrative that defers Black economic and political equality by tying it to the speculative future-oriented workings of market forces sustains an unequal status quo.

Like Baldwin, Tlali suggests that optimism delimited by the retention and acquisition of property—by a logic of equal opportunity—risks complicity and inevitable disappointment for Black people living in white supremacist societies. As the novel tackles how to elide this affective commitment when economic opportunity has felt and feels both necessary and liberatory, it commits to an explicitly anticolonial project that calls not so much for the extension of rights as for the transformation of economic logics. Muriel hopes for economic justice that would manifest within a decolonized nation, having learned that access to property and credit maintain apartheid by falsely leveraging hope. *Between Two Worlds* thus rejects a politics in which individualized economic opportunity is invoked to defer the end of Black thriving. To stay at Metropolitan Radio, Muriel suggests, "I would literally have to trample on my conscience, to gobble it up (as we say in our language)" (165).[59] The idiom of "gobble" evokes Jean-François Bayart's famous elucidation of "*la politique du ventre* (the politics of the belly)," which describes African politico-moral systems that decry processes of accumulation and appropriation that produce satiation in the few while the many go hungry. It marks a refusal to "see 'the market' as a natural force to which human life simply *must* submit" and a tendency to embrace the "insight that markets, prices, and wages are always *human* products."[60] Muriel indeed finally refuses to submit to market logics: to the idea that her aspirations or those of her neighbors may yet be secured through access to property, credit, or a better job.

The much broader scope of her hopes is made clear in the series of events that lead to her resignation. Muriel is greeted with a "HAPPY MORNING" card in the office on the second day of January, while her boss (she pointedly notes) is still on holiday. Black people's celebration of New Year's Day, unlike the celebration of Christmas Day, is unrecognized by the nation with an extra day off, as Muriel laments.[61] She and her Black co-workers are "tired" (212), not just because of the festivities of the holiday season, but also because of the "merciless" month that awaits them financially and no paid rest to begin to see them through it:

> Even if I were to spend the maximum amount of fifty cents per day (if you can imagine such a possibility), I could still not manage with what was left of my husband's salary and mine combined. How on earth was I to make ends meet? (212)

The final reason the novel leaves its readers with for desiring a nation redeemed centers not on equality of economic opportunity, but on equality of rest, where rest is closely associated with the good life. Rest is another demand of the 1955 Freedom Charter, albeit one that, unlike property and housing, is notably absent from the 1996 Bill of Rights: "Rest, leisure, and recreation shall be the right of all."[62] To be sure, Muriel's vision anticipates postapartheid legislative reforms, such as the Public Holidays Act of 1994, which repealed the Public Holidays Act of 1952 and inaugurated official public holidays, such as Human Rights Day, Freedom Day, and Youth Day, that commemorate liberation struggles rather than colonial conquest (as Kruger Day and Founders Day did under apartheid).[63] It further anticipates how the 1994 Act enacted statutory paid holidays, putting an end to apartheid policies such as the Mines and Works Act of 1956, which dictated that Black laborers in the mining industry only had to be paid for four public holidays annually. As Njabulo S. Ndebele noted in 2001, a shared calendar can be an important means of asserting "positive ownership of the entire social and civic landscape."[64]

Yet, Muriel's vision is still more ambitious than these legal reforms. Muriel desires deeply, for herself and for her community, to speak as her white co-workers speak: "of the joys of living, of going away or coming back from holiday" (213). Muriel, who has been employed in white-collar waged labor yet has endured low wages and the constant threat of dismissal, offers a South African dream centered on a Black woman who is a happy vacationer. (Ndebele offers a similar vision in *The Cry of Winnie Mandela*, which ends with its protagonists, all Black women, relaxing on a road trip.)[65] This focus on leisure, in turn, provides a framework for understanding the significance of the form of Tlali's narrative. *Between Two Worlds*, as has been noted, is famous for being the first novel published by a Black South African woman within national borders. In a 1988 interview with Cecily Lockett, Tlali commented on the challenges she faced in accomplishing this feat:

> For a Black woman, I don't think it is very easy unless you have peace inside, which is something that I strive very much to get. You have to analyse situations, and all that needs peace of mind and time. It needs a long time and you have to think about it. And you have to dream about it and black women do not have time to dream.[66]

Tlali returns to the question of time throughout the interview, noting that "most Black people, especially women, do not have the time to sit and read novels" and that "the quagmire of existence in the townships" means that "you are fighting forever at loggerheads with the system, fighting the system of the time in trying to realize your dreams."[67]

Economic dispossession—Tlali notes that her published novel was "still too expensive for Black people to buy"[68]—is also a temporal and gendered dispossession. This is a point that Ndebele makes in his meditation on the challenges of developing a shared South African cultural calendar:

> The calendar of life in a typical township in the worst days of apartheid was all too short. It was a 24-hour calendar. Designed to obliterate any sense of history beyond yesterday, any sense of the future beyond tomorrow. The township was little more than a dormitory, a place of limited social growth.[69]

A famously middle-class form that, as Tlali highlights, requires both analysis of the past and dreaming for the future, the novel itself stands as protest to this calendar and the precarity that underpins it and as a manifestation of aspiration to class mobility. Here it is worth revisiting the fact that Muriel so pointedly leaves Metropolitan Radio without another job lined up. Her South African dream is perhaps twofold: that she should enjoy a clear conscience through pursuing collective action and that she should enjoy some leisure through individual reflection that ultimately takes the form of reading and writing. The two endeavors complement one another, insofar as each is the means to achieving the other. Both ideals cannot be fulfilled in an unredeemed nation, but what would constitute redemption seems clear: a Republic that supports the economic rights of Black people who live within and beyond its borders—not for the sake of national economic progress but because it is right to do so—and a national culture and economy that values and promotes Black women's intellectual and creative labor.

In other words, the "hopes of redemption" that Muriel values most are finally not the privatized domestic hopes of individual families, just as her longing for what is "mine own" is finally not about property ownership as an act of individual possession. Rather, for Muriel the significance of having once had "our own homes" in Sophiatown is the more radical hope that such ownership facilitated within the community. This is the hope that Muriel recalls in a vision of township residents singing to resist removal by calling instead for the removal of white settlers: "*Mabayeke!* . . . (Let them leave . . .)" (150). The confrontation with how a "home full of hope for the future" is a "mockery" under apartheid produces the call not just for the retention of one's own home but for the end of the settler state. The shift is one that Hugh Masekela describes as more broadly characterizing the pan-African ethos of Sophiatown in the years immediately before and after its destruction in 1955:

We Africans were peddled a vision of blacks in the Americas that suggested they were living the high live [sic]—all we ever saw were artists surrounded by glitter and glamour. It came as a shock to my generation, who came to the West in the 1950s and 1060s [sic], to find that wherever black people lived—Europe the Caribbean, America—they were surrounded mostly by poverty, bigotry, squalor, crime, discrimination, and institutionalized murder. This left many of us wildly disillusioned, but it was also the beginning, for many of us, of a commitment to forge solidarity with these communities. (332)

The shock of disillusionment, Masekela suggests, produced a reorientation of hope toward the aspiration of ending a global regime of anti-Blackness. In his compelling 2017 study *Present Imperfect*, Andrew van der Vlies argues that postapartheid South African literature that represents affective and temporal experiences of disappointment and disaffection has the potential to "turn missed appointments and bad feelings into new appointments with the unfolding experience of alternative lives and possible futures."[70] Forms of indeterminate "educated hope" (the term is Ernst Bloch's) may be found in works of fiction that are "informed—crucially— by *past* disappointments."[71] Tlali's novel manifests how an affective experience of disappointment has a longer history in South African letters than van der Vlies charts, while pointing toward how this experience has been entangled in pan-African histories. By envisioning Black economic liberation in terms that prioritize time rather than credit, *Between Two Worlds* dreams of a decolonial South African future that might redeem the anticolonial dreams of Sophiatown.

No Rest Yet

Tlali's novel stages different kinds of optimistic orientations to dreams of postcolonial, postapartheid national becoming. Even as it hopes for a decolonized state measured through time to rest, it is attuned to how the optimistic desire for financial mechanisms such as property and credit are powerful and recurrent under apartheid. Memories of house ownership in Sophiatown bolster aspirational dreams tied to visions of African-American mobility and modernity; the persistence of credit apartheid across South Africa and the US produces the desire for its end and readier access to credit on fairer terms. Tlali's novel reflects on how these hopes and dreams, which persist across decades and are in significant ways life-sustaining under conditions of dispossession, nonetheless set the stage for disillusionment. The novel thinks through how optimism attached to property and credit persists, even when it is known that these are insufficient for ensuring the good life.

In its attention particularly to credit as a locus of desire and disillusionment in South Africa, *Between Two Worlds* anticipates Martjin Konings analysis in *The Emotional Logic of Capitalism* (2015) of the stubborn and cyclical centering of "democratized" credit within US national affect. For Konings, although the American dream is often framed in terms of individual autonomy, merit, and drive, its pursuit has been inextricably bound to individuals' dependency on financial institutions. In the early US republic, Konings argues, the "democratization of credit was viewed as a key term of the new political contract, a way to ensure that money and markets would serve not as sources of corruption but as the institutional foundation of a redemptive republican regime."[72] The economy would be "good," in short, because the white yeoman farmer denied his own property in Europe would be able to access capital to purchase land. Konings shows how this association of the extension of credit with individual and national redemption persisted through twentieth- and twenty-first-century US history, albeit in different iterations. Mid-century New Deal reforms, argues Konings, were designed "not to suppress finance but to reorient credit-creating capacities to the financial aspirations of ordinary [read: white male] Americans and to encourage banks to focus on 'financing the American dream.'"[73] The pattern repeated in subsequent decades:

> Throughout the 1960s and 1970s, the demand for credit grew at a rapid rate. As wage increases became increasingly contested, household debt became a prominent way to secure participation in the American dream, and the baby boomer generation borrowed money for homes, cars, college, and consumption. American policymakers were acutely aware of the increasingly central role of credit in securing social integration and political legitimacy, and they were fully committed to expanding the securitization options available to banks.[74]

The extension of credit in the US has never been democratic, but always racialized, gendered, and classed. Koning's point, however, is that US history evidences an affective cycle whereby the extension of credit is associated with democratization and republicanism, despite the fact that the deepening of the credit economy effectively promotes "the expansion of economy and its penetration into new spheres of human life" that generates the very inequalities that produce crises and calls for a reformed economy.[75] The call for equitable credit in post-1965 Black American rights advocacy is part of this broader US history. US capitalism has been sustained, Konings shows, through "productive admixtures of hope and disappointment, illusion and disillusionment, trauma and the prospect of salvation."[76]

These productive admixtures are everywhere in Tlali's novel, which also tries to imagine a (trans)national future that will diminish their forcefulness. *Between Two Worlds* expresses a desire for rest—for an escape from the exhausting cycle of hope and despair. Yet, its historical awareness of how property and credit have been means of achieving a sense of respite, however brief, foresees the possible continuation of the exhausting work of managing forced removal and debt. In this, the novel anticipates the continuance of postcolonial optimism oriented toward national economic reforms that seek to redress ongoing histories of credit apartheid by prioritizing the extension of property and debt. As the next chapter suggests, turning to Zakes Mda's *The Heart of Redness*, South African literature continues to negotiate the affective pull of the dream of democratized credit, specifically.[77] In an increasingly financialized, postapartheid South African economy, Mda suggests, the market logics of US developmental imperialism gains affective power, such that cycles of hope and despair become an ever-amplified part of South African national life.

Chapter 5

The American Dreams in *The Heart of Redness*

Between Two Worlds, I have argued (chapter 4), dreams of a South African republic where state support for Black people's full economic rights will be subordinate to a broader decolonial project that will lead to rest. In its centering of holidays, Tlali's vision of what a South African republic might offer resonates with the closing scene of one of the great novels of the interregnum, Zakes Mda's *Ways of Dying* (1995).[1] Mda's novel, which begins on Christmas Day, catalogues and mourns horrific instances of violence near the end of political apartheid—instances drawn, Mda reports, from nonfictional news stories he read while living in exile in the US.[2] It ends, however, with a scene of communal celebration:

> At twelve midnight exactly, bells from all the churches in the city begin to ring. Hooters are blaring in all the streets. The settlement people burst into a cacophony: beating pots and pans and other utensils together, while shouting 'Happe-e-e-e New Year!' (211)

The collective first-person narrators report that "two hours after midnight, we are still shouting 'Happe-e-ee!" (211). As in *Between Two Worlds*, it is not Christmas that brings the prospect or realization of the good life, but New Year's, a holiday whose associations with Black people's celebration of emancipation span from Watch Night or Freedom's Eve services in African-American churches to Tweede Nuwe Jaar, or "Second New Year" parades, centered in Cape Town.[3] While referencing the past, the heady description of communal elation also pertains to the time of writing: it evokes the atmosphere of intense hopefulness that accompanied the transition to democracy, historically represented, for example, by the many who celebrated Nelson Mandela's release from prison in 1990 or the long lines that characterized the first elections in the "new" South Africa in 1994. The revelers' creative deployment of kitchen instruments encapsulates a quotidian and localized expression of this sense of national elation. As such, it anticipates the enduring popularity of a New Year's tradition begun in the neighborhood of Hillbrow in Johannesburg in the mid-1990s: that of throwing old furniture out of windows to start the year fresh.[4] The custom arguably asserts Black people's right to property in a way that recalls Tlali's fiction: it defies the systemic restriction of Black people's consumer and property rights. In Mda's novel, as in Tlali's, household goods and holiday celebrations contain resistant potential. Whereas Tlali's novel ends on a ripple of hope, however, Mda's describes sheer euphoria, as a public holiday conveys a sense of well-being that anticipates imminent national liberation.

At the same time, however, this euphoria shares a valence of ambivalence familiar from Tlali's fiction that I argue characterizes postcolonial optimism—hopes for national becoming shaped by US empire—in the South African literary context. Mda stresses the temporariness of liberatory feeling: the "new" year offers a momentary sense of release from an unfree status quo that qualifies the elation surrounding anticipation of the "new" nation. Revelers wish each other "happ-e-ee," but the intensity of their shouts betrays the strain underpinning the wish. The burning tires that illuminate the New Year's celebrations suggest the proximity of histories of violence and ongoing dispossession. The collective narrators note that the fires do not emit the "sickly stench of roasting human flesh" but of "pure wholesome rubber" (212). Of course, the rubber is not wholesome at all, and its burning marks ongoing environmental racism. The sentence also makes clear that burning tires viscerally recall the lynchings of community members. South Africans may celebrate freedom, but they do so in a context of unfreedom that persists into the postapartheid era. To return to the New Year's celebrations in Hillbrow: they see numerous people hurt each year, and an increased police presence has become par for the course. Inequality, dispossession, bodily risk, and state violence are woven into the scene of collective celebration, as they are in Mda's novel. The euphoria described at the end of *Ways of Dying* thus aligns with the etymological sense of the term, whereby euphoria is a flush of well-being experienced by those who are sick, a sense of optimism that is "based on over-confidence or over-optimism."[5] Here again is postcolonial optimism that feels inevitably bound to disillusionment. Mda's euphoria, while marking an amplification of intensity of feeling, is continuous with Tlali's hopefulness, I suggest, insofar as it invites an examination of the magnetism and the insufficiency of national aspirations for the good life.

In Mda's subsequent work, the affective structure of postcolonial optimism encompasses a hope that Muriel holds dear in *Between Two Worlds*: a hope that a new republic might realize time for Black leisure and creativity. To the degree that such hope has been achieved in the postapartheid nation, Mda suggests, it has also been betrayed. In *The Whale Caller* (2005), for example, the "rainbow nation" manifest in the seaside resort town of Hermanus is an opiate that, like the fiction's other pharmakons, both eases and jeopardizes day-to-day survival:

> The Whale Caller negotiates his way among the rainbow people. People of what is fashionably referred to as the new South Africa, even though it is ten years old. Ten years is a second in the life of a nation. Rainbow people sport rainbow hairstyles. Heads looking like frosted birthday cakes. Black hair with silver stripes. Orange and blue hair with golden stripes. Peroxide blondes with black polka dots. Leggy model-types and stout granny-types. Broad-shouldered bare-chested men in wet Bermuda shorts, wearing green, blue, black, purple, and yellow serpent or dragon tattoos on golden brown tans.
>   Hair. It is a blight they must carry on their heads, exposing the position each head occupied in the statutory hierarchies of the past. The troubles of humanity are locked in the hair. Yet the people have managed to disguise their shame by painting it in the colours that designate them all a people of the rainbow. Without exception. Without a past. Without rancor. Without hierarchies. Only their eyes betray the big lie. In these eyes you can see a people living in a daze. Rainbow people walking in a precarious dream that may explode into a nightmare without much warning. (18)[6]

The holiday scene suggests how the forms of rest made possible by the end of political apartheid exist alongside ongoing histories of racialized inequality. Njabulo S. Ndebele suggested in a 1999 essay that "the liberation of leisure is an essential aspect of the new experience of freedom."[7] As Barnard notes, the postapartheid spread to Black communities of key government services, such as electricity and running water, did change day-to-day lives; Black women could report having "time to rest."[8] If leisure is to be truly liberated, however, Ndebele, like Mda, makes clear it cannot reproduce the inequalities of colonial culture but requires a "shared culture of leisure between the worker and the tourist."[9] Otherwise, as Mda shows, the high of the "new" is little more than a fig leaf for ongoing shame, including, for example, the continuance of state policies that effectively distribute property rights along racialized lines. There may be more Black tourists among the beach-goers, but the child Lunga Tubu sings on the streets to earn money for school fees after his family is disqualified from the indigent tariff for owning "a range of electrical appliances and gadgets" (87). The high of new nationhood might be sustained and renewed (for ten years and more), but the comedown is built in. The feeling that South African dreams of collective liberation have been redeemed with any singular political event forecloses confrontation with ongoing shameful histories and ongoing real inequalities. Mda's fiction, like Tlali's, not only exposes these unjust realities but also explores why optimistic attachments to visions of postcolonial, postapartheid nationhood—and especially those bound to property and credit—become a way of surviving them.

Nowhere in Mda's oeuvre is this exploration of postcolonial optimism more evident than in *The Heart of Redness* (2000), which explicitly depicts intoxicating feelings around visions of economic opportunity that seem about to be realized in the years following 1994.[10] For the many dreamers in this novel, the past is vividly present and the "new South Africa" is already here, as various forms of investment and lending make individual and collective thriving seems just within reach. Critics have celebrated the proliferation of dreams in *The Heart of Redness*, as well as the way the novel's many paths to economic "development" seem to recalibrate aspiration away from the nation to scales of the local and global. I argue against the grain of these readings by highlighting how the novel's aspirations are intimately tied with idealizations of the US, as well as with South African diasporic exposure to the market tenets of US empire. To be sure, there is plenty of disaffection with both the South African and US nation in the novel. This disaffection, however, belies the continuance of a millenarian temporality and euphoric affective structure that the novel associates with claims of national exceptionalism. As disillusionment with the nation produces visions that the democratization of investment and credit will finally manifest the exceptional nation as it was foreseen to be, the nation is not so much relinquished as remade according to a more neoliberal template.

Charting the entangled double helix of South African and American dreams in *The Heart of Redness*, I show, clarifies the novel's profound concern with the hegemony of postcolonial optimism in postapartheid South Africa. Within the fiction's amaXhosa community, there are multiple visions of what the future ought to be, including those that explicitly embrace or decry US imperialism. Yet, these dreams are similar in that they look forward to a redeemed economy in which credit and real estate accrue to meritorious individuals who work hard. They are all, in other words, dreams of redemption that are often conceived in terms resonant with US proclamations of national economic opportunity (although the novel suggests how they are also deeply woven into amaXhosa history), whereby the hard-working and self-denying individual receives just rewards. In Mda's fiction, such dreams are precarious indeed and threaten to explode into a South African nightmare of debt and despair. *The Heart of Redness*, like other South African fiction of postcolonial optimism, thus unsettles a chronology that narrates progressive disillusionment with ideals of South African exceptionalism. It shows instead how national myths of exceptional economic opportunity proliferate forms of euphoric hope, an optimism that is over-optimistic. Mda's euphoric postapartheid work does not fail to anticipate coming disillusionment, and it does not stand apart from future disaffection: rather, it shows how disillusionment underpins and delimits the very moment of hopeful anticipation. At the same time, while Mda's novel registers this affective constellation of national exceptionality, it also writes against it. The dream-like aesthetic of *The Heart of Redness*, after all, seems far from instantiating a redemptive work ethic: it celebrates indulgence and dependency rather than austerity and autonomy. Mda's novel dreams of having collective time for dreaming, and for the renewal of creative energies and expansion of aspirations that such a luxury would afford.

The Highs

A central conflict in *The Heart of Redness* revolves around the question of what kind of investment will be best for the Eastern Cape village of Qolorha-by-Sea. In 1998, a flashpoint of controversy is the proposed construction of a casino and water park. One prominent community member, Bhonco, argues that the presence of wealthy people will benefit the community as a whole: "The new developments will bring tourists. The new developments will create employment for us all. The new developments will bring people from all over the world. From America!" (92–93). Prominent among critics of this dream is Camagu, a visitor to the village—and the novel's main protagonist—who argues that the proposed development will in fact produce few jobs, deprive the community of access to the sea and its resources, engender dependency, and benefit shareholders and government officials (200). In its place, Camagu proposes a new "dream": "The promotion of the kind of tourism that will benefit the people, that will not destroy indigenous forests, that will not bring hordes of people who will pollute the rivers and drive away the birds" (201). As Camagu ecstatically realizes that Qolorha has the potential to "even create our own electricity! From the sun!" (239), he believes that he and the villagers might establish their own local infrastructure.[11] Here is a dream that prophesies a prosperous future in the "new" South Africa if only energies are invested in starting local cooperatives (as Camagu eventually does) rather than attracting foreign developers.

Importantly to the novel's structure, both sides of this dispute ground their faith in what is best for the community in what Jennifer Wenzel describes as a sense of the "vitality of incomplete pasts."[12] More specifically, both supporters and detractors of the resort complex rehearse the history of the events of 1856–57 in kwaXhosa, when followers of the prophet Nongqawuse slaughtered cattle and halted cultivation because she had foreseen that, in Mda's words, "the whole community of the dead" would arise with new livestock and animals (54–55).[13] Supporters of the waterpark, including Bhonco and other "Unbelievers," look on this history with "shame" and as evidence that liberation is not to be found in amaXhosa knowledge (68). Those "Believers" who oppose the casino complex find sustenance for anticolonial resistance in this same history. As Wenzel argues, *The Heart of Redness* depicts what Dipesh Chakrabarty calls "heterotemporality," or "a plurality of times existing together."[14] This emphasis on simultaneity means that the novel's oppositions are continuously undercut. In the nineteenth-century storyline, for example, some followers of Nongqawuse are very much like 1998's Unbelievers looking forward to the arrival of the Americans, insofar as they have faith that "our ancestors" may arise as "Russians," who were believed to be a "black nation" because they had successfully defeated British colonizers in battle (82–83). AmaXhosa identity is always already transnational, and amaXhosa Believers turn to other nations in the name of autonomy. Such imbrication of the global and local is also true for the twentieth century. Bhonco, for example, though he may seek salvation in foreign investment, is finally like the historical followers of Nongqawuse in his full commitment to amaXhosa community. The youth of Qolorha-by-Sea, we are reminded multiple times, are leaving the village for cities such as Pretoria, Cape Town, and Johannesburg. Their opportunities seem to lie not with village cooperative societies but with centers of international capital, so, by advocating for the complex, Bhonco advocates for generational continuity. (As Bhonco loses the casino complex, he also loses his daughter Xoliswa Ximiya, who moves to Pretoria.) By depicting the entanglement of the local and global, Mda's novel defies essentialist notions of culture and traditions, as well as what Matthew Eatough describes as the either-or logic of the global capitalist marketplace.[15]

Several of Mda's readers have identified what is bracing in this poststructuralist representation of the postapartheid nation, in which, as Wenzel puts it, the novel offers only "tenuous solutions cognizant of their own provisionality."[16] By detaching "utopian promise" from a strictly national imaginary and recalibrating "dreams of liberation" to the scales of the local and global, Wenzel argues, the novel renews those dreams.[17] As Rita Barnard notes, the novel preserves an openness to liberatory potentialities, as orientations toward autochthonous heritages and global networks are often "undecidable and contradictory."[18] Mda's work in these respects follows what Wenzel describes as a "logic of proliferation rather than resolution" that from a certain perspective stands as a potentially refreshing counterpoint to singular dreams of national development.[19]

I want to suggest, however, that in another respect this openness, provisionality, and anti-essentialism points toward a disturbing sameness in the aspirations that Mda depicts, which I contend are hegemonically expressive of the condition of nation-building under empire. The oppressive permeation of the US throughout Mda's novel has not been fully discussed, but it is readily apparent, particularly in the figure of Xoliswa Ximiya, Bhonco's daughter. Xoliswa works as the school principal in the village, but her biggest point of pride is that she has been to Athens, Ohio for six months and hopes "to go back one day"; she thinks of the United States as "the best country in the world" (65). She proclaims it "a fairy-tale country, with beautiful people. People like Dolly Parton and Eddie Murphy. It is a vast country that is highly technological" (64). Much like her father, her unabashed dream for her community is that the planned resort makes her home village more like an idealized America: "this is a lifetime opportunity for Qolorha to be like some of the holiday resorts in America. To have big stars like Eddie Murphy and Dolly Parton come here for holiday" (67). Dolly Parton, famously, was born into poverty before achieving massive fame as a country singer. In *Dream More*, she proclaims of her fortune: "I know that I am living the all-American dream."[20] Eddie Murphy has described his family growing up as "struggling-class black folks," and his starring turns in *Trading Places* (1983) and *Coming to America* (1988), along with his own stardom, likewise seem to affirm "America" as a place of opportunity and class mobility.[21] Xoliswa's hope is that the opportunity and success that her favorite celebrities embody will be made available to Qolorha. After all, though Xoliswa's father, Bhonco, brags about his daughter's "great achievement" of having acquired "two hot plates" after the school became one of three "places in the village that have electricity drawn from Butterworth" (93), this development clearly does not satisfy Xoliswa's desire to access the "highly technological" (64). The holiday resort, however, promises better infrastructure, and better infrastructure means Xoliswa might be able to enjoy luxuries in Qolorha that exceed a few hot plates.[22]

At first glance, Camagu's plans for infrastructural development and community investment seem opposed to this vision, not least because

Camagu himself does not hesitate to set himself up as a critic of US imperialism. Camagu, who lived in the US for thirty years before returning to South Africa to vote, associates the US with "racial prejudice and bully-boy tactics toward other countries" (66).[23] He rejects the Cold War fantasy of American exceptionalism that, as Donald Pease states, produced "the structuring disavowal of imperialism as an American way of life."[24] For Camagu, the US is nothing to aspire to, and the dream of opportunity associated with it is nothing more than a dream. The proposed development, he maintains, would only perpetuate the reality of racialized inequality in South Africa and further US power.[25] Yet, regardless of his disdain for the US, Camagu is undoubtedly an agent of US influence. He has a doctoral degree in "communication and economic development," earned while working for an international development agency in New York (29). His "local" co-op is thus led by a man who has spent most of his life in the US and whose commitment to "grassroots," "sustainable" development programs that purportedly empower women reflects ideological orthodoxies within US universities since the 1970s.[26] Camagu returns to South Africa after thirty years absence "as a pedlar of dreams" (36), ready to sell the gospel of sustainable development that, in its commitment to privatization and competition, is not as distinct from the proposed casino development as he might imagine.

I read a uniformity, in other words, across aspirations for Qolorha's future that are perhaps too easily read as distinct: a postcolonial optimism, shaped by conditions of US empire, that invests in so-called economic opportunity as a means of redeeming the yet-to-be-realized promises of the "new" South Africa. This feeling, the novel emphasizes, is millenarian in character, insofar as the experience of heterotemporality is paradoxically persistent across time: in both the mid-nineteenth and late twentieth centuries, the present overwhelms the past and the future, such that ancestors are living and prophecies of imminent salvation are forceful. Bhonco and Camagu, after all, are very like their nineteenth-century counterparts who foresee redemption in the arrival of Russians and/or ancestors. They differ from amaXhosa forebearers only in the fact that the US, rather than Britain, explicitly or implicitly shapes their sense of what future is possible in the "new" South Africa.[27] That their optimism resonates with a structure of feeling commonly associated with the US is no coincidence, for what is the idea of America if not a millenarian prophecy? Going back to John Winthrop's 1630 sermon "A Modell of Christian Charity," which proclaimed that the preacher and his fellow settler colonists must be "as a city on the hill," for the "eyes of all people are upon us,"[28] a foundational myth of the nation that becomes known as "America" is the idea that the present is always the moment to fulfill past hopes and usher in the promised future.²⁹ Whether in South Africa or the US, the occasion for millenarian dreams that reach to the past to imagine a better future *is* the "new" nation.

Rather than sidelining the nation, then, Mda's fiction depicts how the centering of aspirations on global and local economies is symptomatic of the ways in which the "new" South Africa exists within a US-dominated imperial regime in which the millenarian, exceptional nation seeks redemption through the market. As I detail in the next section, the fiction suggests how the postcolonial, optimistic persistence of these aspirations is in no small part fueled by disillusionment with the nation—a disillusionment that redoubles a euphoric sense that a capitalist economy that is conceived as working apart from the state may yet manifest an exceptional national destiny of prosperity. South Africans, Mda suggests, like Americans, are in a state, in the sense that Jacqueline Rose plays on the term in *States of Fantasy* (1998): they share a psychic condition (they are "in a state"), an affective orientation toward the polity that is necessary for the nation-state's legitimation.³⁰ This state alternates between euphoria and despair, as high hopes for economic growth produce the conditions for their own betrayal. For all that Mda's fiction privileges local and global flows, the novel is yet preoccupied with South African nationhood, particularly as it has become increasingly bound to the dreams and prophecies of US empire.

With the Lows

Hopes and disillusionment bound to twentieth-century accounts of the mythically exceptional nations of America and South Africa are crucial to Mda's exploration of the postapartheid feeling I am describing as postcolonial optimism: an ongoing optimistic investment in the instruments of capital as means to national becoming that has known and ensures the recurrence of despair. Even if the transition to democracy did not indicate the "completion" of redemption, it did signal, per Wenzel, a revival of hopes that decolonization in Africa might be achieved in the "new" nation.³¹ By 2010, however, Gareth Cornwell posited that "it would seem that South Africans have lost that sense of exceptionalism that the more or less peaceful transition of power in the early 1990s conferred upon them, in the eyes of the world, as well as their own."³²

In Mda's fiction, both Bhonco and Camagu feel in 1998 that the nation has already failed them—but this does not mean they have given up on dreams of redemption. Bhonco is bitterly disappointed that the government "refuses to give me my pension," despite the fact he has had endless troubles "working for his country" at a textile factory, dairy, blanket factory, and Cape Town docks (10):

> Why won't the government give him nkamnkam like all the old men and women of South Africa who are on old-age pensions today? Is it fair that now, even though ravines of maturity run wild on his face, he should still not receive any nkamnkam? (10)

Camagu also feels that the "new" South Africa has been unjust. After being "swept up by the euphoria of the time" and searching for a job with the new government with the aim of contributing to "the development of his country" (29), after four years he is only able to find a job teaching part-time at a trade school (31). He is deeply disillusioned by a nation that he judges to be run by the "Aristocrats of the Revolution" via a system of "what he called patronage" (33). Both Bhonco and Camagu's ecstatic hopes for the future (jobs for all! electricity for everyone!) are grounded in their bitter disappointment with the nation, which seems to offer no material reward for service to one's country and no opportunity to serve one's country. It appears complicit with, rather than a ward against, a corrupt extractive economy that enforces migration to urban centers and ensures that the profits and pleasures of natural resources accrue largely to outside developers and tourists.

The myth of the "new" nation thus produces both disillusionment with national governance and overly-confident hopes for national redemption that ostensibly do not depend upon government action. More specifically, Camagu and Bhonco both embrace an ethos of austerity and independence in their visions of Qolorha-by-Sea's future. Camagu contends that the postapartheid South African regime has betrayed the freedom promised in the new republic: "notions of delivery and upliftment have turned our people into passive recipients of programs," and "people are denied the right to shape their own destiny" because "a dependency mentality is reinforced in their minds" (180). Rural Qolorha fulfills his "search" for a "dream" because "here people were now doing things for themselves, without any handouts from the government" (172). Likewise, although Bhonco's critics believe he has "led a careless life" based on his absence of savings, others recall that he too has lived a life of self-discipline and austerity (144): his efforts to educate his daughter through university "swallowed even the money he had accumulated in his younger days" (145). If Bhonco desires both a government pension and a modernized job for his daughter, it is because he believes he has worked hard and sacrificed much for both.

This commitment to defining merit in terms of autonomy and discipline aligns with the neoliberal logics adopted by Mandela's ANC government and enacted through measures such as voluntary structural adjustment and a shift from prioritizing poverty alleviation to market-based growth in programs from housing to land redistribution. It also aligns with the affective pattern that Martjin Konings argues in *The Emotional Logic of Capitalism* (2015) best characterizes the founding and imperial expansion of the US: one of "intense resentment and the prospect of redemption."[33] This pattern, Konings notes, is grounded in a tradition of salvific Protestantism, which figured the "New World" as the place where the "moral corruption" of the "Old World," defined in terms of "indulgence" and "dependence," might be purged.[34] This purging has been continuously imagined in terms of "personal independence and self-help," such that proper "discipline" will redress the potential betrayals enacted by state-sanctioned "permissiveness and paternalism."[35] Near the turn of the millennium, Bill Clinton invoked this long rhetorical tradition as he cut funding for welfare and public housing.[36] His administration looked for equality through the revitalization of Richard Nixon's black capitalism framework, creating incentives for companies to invest in impoverished Black communities. The policies were informed by a broader intellectual and political milieu, evident in Camagu's beliefs, that "poverty was just a result of misaligned market incentives" that could best be addressed through the pursuit of "economic self-interest."[37]

Konings's analysis draws attention to how Mda highlights South Africa's own history of Protestant traditions glorifying autonomy and discipline. In Mda's telling, Nongqawuse's uncle Mhlakaza, a convert to Methodism then Anglicanism also known as Wilhelm Goliath, attests to the truth of his niece's visions (48).[38] These visions link salvation to enacting a particular regime of tremendous self-discipline: "all cattle now living must be slaughtered . . . the fields must not be cultivated, but great new grain pits must be dug, new houses must be built, and great strong cattle kraals must be erected" (54). In South Africa as in the US, the dreams that would eschew the nation are yet very much part of a national ethos that embraces privatization, self-discipline, and entrepreneurial endeavor.

Yet more specifically, as Konings argues regarding the US, so South African literature of postcolonial optimism suggests is true regarding South Africa: disillusionment with the purportedly exceptional nation leads to a desire for a purified financial system that is repeatedly expressed in calls for the democratization of credit. As shown in the last chapter, Tlali's *Between Two Worlds* emphasizes the importance of credit (and the property that can be purchased with it) in dreams of Black liberation that responded to the injustices of an apartheid economy. With the transition to democracy, these dreams were to some degree fulfilled. As Deborah James examines in *Money from Nothing* (2015), in the years following 1994, "the offering and taking up of credit was expanded and 'democratized' in an unprecedented way."[39] This expansion "arguably offered considerable advantage," especially insofar as it "enabled the expansion" of the Black middle class and "unleash[ed] the inventively hybrid novelty and creativity of a new generation of consumers."[40] From this perspective, "the money householders were able to borrow was thus of crucial importance in the story of South Africa's transition, perhaps much more than what anyone expected or realized."[41] At the same time, however, a system of credit apartheid remained in place, and *The Heart of Redness* is keenly attuned to credit's unequal distribution. Without a pension, Bhonco constantly struggles to make purchases on credit from John Dalton's Vulindlela Trading Store. And Camagu repeatedly laments that his dreams are limited only by his limited access to capital: "The cooperative society is not doing badly. Business would be booming if the banks were interested in assisting small-business people" (178). Survival depends on expansion, and expansion cannot happen without a loan. Thwarted once in his attempt to open his own consultancy by the refusal of a bank to issue a guarantee, Camagu fears that "history is repeating itself. His cooperative society is on the verge of success. But the South African banks are determined that it should not succeed. So much for black empowerment!" (179). The extension of favorable credit to Black people in the "new" South Africa has created new forms of inequality to which Bhonco and Camagu are attuned. To remedy this inequality, they call for credit's further expansion. The logic here is notably like that which produced the Black Economic Empowerment (BEE) programs designed precisely to extend entrepreneurial opportunities to small businesses.

Far from even provisionally promoting such policy, Mda's novel makes the paradoxes of this progressive logic wildly apparent by stressing how visions of redemption (both South African and American) at the turn of the millennium require the ongoing servicing of debt. For both Bhonco and Camagu, calls to self-sufficiency hinge on the opportunity to enter relationships of financial dependency and debt, and calls to self-discipline are inextricably linked with ready access to credit. Konings summarizes the effects of recurrent calls to democratized credit in the US: "in each case, the effect of such iconoclastic demands has been to deepen the economy, to promote the expansion of financial markets, and to shore up the dollar standard."[42] "Modern capitalism's signal achievement," Konings argues, is "to have converted awareness of its problematic aspects into a motor of its further expansion" through "productive admixtures of hope and disappointment, illusion and disillusionment, trauma and the prospect of salvation."[43] South African dreams, Mda's fiction suggests, have been and have become more like American dreams (and vice versa), as they have sought to redeem the purportedly exceptional nation through the entrenchment of capital. The pattern is one that the novel represents as nascent in nineteenth-century amaXhosa history, whereby disillusionment with Nongqawuse (who has imagined the amaXhosa as those who will free the Eastern Cape from colonial influence) leads some amaXhosa leaders to support a policy whereby "chiefs would henceforth receive a monthly salary in colonial money" that, they believe, will help to secure their "status," although, as their critics note, this will also mean chiefs will "owe their loyalty" to the British (134). Governmentality is secured, not destabilized, through the expansion of relations of indebtedness mediated by capital. The "logic of credit and debt" is, as Konings observes, and as colonized nations have long known, a "crucial technique of government," especially "in an era that has seen a rapid growth of poverty and inequality."[44] The novel's proliferation of dreams that yet hegemonically require access to credit is symptomatic of how "capitalism does not so much stomp on us when we're down" as enable us to "access new powers and to deploy these to restore and elaborate the metaphorical modalities of our subordination."[45] It promises that inequality and exploitation may yet be overcome through the self-sacrifice and self-discipline that makes citizens good debtors. So far as Bhonco and Camagu have any dreams attached to the collectivity of the South African nation, they are only that the nation become a more reliable and efficient bank, which, of course, is no dream of collectivity at all. It is, rather, a form of euphoria, a fever-dream that is always also a nightmare.

Dreaming the Rainbow Nation

The potent imagined connection between an austere morality and redeemed economy, which is, Mda suggests, not only American, is one that in *The Heart of Redness* profoundly affects postapartheid visions of futurity, wherein conceptions of moral merit tend to be inextricably tied to regimes of economic credit. Mda's novel foregrounds entwined transnational histories that culminate, by the late 1990s, in a fervent belief that the future of the nation depends on self-discipline and market growth. If, as Eric Cazdyn has argued, the time of globalization might be described as the "new chronic,"[46] such that the future is overwhelmed by a sense of continuously managed crisis in the present, then Mda's fiction shows how the affective register of that temporal experience of ongoing crisis is not necessarily bound to "bad" feelings of anxiety and disaffection. The time of globalization might also be conceived as a time of chronic euphoria. The nation in crisis is always also the nation that may yet be redeemed: disillusionment with the purportedly exceptional nation produces a desire for the redemption of national hopes that yet evacuates the nation as a primary site for imagining or enacting collectivity.

The potentially catastrophic effects of this evacuation were registered by Njabulo Ndebele in his curious 2001 meditation titled "South Africans in Search of Common Values."[47] Ndebele observes that "six years into democracy, we still lack a national consciousness. Our communities still need common values in order to create a unifying framework within which democracy can operate."[48] Ndebele clarifies what he means by national consciousness in a series of his signature, quietly unnerving questions:

> If 50,000 South Africans of various races, classes, ethnic groups, and religions were airlifted into New York, right now, what is it, once they have settled, that would make them gravitate toward one another? What is it that would distinguish them from other nationalities in such a way that their distinctiveness becomes a basis on which they might become economically or culturally useful to New York?[49]

Geographical borders, a constitution, and a "replicated landscape of major commercial chains" are not enough to comprise a national identity, which, Ndebele implies, is necessary for the survival of local cultures in a globalized world.[50] Being "useful to" New York, after all, means having the economic and political capital necessary to ensure the transmission and protection of culture and so "survive as a cultural entity" in a "world city," which is not coincidently the US's financial center.[51] The point resonates with Timothy Brennan's contemporaneous, practical defense of the nation in "Cosmo-Theory": "within the framework of a world system of nations in which enormous disparities in national power exist ... the nation protects the weak and is their refuge."[52] Mda's novel, like Ndebele's essay, registers how the South African nation at the turn of the millennium is, to adapt Brennan's diagnosis, "less nation but more state, but a modified state, not one that micromanages corporations or regulates business enterprises at the expense of growth."⁵³ A state, that is, that is akin to the US.⁵⁴ As Ndebele suggests, in the US-dominated global political order of the early twenty-first century, a robust national culture that maps onto the boundaries of the state may be key to defending sovereignty.

The Heart of Redness is a South African novel that registers the shrinking of a public national imaginary in the "new" South African state. It also, I think, strives to imagine the nation beyond these limitations—beyond the constriction of a nation to a state that manages debt—and it does so at the level of formal innovation. The fiction conjures South Africa outside logics of development at the level of what I have described elsewhere as a prismatic aesthetics.⁵⁵ Even though the "rainbow nation" has betrayed its promises of justice and equality, it yet is startlingly referenced in the artistry of Qukezwa's double-voiced singing:

> Qukezwa sings in such beautiful colors. Soft colors like the ochre of yellow gullies. Reassuring colors of the earth. Red. Hot colors like blazing fire. Deep blue. Deep green. Colors of the valleys and the ocean. Cool colors like the rain of summer sliding down a pair of naked bodies.
>
> She sings in soft pastel colors, this Qukezwa. In crude and glaring colors. And in bright glossy colors. In subdued colors of the newly turned fields. (193)

In its many hues, the song evokes the "rainbow nation," which is here comprised of colors associated with isiXhosa costume (ochre and red), as well as those of international capital ("crude and glaring colors"). Like Mda's novel, the song presents a collectivity characterized by a distinctive constellation of different spatial scales. This "rainbow nation" is defined not by ideals of racial harmony but by varied assemblages of Indigenous and international networks. The vision of the exceptional nation tied to a temporality of liberatory progress thus yields to the expression of a multiply-valanced present that encompasses the local, global, and national, albeit the national as it is expressed by Black women. The South African culture that Mda intimates is one that provides time and space for Black women's creativity. As in Tlali's novel, this grounding is, perhaps, fresh soil for a decolonized nation.

The singing marks a distinctive conception not only of nation but also of empire. The crude, glossy hues associated with US capital and consumerism throughout the fiction are proffered in the song as interwoven in the fabric of the collectivity being sung. They are neither embraced as redemptive nor abjected as prohibiting redemption. They evoke, rather, a facet of living history that co-exists with the reds of amaXhosa self-definition and the blues of the geological history of landscape and ocean. As part of a series of passages in which it becomes increasingly unclear whether the Qukezwa singing is of the nineteenth or twentieth century, the glaring colors are rendered an inextricable part of a longer history of colonial incursion, in which amaXhosa resistance has been neither completely realized nor completely suppressed. Across the gulf of time separating the two Qukezwas stands the violence of colonialism and apartheid, as well as the resistance and persistence of amaXhosa community.

The synesthesia of the passage, along with its blurring of temporalities, is exemplary of why Mda is sometimes identified as a writer of magic realism, a genre often defined in terms of aesthetic commitments to revealing what is fantastical in history. Mda's work is even more effectively located in the genre, however, based on what Fredric Jameson has suggested is the "political realism" of "magic realism": its staging of the "archetypal repression which allows all of us to survive history's immemorial nightmares."[56] Qukezwa's singing registers this repression in its sublimation of histories of imperial domination. Mda's novel does the same, beginning with the prefatory genealogy that designates those who lived and died during colonialism and apartheid simply as "The Middle Generations," and through to the fact that the contemporary narrative barely mentions life under apartheid. The permeation of (neo)colonial violence is both everywhere and everywhere unacknowledged, such that its repression, often through the maintenance of euphoric hope, is all the more fully expressed. If Jameson's suggestion is that the formula of "baroque disorder and excess" is inadequate to describe the style of magic realism, his suggestion that the politics of magic realist style has been tied to registering the ongoing repression of imperial (and, in his analysis of Gabriel García Màrquez's *One Hundred Years of Solitude*, specifically US) violence in national imaginaries is more than adequate to describing Mda's novel. Put in other terms, in Jameson's account of magic realism, repetitive synchronicity (across generations of the mythic family as nation) coexists with a diachronous history of continually repressed violence. Heterotemporality does not produce a sense of multiple futures so much as it marks the sameness of life under empire. Hence, Jameson's reading of García Màrquez situates its famous, relentless "association of events" not with the fantastic or excessive but with the production of a kind of boredom that signals "the absence of the miraculous event." I have argued a similar structure is to be found in Mda, where the proliferation of euphoric hopes and prophecies of eminent redemption across timelines index the monotony of life in the shadow of imperial economies.

As my reading of Qukezwa's double-voiced singing suggests, however, I also think that Mda's novel imagines what the nation might do and be under conditions of empire: its project is not only of exposure. The novel, that is, offers reason for optimism that is delinked from aspirations bound to the expansion of credit and debt and their accompanying ideologies of individual responsibility and collective austerity. Alongside euphoric visions of economic development that repress imperial violence, the fiction's action, again and again, takes shape because other kinds of dreams inaugurate new forms of relationship that defy all attempts at self-control: as characters sleep, daydream, and rest, unexpected temporalities and affects come into being. These dreams are miraculous, albeit still quotidian, events that disrupt an individualistic status quo. Ancestors visit namesakes in dreams (42), descendants dream of ancestors (47), strangers dream of strangers, and dreams are "invaded" by new acquaintances (264). These dreams register experiences, sometimes unwanted, of being given over to or taken over by others. Camagu, for example, first arrives at Qolorha-by-Sea with no thought of becoming an entrepreneur. Rather, he has apprehended that NomaRussia, a woman he hears sing in Johannesburg, is a "mothering spirit" (28). She features in a "recurring dream" wherein "he was the river, and NomaRussia was its water" (60). The dream resists any simple allegorical reading, and NomaRussia, who is dying of cervical cancer, offers no nurturement when Camagu finally meets her. Dreams are not a source, then, of new dreams tied to the aspirational and redemptive logics of nation and market. They do, however, oppose redemptive economic logics premised on self-discipline and austerity, as they defy understandings of the self as ever even potentially autonomous. David Marriott, noting that Western anti-Black discourse associates whiteness with restraint, industriousness, and thriftiness and blackness with excess and decadence, suggests that, rather than summoning a dialectical desire for "discipline and subjection," it is possible to posit "a reading of decadence that is itself decadent."[57] The decadence of Mda's dreams, their excessiveness to understandings of the singular, sovereign self, offer such a reading.

Sharon Sliwinski argues in her theory of dreaming developed through attention to Nelson Mandela's dreamlife that dreams are "one of the principal means of transport for a unique form of knowledge that each subject carries but that remains vexingly other."[58] They are an "alternative thought-landscape" that provide "vehicles for otherwise unthinkable thoughts," including unspoken conflict and ongoing conditions of unfreedom. They are "an everyday means to carry out an examination of one's social moorings."[59] They are, in short, full of political potential that can manifest through acts of narrative (the disclosure of dreamlife) and interpretation (the sustenance of the public sphere). *The Heart of*

Redness celebrates the dreams that come in sleep, with rest, and through history as excessive to dreams of individual and national redemption via autonomy and self-discipline, insofar as they keep understandings of collectivity in flux by reconfiguring the self's relationship to others. If Camagu brings to Qolorha dreams of sustainable development and a "better" Black capitalism, *The Heart of Redness* brings to US readers an invitation to revisit dreams of, and dream anew, the long histories and surprising connections that support anticolonial and anti-imperial pan-African struggle. An antidote to (inter)national chronic euphoria, Mda suggests, may be fiction's capacity to sustain and proliferate such dreamscapes of past, present, and future dependencies; at least, this is the antidote offered by this heady and brutal novel.

From Rainbow Nation to *Black Diamond*

Mda's fiction has continued to track how South African hopes and dreams have been pinned to property and credit. The 2009 *Black Diamond* follows Don Mateza and his girlfriend Tumi, as the latter does her best to establish the networks and investment that will see herself and Don transformed into "Black Diamonds—as the fat-cat BEE beneficiaries are called" (15).[60] As the moniker acknowledges, the accomplishment is a rarity. In the novel's telling, aspirations to middle-class standing will be disappointed, despite all efforts, particularly if one's revolutionary credentials fall short or proximity to whiteness is not established. The exemplar of success as a Black Diamond is Molotov Mbungane, or "Comrade Deal-a-Minute," who is an expert in converting "political capital" gained during the anti-apartheid struggle into "financial capital and equity" by working with the white elite; he has "put together consortia that acquired huge stakes in the mining industry" (21). For Tumi, Mbungane is a role model who embodies the potential outcome of "positive thinking" and relentless networking (22). For others, including Don's former comrades in the struggle, and increasingly Don, he is a reason for despair: "they are so disillusioned with life, with what they call crony capitalism in South Africa, and with the betrayal by such comrades as Molotov whose mantra is that 'accumulation cannot be democratized, comrades,' that they have given up trying" (47). Hopes that Tumi will secure an investment for her business or that Don will secure a promotion are cut through with the irony of the mantra, whose empty gesture of solidarity glosses over an unequal status quo. Past betrayals anticipate future betrayals, even as the affective forcefulness of the promise that economic mobility and opportunity remain possible in South Africa holds strong. The dream that accumulation might yet be democratized runs through not only Don's and Tumi's hopes but also in the novel's satire of the state's current failings. The fiction reflects Mda's contemporaneous call in the *New York Times* that the renewal of Mandela's dream requires that, contra Jacob Zuma's patronage politics, economic benefits be extended beyond the "white establishment and black elite." Dreams of redemption remain here attached to visions of wider economic opportunity.

That postcolonial optimism persists in post-transition South Africa under conditions of US empire is registered in the novel by the fact that Mbungane is a clear stand-in for Tokyo Sexwale, a former member of Umkhonto we Sizwe who was imprisoned by the apartheid regime on Robben Island and who has, in the words of *Africa Report*, emerged as "one of a new and ambitious breed of power-brokers and one of South Africa's wealthiest postapartheid entrepreneurs."[61] Sexwale has been hailed not only as "Mr. Deal-a-Minute" but also as the "face" of Black Economic Empowerment.[62] *Fortune* magazine has proposed that his "improbable life story reflects the transformation of his country."[63] A politician frequently floated as a potential candidate for the presidency, Sexwale's fortune was amassed through Mvelaphanda Holdings, a mining company "with tentacles reaching into many strategic sectors including energy, transport and communications, property, hotels, engineering, health, banking and financial services."[64] Mvelaphanda, a Venda word that roughly translates as "progress," models a market-based version of development that, to be sure, promises the democratization of credit and debt, rather than of wealth itself. It is not surprising, then, that Sexwale's vitae includes a short stint as host of *The Apprentice South Africa*. Airing for only one season in 2009, *The Apprentice South Africa* purportedly gave viewers the opportunity to witness the dream of nationhood embodied by its face, as the winning candidate would be rewarded with a job at Mvelaphanda. The program, like government actions such as BEE, promised that after apartheid individual talent and drive could be sufficient for securing prosperity. An individual only needed to be adaptable and innovative enough to operate within a system characterized by the privatization of industry, the deregulation of capital, and the growth of the financial sector. In this, the show was like its original US program, hosted by Donald Trump, and symptomatic of the privatization of the nation.[65] It stands as a cultural object that speaks to the globalization of US capital and governance and the affective cultures that accompany it.

At the same time, Sexwale, like his fictional counterpart Mbungane, was at pains to connect his commitment to market entrepreneurialism to the anti-apartheid struggle and a longer South African history of advocating for economic rights. Write-ups of the show were careful to note that Sexwale, reportedly in a nod to South African labor laws designed to "protect employees against arbitrary layoffs," preferred the purportedly gentler "You're dismissed!" to Trump's "You're fired!" and that he "was criticized for hiring both finalists."[66] The host himself sought to highlight that he was "no Trump clone": "'We're looking for a leader. So remember ethics, ethics, ethics,' the soft-spoken Sexwale told the 16 original contestants. The would-be moguls competed to help a Johannesburg street vendor of vegetables develop a sustainable business model."[67] In South Africa, the show suggested, the mining magnate and the vegetable vendor are both "entrepreneurs," and the former is ready to help the latter succeed: they are still comrades, if unequally wealthy ones. Of course, Sexwale's exhortation to "ethics, ethics, ethics" arguably appears as self-evidently rhetorical, as transparently fantastical as Trump's invocation in the 2016 US general election to "make America great again." Yet, as the next chapter continues to explore, to dismiss ongoing exhortations to an "ethical" postcolonial optimism in a period of general disillusionment as only rhetorical is to risk downplaying the ongoing affective and moral appeal of discourses that, at their heart, promise the redemption of national dreams that have been shattered, deferred, or derailed.

Chapter 6

The Last Best Hope of *White Wahala*

Zakes Mda's *The Heart of Redness*, I have argued (chapter 5), critiques a form of postcolonial optimism that attaches the redemption of national ideals of exceptional equality and justice to the democratization of credit. Mda's fiction shows how salvific hopes that deepen dependency on financial institutions, even as they disavow other forms of dependency, are euphoric: they are sustaining illusions that cannot be sustained and thus yield despair. Mda's novel has proven prescient in its perception and anticipation of disillusionment. In South Africa, the hopeful proliferation of development schemes in the late 1990s that trumpeted the efficacy of microfinance and other forms of lending has increasingly given way to a crushing sense of ongoing indebtedness. US capitalism, Martjin Konings notes, has historically promised "the comfortable enjoyment of the conveniences of consumer capitalism" but produced for most people "an anxiety-driven integration into disciplinary mechanisms of credit and debt in a context of stagnant wage growth and rising unemployment."[1] The characterization does not badly capture the postapartheid South African situation, where, Deborah James shows, anxieties concerning widespread indebtedness were expressed vocally in the 1990s well before they were echoed in the US following the 2007 global recession.[2] Such anxieties, Mda's fiction suggests, do not foreclose the cultivation of optimism centered on access to capital, thus amplifying the stresses of debt that see dreams collapse into nightmare.

Whether in the US or South Africa, in the first decades of the twenty-first century the democratization of credit, rather than generating equality of opportunity, marked a technique for both managing and exacerbating unequal opportunities that were continuously racialized in a financialized global economy with high rates of unemployment. While the democratization of credit has often seemed a progressive way of financing national dreams, as Konings is at pains to show in the US, it has effectively proliferated regimes of austerity and privatization. This outcome supports Walter Benn Michaels's observation that "the commitment to antidiscrimination" can be found at the "foundation" of neoliberalism, insofar as prioritizing "equality of access" to markets is not the same as committing to "equality embodied in redistribution."[3] At the same time, the effects of ever-expanding credit regimes are undoubtedly racialized. As Mehrsa Baradaran shows in her discussion of the US 1970 Fair Credit Reporting Act and the 1974 Equal Opportunity Act, which "eliminated race and gender identification from loan applications," these antidiscrimination policies did not address the "plethora of other conditions" that affected the default risks of Black Americans who were poor in income and poor in assets living in segregated communities, whose access to credit continued to come at disproportionate cost.[4] Later policies built on a similar model of fostering "black capitalism," such as Bill Clinton's support for Community Development Financial Institutions, also necessarily failed to yield equality: "the only way to eliminate the drastic credit disparity was to eliminate the wide disparity of wealth" through techniques such as the integration of credit markets.[5] Short of this redistribution, racialized inequality has been maintained through credit's expansion. Jackie Wang is persuasive in her argument that "predatory lending" is one of the "main modalities of contemporary racial capitalism" in the US: the extension of credit is a "method of dispossession."[6]

A comparable pattern of dispossession is evident in South Africa. Achille Mbembe observed in *African Futures* (2016) that, while the logic of extraction that characterizes the South African "raw economy" is different than the "logic of industrialization that seems to partly characterize Northern economies," both have "quickened the accumulation of surplus populations."[7] This quickening marks how, globally, the "wellspring of wealth" has become finance rather than labor.[8] Mbembe described the resultant "emerging international politics of public debt," whereby

> global capital increasingly requires that the 'average citizen' pay—for the consolidation of public finances, the bankruptcy of foreign states, the rising rates of interest on public debt, and if necessary the rescue of national and international banks—with his or her private savings and through cuts in public entitlements, reduced public services, and higher taxation.[9]

As Anne-Maria Makhulu argued, in the growing absence of formal wage labor, the avoidance of "the ultimate risk of total destitution"[10] requires "another kind of labor" that centers on "the forging of relations of borrowing, lending, and the extension of credit."[11] In the contemporary South African economy, the quest for "economic sovereignty," in Makhulu's words, is paradoxically tied to establishing relations of credit and debt that in turn engender narratives of "frugality and self-restraint."[12] South Africa's "credit-debt revolution," James noted, coming as it did "on top of the credit apartheid" that preceded it, "was bound to have effects that were racially skewed": "As the banks did with the poor housing purchasers in the subprime mortgage market in the United States, so a far wider spectrum of lenders does to a wider spectrum of borrowers in South Africa."[13] Financialization has depended on racialized forms of precarious and exploited labor instituted under colonialism and apartheid, and expanded access to credit markets has perpetuated this precarity and exploitation.[14]

The misery of indebtedness has contributed to shifting affective relations to the nation-state. Dreams of development have increasingly given way to a sense of precarity that renders the future indeterminate, such that Mbembe described a continent-wide "generalization and radicalization of temporariness."[15] The "horizon of liberation" is no longer freedom from exploitation, he argued, but a longing to "escape the traps of temporariness": of not even being consistently exploited through a relation of wage labor.[16] This new sense of a non-future in turn inflects the past. Makhulu noted that some South Africans feel nostalgic for the imagined certainties of apartheid-era "migrant-dependent wage work," even as this nostalgia itself depends on neglecting a longer history of "wageless life."[17] A similar sense of uncertainty and nostalgia has emerged in the US, where anxieties about the gig economy and longing for the imagined security of mid-century waged work proliferate.[18]

As we have seen, however, it is precisely at moments when national dreams seem exhausted and archaic that they are also ripe for redemption. South African literature of postcolonial optimism suggests that this is especially true for those national dreams that are sustained by faith that credit markets might be "regulated" or "deregulated" differently such that economic justice might yet be achieved. Thus, even following the failures of structural adjustment to address inequality and the global recession of 2007–08, dreams of national redemption, in both South Africa and the US, remain attached to ideals of economic reform. This, at least, is one implication of Ekow Duker's 2015 *White Wahala*, a sardonic novel that has drawn little attention from critics but is of interest both for its sustained send-up of South African credit markets in the 2010s and for its representation of South Africa as a nation that exists under conditions of US empire.[19] Duker's picaresque fiction is set in Johannesburg in 2014, the year in which a contraction in the South African housing market made the insufficiencies of the National Credit Act of 2005 painfully obvious. As the novel satirizes the ongoing reality of credit apartheid in broad strokes, it explores how credit remains a locus of hope despite also being a source of ongoing pain. In so doing, it demonstrates once again how South African literature seems particularly adept at identifying the affective dynamics that attend the expansive, unequal debt that characterizes national life under US empire. The affective heart of *White Wahala*, I suggest, is the massively exploitative credit kiosk known as the "Last Best Hope Financial Service": consequently hope, along with the desperation implied by "last best" hope, is tied both to never-ending debt and to historic speeches by US presidents that affirmed "America" as the "last, best hope" for freedom. As *White Wahala* charts the triumphs and tribulations of the kiosk's owner, Cash Tshabalala, it shows how South African credit markets, like those in the US, promise progressive equality by reproducing an unequal, anti-Black status quo. The novel thus doubles down on how a pan-African sense of temporariness produced by a financialized economy can be exhausting: not just because precarious debt has usurped regular wages but also because ongoing indebtedness is presented as how national dreams will be redeemed.

The episodic, non-developmental form of *White Wahala* reflects the exhausting stasis of national imaginaries in which Black residents are perpetually owed their futures. From this exhaustion, the novel offers no respite. It does, however, consider the disruptive potential of democratizing credit in new ways. There are certain kinds of democratized debt, the novel suggests, that are readily accommodated, if only in principle, by US and South African credit markets. The US presidential speeches alluded to in *White Wahala* profess "America" to be the "last, best hope" because of a national dream whereby all ought to have equal opportunity: in principle, the state owes its citizens, including its Black citizens, economic justice. South African officials in the novel build on this language of debt by explicitly stating that freedom will only come when white South Africans have paid what they owe to Black South Africans after the pillage wrought by colonial and apartheid governments: in principle, redistribution must be implemented. *White Wahala* shows how these principles are both incorporated into and betrayed by credit markets. What these markets cannot incorporate, however, even in principle, is the story at the heart of the novel's own extravagant plot: a rich white man borrowing money on the same terms as poor Black people. The novel thus proposes a shift from imagining what is owed to Black people in principle to envisioning the democratization of borrowing from Black-owned institutions in practice. It dreams of an end to credit apartheid, not through the expansion of credit, but through the thorough desegregation of debt.

The Postapartheid Picaresque

Ekow Duker's *White Wahala* was shortlisted for the 2011/12 European Union Literary Award (renamed the Dinaane Debut Fiction Award in 2015). The South African literary award, supported by EU embassies and commissions, adjudicates unpublished works of fiction by first-time authors that are written or translated into English.[20] Although Ashraf Kagee was awarded the cash prize and publication deal the year Duker's first novel was shortlisted, Duker signed a three-book contract with Picador Africa, and *White Wahala* was released alongside *Dying in New York* in 2014; *The God Who Made Mistakes* followed in 2016. Duker describes himself as an "oil field engineer turned investment banker turned part-time author" who, "since leaving the oil field," has worked "mainly as a corporate strategist and in investment banking," an occupation, he notes, that "draws heavily on storytelling."[21] Raised in Ghana and educated in Ghana, the UK, the US, and France, Duker maintains dual Ghanaian and South African citizenship and has settled in Johannesburg, where he has been employed at the data expertise firm Ixio Analytics. He remains a self-described "happy dabbler" who declines to call himself a writer "because I write primarily for pleasure."[22] While Duker has been active in the South African literary festival and book club scene, *White Wahala* has received only a few reviews. Karina M. Szczurek called the novel "a modern tall tale with a dark South African twist" that "has the potential to generate a lot of debate."[23] Relebone Rirhandzu Myambo, writing for *The Con*, was more critical, judging the fiction "a messy attempt at social commentary" that has a "dumbing effect."[24] Myambo especially notes that the novel proliferates stereotypes, an effect compounded by the fact that its "exaggerated characters," to borrow Szczurek's phrase, tend to espouse racist and sexist views.

Yet, the broad strokes of *White Wahala*, I propose, seem apt for describing what emerges as the novel's main satirical focus, namely the South African financial industry with which Duker is intimately familiar. The novel is set just after the "demand for residential housing collapsed spectacularly" in 2014.[25] That year saw the implosion and $1.6 billion bailout of African Bank, a registered commercial micro-lender that specialized in providing unsecured credit to poor people. Following the collapse of the subprime loan market in the US in 2007, South African financiers and regulators believed they had avoided a similar fate.[26] The National Credit Act, passed in 2005 and fully implemented in 2007, was a comprehensive legislative overhaul of the credit industry that, among other things, sought to "promote a fair and non-discriminatory marketplace for access to consumer credit" and "to promote black economic empowerment and ownership within the consumer credit industry."[27] Its provisions included the establishment of the National Credit Regulator, the National Consumer Tribunal, new credit industry regulations (including registrations requirements for credit providers), the establishment of consumer rights when applying and signing for credit, and regulation for debt enforcement. The Act was designed specifically to protect borrowers from a booming microfinance industry, which expanded dramatically as white Afrikaners formerly employed in public service sought to profit from diverting state monies "flowing into the bank accounts of black civil servants."[28] Yet, as T.O. Molefe explains, "to make providing credit to low-income earners an attractive business proposition," the state "left a gap—allowing lenders to provide unsecured credit at higher interest rates . . . and over longer repayment periods."[29] The risk of this form of financial inclusion was deemed "acceptable" on the grounds that it would "amplify the economic potential of low-income earners," but "in reality, borrowers' incomes hadn't grown fast enough to keep pace with the extremely high interest payments and fees after they had paid for basic needs." The only option was to borrow more, leading to inevitable default.[30] The dynamic recalls the introduction of revolving debt in the US in the 1970s. As Konings describes it, US citizens were, for the first time, able to "acquir[e] a piece of the American dream, not by promising extinction of the principle but on the basis of indefinite penance . . . even a modest amount of credit could entail a lifetime of indebtedness."[31] The National Credit Act, in other words, might be understood as an expression of the chronically renewed South African optimism that national ideals might be redeemed through credit's "democratization." Duker's fiction, however, conveys profound disillusionment with this dream, even as it dissects the affective politics through which it is maintained. As in the work of Tlali and Mda, the fiction engages the curious cycle of redemptive hopes and deep disillusionment that I have argued is distinctive to South African literature of postcolonial optimism.

In *White Wahala*, credit apartheid is not only alive and well, but its continuance also seems assured. In this and other details, it reflects historical fact. By the late 2000s, James notes, there were "three distinct lending sectors" in South Africa: "the mainstream or formal financial sector," historically dominated by an "oligopoly of British-owned banks"; "the new microlending sector . . . mostly run by Afrikaans-speaking former civil servants . . . who engaged in practices that were later prohibited" under the National Credit Act; and "the *mashonisas*, or neighborhood moneylenders . . . [whose] protagonists were defined as loan sharks because they remained unregistered under the act."[32] These sectors are neatly evoked in Duker's novel through its principle characters.

Alasdair Nicholson works as a credit analyst at Megabank. His Scotch-inflected first name complements that of his co-worker and friend Sean, who identifies as Irish, though his settler family recently "came from Zambia" (20). These Anglo-employees chafe under the management of Mr. Viljoen, an Afrikaner who comes to agree with his wife Marietjie as to the preferability of an Afrikaans bank, as "the Engelse will screw you in the end" (281). Finally, the novel's anti-hero, Cash Tshabalala, is a *mashonisa* who runs a money-lending service in the fictional former township of Scottsville in Soweto.[33] Other characters represent additional local sources of financing: the President of the Scottsville Tomato Sellers' Association (99), for example, or Mrs. Simelane, who runs a burial society and later loan service in direct competition with Cash.[34] Taken together, the cast of characters obviously reflects what James called "the ethnic and racial divisions of South Africa's past and of its new dispensation."[35] The cast also represents the transformed opportunities for South Africans to access credit in the twenty-first century and attests to how anxieties around credit have only sharpened. As Makhulu argued, in contemporary South Africa, "heavily indebted households shore up finances in the absence of steady wage work" by managing a "dizzying array of both formal and informal financial instruments, which enable survival from one financial year to the next."[36]

The seeming intractability of the racial and class divisions enforced by an evolving credit regime are conveyed by the fiction's convoluted plot, in which boundaries are crossed only to be re-established more firmly than ever. To summarize this plot as briefly as possible: after Sean gives Alasdair a new drug, tok, at work, Alasdair becomes determined to seek out more in Soweto. (The blue powdery "tok" is a more powerful version of "tik," a slang term for crystal methamphetamine.) When purchasing the drug from a woman named Lerato, he is dismayed that he doesn't have enough cash on hand and that "no one in Scottsville goes to the ATM after dark" (56). Lerato directs him to Cash's kiosk, where Cash agrees to lend Alasdair the cash, on the condition that Alasdair revisits the loan application that Cash's sister, Gladys, has made to Megabank so that she can finance her tomato stand. Alasdair repays the money to Cash but throws out the application. After Gladys is killed in a traffic accident, Cash blames Alasdair: Gladys would not have been hit, he thinks, if she hadn't been visiting her brother to beg for financing. (Cash refuses to lend to his sister because his business depends on beating up defaulters.) Looking to hold Alasdair accountable, Cash and his two partners, S'bu One and S'bu Two, show up at Alasdair's home, where they interrupt a book club run by Alasdair's mother, Agatha. Events escalate, the police arrive, and shots are fired; book club member and renowned lawyer Tasmin Khan is shot in the neck. Cash and the Sbus are thrown in Sun City Prison (as the Johannesburg Correctional Center is known). Alasdair's sixteen-year-old sister Ghislaine visits Cash, with whom she has become enamored, in prison. At Cash's urging, Ghislaine contacts Angie Khumalo, the one Black book club member who witnessed the confrontation. Angie in turn brings Cash's situation to the attention of her husband, Terry, "the man all the bankers and politicians called when there was an important deal to be done or some complex negotiation to be brokered" (178). Terry contacts Elvis Thikaya, the leader of the ANC Youth League who is running for re-election and in need of a cause. Elvis leads a movement to protest Cash's imprisonment, as well as Megabank: "Our brother came to this bank to ask for a loan. Instead of to give him money, Megabank arrested him and threw him in prison" (186). When a man in a "revolutionary rapture" rushes Alasdair at the protest, Alasdair accidently shoots Elvis. Agatha pays off Elvis, who secures Cash's release and does not charge Alasdair in the name of "reconciliation" (226). Cash is feted as the "symbol of the struggle" (241). Ghislaine finds him, and they have sex and torment and torture Cash's customers together. Alasdair and Agatha seek out Ghislaine in the kiosk; Agatha confesses to murdering her husband Thor, who has been "missing" for two years. A mob threatens to burn down the kiosk but doesn't. In the end, the Nicholsons return to their mansion, and Cash remains in Soweto.

The complex networks of indebtedness upon which the plot hinges, the novel affirms, have been produced through the regime of credit apartheid that, in James's words, has been "implanted in capitalist arrangements of a widespread and thoroughgoing character," as well as by "a South African system of race-based exclusionary justice."[37] If, per Konings, the proliferation of credit and debt produces "an intricate pyramid of social obligations and promises," in South Africa as in the US, racism has remained integral to their design.[38] As Cash proposes, lending money turns out to be "much more personal" than simply checking credit histories: "The real question is whether I'm happy for my life to be mixed up with his" (268). Cash is reluctant to mix his life up with Alasdair's, as white people in the past have brought nothing but police brutality to Scottsville and interruptions in business and no hope of compensation—Cash still holds a Swiss diplomat responsible for his loss, in 1998, of eleven thousand seven hundred and fifty rand and thirty-five cents, for which he billed the Swiss embassy to no avail (38). Yet, Cash risks white wahala (a multi-lingual Nigerian word for "trouble" or "shit") to help his sister. Alasdair, however, though he agrees that Megabank may "in principle" provide a loan to a tomato seller, throws Gladys's application out his car window without a second thought; he is not prepared to do business with a poor Black woman (63). White wahala exists because promises of fair opportunity and treatment "in principle"—by big banks, by the police—continue to be an effective way of denying it in practice.

The Orgastic Future

And yet, despite the manifest troubles of credit apartheid, hope persists—at least in principle. The center of this hope in Duker's fiction is, ironically, Cash Tshabalala himself. Cash, to be sure, is a loan shark, but in contrast to white bankers, he is at least upfront about the injustices he inflicts on borrowers: he promises and delivers on the arbitrary extension of loans, exorbitant interest rates, and brutal reprisals for defaulters. This grim business is offered under the moniker "The Last Best Hope Financial Service." The name of Cash's kiosk on the one hand is ironic, insofar as it suggests the desperation of his customers, who turn to Cash with extreme reluctance when they have no other options. As Gladys remarks, the name in some respects "doesn't ring true any more. It's become like one of those adverts for the lotto. You know in your heart you're never going to win" (92). On the other hand, the name rings true, albeit briefly, as a metonym for temporarily resurgent national dreams that seek to redress the ongoing inequities of colonialism and apartheid. After Cash is arrested and his cause is taken up by the ANC Youth League, he is celebrated in *The Sowetan* as "the Robin Hood of Scottsville" (208). Ghislaine sums up the media coverage: "I mean The Last Best Hope Financial Service? That's what Black Economic Empowerment was really intended for, wasn't it?" (209). As a Black businessman serving a Black community, Cash Tshabalala is proclaimed a "man of the people" (214), a "symbol of the struggle" (241). The specifics of his brutal and unfair business practices, as well as the systemic reality of ongoing credit apartheid, are forgotten as Cash is hailed a national "hero" (298). As in Mda's *Heart of Redness*, in which dreams of so-called development hinge on industrious individuals' access to capital (chapter 5), the last best hope of postapartheid dreams in these wildly optimistic formulations is that Black "entrepreneurs" such as Cash are earning a comfortable living by "helping" others live out their dreams in the "new" South Africa. As Cash—and his customers—are keenly aware, however, the optimism produced by this rhetoric is transient at best given the economic reality. Cash's business may fleetingly make people "feel good about themselves," but since you can't "pay for food with good feelings," and since the terms of his services are both harsh and racialized, disillusionment is inevitable: "I didn't change anything," he says (298). As in Tlali's and Mda's literature of postcolonial optimism (chapters 4 and 5), *White Wahala* registers a South African affective cycle of hoped-for redemption and collective disillusionment that turns on the ambivalence of access to credit, which is to say the vulnerability of debt. Because of this ambivalence, disillusionment is built into a postcolonial optimism that persists despite the knowledge that it has been continually betrayed.

Also like Tlali and Mda, Duker explicitly draws a connection between this affective cycle and nationalism as it has been propagated under US empire. As numerous characters remark, "The Last Best Hope Financial Service" borrows its name from a speech by Barack Obama, who, characters note, lifted it in turn from Abraham Lincoln. Obama's 2008 nomination victory speech promised to "restore our moral standing"—a highly-coded reference to the crimes against humanity perpetrated by the US during its twenty-first-century wars against Iraq and Afghanistan—so as to make America "once again that last, best hope for all who are called to the cause of freedom, who long for lives of peace, and who yearn for a better future."[39] Lincoln's 1862 annual message to Congress proclaimed the end or continuance of slavery as key to whether "we shall nobly save or meanly lose the last best hope of earth" and thereby assure or jeopardize "freedom to the free."[40] The speeches evoke a long history of American exceptionalism that prophecies freedom as imminent. The central allusion to the speeches in *White Wahala* gestures toward how this rhetoric of exceptionalism has been globalized in the "new" South Africa, where the nation also promises freedom that is always deferred.

The fact that the allusion to a "last, best hope" is pinned to Cash's kiosk—a site of racialized violence and exploitation—in turn invites critique of the rhetoric of American freedom that has positioned the US as a supposed model for the world and thus attempted to justify its imperial ambitions. In other words, while "freedom" is the explicit endpoint of the "last, best hope" in US presidential speeches, the name of Cash's kiosk invites a reading of these presidential remarks in terms of the brutalities of the market and US histories of credit and debt. How is American hope to be paid for? Lincoln's annual message proposed that "freedom" be financed through the extended enslavement of Black people, the dispossession of Native Americans, and the taxation of settler immigrants. In the same speech where he held up the nation as a final hope, Lincoln counselled "compensated emancipation" over the course of thirty-seven years, on the grounds that those who claim people as property may be more cheaply compensated for that claimed property over time, so long as the white settler population continued to increase as expected.[41] "No ready cash" would be necessary for the project, as Lincoln maintained that at the end of thirty-seven years, "we shall probably have a hundred millions of people to share the burden, instead of thirty-one millions as now."[42] That "the Indian tribes upon our frontiers have during the past year manifested a spirit of subordination" may be "profitably" remedied, Lincoln suggested, through a "remodeled" "Indian system."[43] "Freedom to the free" can be assured, Lincoln argued, by continuing to profit from the systems of enslavement and conquest.[44] White settler freedom, the speech made clear, depends upon the maintenance of an economy that dispossesses Black and Indigenous people.

In a speech that, like his presidential campaign, repeatedly promised "change," Obama envisioned a freedom that would ostensibly be paid for differently. In the place of an "old, discredited" philosophy of "up by your bootstraps," Obama offered an "American promise" that would "ensure opportunity not just for those with the most money and influence, but for every American who's willing to work":

> It is that promise that has always set this country apart—that through hard work and sacrifice, each of us can pursue our individual dreams but still come together as one American family, to ensure that the next generation can pursue their dreams as well.[45]

Freedom—or at least the freedom to work for a better future—will come, not by the state subsidizing slavery and promoting colonization, but by "closing corporate loopholes and tax havens" and "eliminating programs" that are inefficient.[46] The only cost to the proverbial average American, Obama implied, is a commitment to work and a readiness to believe "that together, our dreams can be one."[47] Such a belief, Obama suggested, can be found in Martin Luther King, Jr.'s famous 1963 address at Lincoln's memorial. Obama's reading of that speech, however, pointed to the additional costs of his imagined future that remain only implicit in his own address:

> The men and women who gathered there [at the Lincoln memorial] could've heard many things. They could've heard words of anger and discord. They could've been told to succumb to the fear and frustration of so many dreams deferred. But what the people heard instead—people of every creed and color, from every walk of life—is that in America, our destiny is inextricably linked.[48]

Obama acknowledged that the message of King's speech varied depending on the ear of the listener; in so doing, it unintentionally highlighted what is omitted in hearing King's dream as one of unity rather than one bent on acknowledging and redressing the "fear and frustration of so many dreams deferred." It was, after all, exactly forty-five years earlier at the March on Washington that King asserted "we've come to our nation's capital to collect a check" for "the unalienable rights of life, liberty, and the pursuit of happiness."[49] Obama in effect called on *his* listeners to not hear the disunity in King's contentions: that it is "obvious today that America has defaulted on this promissory note insofar as her citizens of color are concerned."[50] Implicitly for Obama as for Lincoln, the "last, best hope" for future freedom is to be paid for by ongoing racialized injustice and unfreedom.

Notably, Obama's speech was delivered during a financial crisis that was caused in part by creditors aggressively marketing subprime mortgages to Black people historically discriminated against in the housing market. As Baradaran writes, this crisis "disproportionately affected segregated black communities and turned the persistent racial wealth gap into a chasm" by wiping out "53 percent of total black wealth."[51] Yet, the Obama administration "did not specifically target the racial wealth gap, nor did [it] advocate a race-based economic agenda."[52] It did extend the two wars that Obama suggested had jeopardized the US's "moral standing," and financed those wars through national debt. The "last, best" hope for freedom, once again, is that change will come after nothing really changes.[53]

The final lines of *White Wahala* emphasize that the form of hope available through South Africa's credit economy is precisely as attenuated as that proffered by the American dream of ever-deferred freedom. Cash, alone in his kiosk, ponders its moniker: "The neon sign flickered for a moment, then held defiantly. He gazed up at it proudly. It was a crimson ribbon against the morning sky. The Last Best Hope Financial Service. Now *that* was something he could believe in" (303). Cash has no faith in Obama's promise: "change you can believe in." Rather, he only has faith in himself: in Cash and the cash he provides, which is to say in the continuance of the status quo that forever holds out the promise of the freedom of the last best hope. In other words, after hopes for revolutionary heroes and transformative entrepreneurs have (temporarily) passed, a belief in the fiction of money persists, so that those hopes might one day be renewed. The crimson of Cash's sign complements the violet logo of Megabank and the striking blue of "tok." Taken together, these vivid, repeatedly mentioned colors evoke the primary palette of South African rand notes. By linking banking with a powerful drug,

While Wahala, like *The Heart of Redness* (chapter 5), suggests how the promise of credit is akin to the experience of intoxication. The process of managing debt is, in general, arduous: "Time passed more slowly for Alasdair than a credit application crawling its laborious way through multiple levels of approval" (44). The hit of cash, like the ecstasy of "tok," however, provides a fleeting sense of temporal escape: something is happening, something *could* change. It's the kind of faith that Nick Carraway describes at the end of Fitzgerald's famous novel, where the glowing light is green rather than crimson:

> Gatsby believed in the green light, the orgastic future that year by year recedes before us. It eluded us then, but that's no matter—tomorrow we will run faster, stretch out our arms farther . . . And then one fine morning—o we beat on, boats against the current, borne back ceaselessly into the past.[54]

Credit, like a drug, beams out an "orgastic future" whereby a moment of remembered happiness and ecstasy might one day be attained and preserved. *That* is what Cash believes in: not the orgastic future, per se, but the capitalist processes that produce it. He will continue to profit because he is others' last, best hope, in all the ecstasy and desperation the phrase implies.

Cash entertains the possibility that the hope and optimism he offers is "plagiarism" of US originals (117)—his kiosk lifts its name from Obama as *White Wahala* lifts its ending from *The Great Gatsby*. The lawyer Tasmin, however, troubles this account: "Even if the American president did use that phrase, neither he nor anyone else can lay claim to ownership" (118). It follows that the South African dream that credit will bring freedom does and does not mimic its American counterpart. Duker's fiction walks a familiar fine line (in this project) in reckoning with South African histories of aspiration in relation to US imperialism. On the one hand, the centrality of US nationalist discourses to *White Wahala* points to US influence on postapartheid policies that has continued to emphasize market growth and celebrate microfinance. USAID, for example, managed in 2020 "a total portfolio exceeding $100 million" in credit guarantees with local banking institutions in South Africa, and it actively supported the "development of new financial products to meet the needs of small and medium-sized enterprises."[55] On the other, Duker's novel emphasizes how granting US "ownership" over forms of aspiration related to financial opportunity simplifies entwined yet particular national histories. Cash speculates, for instance, that the specific humiliations of apartheid have much to do with his periodic lionization: though he is "cruel," he at least spares prospective borrowers from having to ask for money from white people and thus risk remembering "the countless other hurts life has thrown at them" and their families (299). Postcolonial optimism, South African literature suggests, not only reflects but also reflects on the American dream. As an affect, it knowingly spotlights the pan-African racialized desperation borne of revolving debt that has been integral to (trans)national dreams of endless credit.

"In principle . . ."

Given how credit produces a continual cycle of hope and disillusionment, despair and redemption, it is no wonder that most people who depend on it in *White Wahala* are exhausted. Facing adoration and need that quickly converts to contempt and then back again, Cash, who is in his forties, has a favorite refrain: "He really was getting too old for this crap" (40). Indeed, the enduring greatest hope of multiple characters is to weather bouts of collective hope and disillusionment and make it to retirement. This individual option seems especially appealing given that, when a loan from a *mashonisa* is the "last, best hope," there seems to be little room for collective action. The mass protest to release Cash from prison, organized by Elvis Tshikaya, has nothing to do with systemic change; rather, it centers on one individual who can be upheld as symbolic of freedom (Cash) to the benefit of another (Elvis), who, like the manager of Megabank, is able to orchestrate events surrounding Cash's imprisonment to his own political and financial gain. The crowds looking for Cash's release sing to "break down the doors of oppression and let freedom in" (235). What constitutes "freedom" apart from the release of a man and his friends remains unclear (and, as we've seen, Cash's freedom is closely bound to others' peonage). Similarly, Elvis speaks to the media of Cash's release as being about "reconciliation" and "justice" (226), yet the terms' application to the situation seems abstract at best. To be sure, Cash and his henchmen have been unjustly assumed guilty of shooting Tasmin; they have also assaulted, without consequence, innumerable other people who have defaulted on their loans. The songs and rhetoric of the anti-apartheid struggle are remembered, invoked, and even deeply felt, yet there is something exhausted about them, as they simplify rather than clarify what would comprise "reconciliation" and "justice" after the transition to democracy. Minister Ndebele is eager that Cash's release recall Mandela's and carefully coaches him on the proper gestures: "But Cash forgot to clench his fist and in the morning papers the next day, he looked as if he was directing traffic or waving to a friend he didn't really want to see" (244). The failed attempt at a Black power salute captures the ambivalent way in which Cash represents Black power as an avatar of black capitalism. Mandela's release heralded the end of political apartheid and the acceleration of credit apartheid, while Cash's release heralds only the ongoing hope that something might change, one day, but that any change will bring its own disappointments. Remembered futures, *White Wahala* suggests, are not necessarily liberatory in their potential. Indeed, their exhaustive rehearsal—the rehearsal of what I am calling postcolonial optimism—can emphasize how the realization of hopes has produced and will produce conditions of disillusionment.

Given both its rakish hero and a story that ends where it began, *White Wahala* is best classified as a picaresque. This genre, as Stacey Balkan has argued, is well-suited for subverting "popular narratives of economic development—either individual enrichment or societal progress ... in part because of its form: a series of episodes with no discernible resolution."[56] The unresolved and episodic, we have seen, are characteristic of South African literature of postcolonial optimism. Tlali's protagonist prefers an unknown future to ongoing employment in the loan industry, her hopes tempered by an awareness of their proximity to past disappointments. Mda's magic realism rehearses the monotony of colonial oppression across centuries, including its manifestation vis-à-vis microfinance. Similarly, *White Wahala*'s non-developmental structure subverts the national narrative that would associate credit reform with progress: such reform, though it may foster and sustain inclusion in networks of indebtedness, remains relentlessly racialized based on pre-existing income and assets. In highlighting this essential stasis, the novel exemplifies what Jens Elze calls the postcolonial picaresque, wherein "any change of status" achieved by the picaro (in this case Cash) is "highly precarious."[57] This precarity, Elze argues, exposes the paradox of what he calls cosmological capitalism: ideologies of self-reliance and meritocracy are delimited by "the effectively impenetrable imperialistic and neoliberal structures that replaced official colonialism only to secure the very same hierarchies under another guise."[58] *White Wahala* enacts such exposure. At the same time, the novel offers a significant variation of the genre Elze describes in that its picaro offers no first-person confession that centers the "cruel optimism" of individual "hopes and efforts" invested in "a capitalist promise of permeability."[59] Instead, the third person account emphasizes a collective, wearied sense of cyclical hopes and inevitable disillusionment. The narrative thereby not only exposes but also demands accountability for the ongoing precarity engendered by the form of cosmological capitalism described here as credit apartheid.

This is to say that the novel does not entirely despair of the future, and its satire of how credit apartheid has not been systemically addressed develops into a systemic critique. In this respect, Cash Tshabalala really does emerge as something of a hero: not because he (precariously) represents Black liberation but because he challenges the limits of how it has been imagined on a national scale. Cash's grief and fury at his sister's death prompts him to confront Alasdair directly about what Cash rightly perceives as hypocrisy. When Cash initially seeks assurance from Alasdair that Gladys might be approved for a loan from Megabank, Alasdair responds: "In principle, if all the boxes were ticked, then I could recommend a loan" (63). Cash takes the assurance as a promise before lending Alasdair the money he needs for drugs. When Cash invades the Nicholson home after Gladys's death, he offers a scathing take-down of Alasdair's "in-principle response" (123). He does so, surprisingly, through a close reading, in a moment that invites metafictional analysis. Agatha's book club has taken up a collection of short stories set in Scottsville that is "daring and provocative" with a "lighter style and an understated irreverence" (109)—descriptors that might apply to Duker's fiction. Cash is familiar with the collection and interprets, for his literally captive audience, a "piece about an old man running from a mob" (123):

> The community decided that the in-principle agreement they had with the old man didn't matter anymore . . . one day they realized the man was too old, too poor, too much of a burden, or perhaps too much of an inconsequence. So they conveniently forgot about the in-principle agreement they had with the old man, the agreement that had allowed him to live his life in peace for so many years. (124)

The "in-principle" agreement, Cash suggests, is made to be broken, as Alasdair broke with Gladys. In South Africa, credit is offered "in-principle" based on merit, just as rights are guaranteed "in-principle" to all by the South African constitution. Megabank's wealth can be claimed "in-principle" by Elvis Thikaya as rightfully belonging to the "we" who "dug [it] out of the ground" (186). In practice, however, the differential application of these "in-principle" agreements is a matter of life and death in Scottsville. While Cash confronts the violent consequences of his actions every day—he is periodically the man chased by a mob, not because he is "too poor" but because he has rendered others so, often by force—Alasdair is only made to confront such consequences after Cash tries to hold him to account. In other words, Cash's reading of a literary fable foregrounds the violence of white-owned banking institutions that would distinguish themselves from the criminalized *mashonisa*. The reading, as Cash applies it to his own situation, further underscores the casual racism that allows for such imagined distance. Alasdair has proven himself incapable of believing that he *in fact* owes a loan to Cash and his sister; he is not happy for his life to be "mixed up" in theirs (268). The continuance of credit apartheid does not hinge on whether there are Black employees at Megabank (there are) or whether poor Black people can access credit (they can): it is a matter of who borrows from whom on what terms. Cash, it is noted, has plenty of money to seek the safety of a house in a mostly white suburb; he would not and could not, however, sustain a business there.

White supremacy is the white whale of *White Wahala*, and Cash, in the moment he forgets the profitability of his kiosk out of grief for his sister, takes on the role of Ahab. Toni Morrison's famous reading of *Moby-Dick* posits the white whale as the "ideology of race" in the US that coalesced at the moment of Herman Melville's writing, the parasitical whiteness that asserts the notion of racial superiority. Morrison's analysis finds in the novel suggestions of a "different Ahab" than the familiar tyrant: "the only white male American heroic enough to try to slay the monster that was devouring the world," which is to say "whiteness idealized."[60] Cash tries and fails to slay such a monster. Against the exculpatory logic of the "in-principle," Cash asserts that "it's all about the principle," which is to say it's all about the practice of who pays down a principle to whom (89). Cash is a man who maintains that he lays his "own tracks" (91), as Ahab asserts "the path to my fixed purpose is laid with iron rails, whereon my soul is grooved to run."[61] Alasdair owes him more than rand, and Cash comes to collect what is owed him out of principle. To be sure, Cash's principles are merciless, but they are at least explicit about the potentially violent consequences of giving or denying a loan. There is no clear vision of a redeemed market here, no suggestion that the principles of freedom or equality that comprise South African or American dreams may be realized through The Last Best Hope Financial Services or any other institution. There is, however, a call to acknowledge responsibility for the racialized violence engendered by "in-principle" agreements of convenience that promise freedom but ultimately serve and preserve whiteness. The beginnings of such responsibility, the novel suggests, requires that white people willingly practice being "mixed up" in the lives of Black people from positions of vulnerability, not as lenders but as debtors. Alasdair accepting his debt to Cash is the slightest example. Achieving an end to credit apartheid and the optimistic anticipation of economic equality that sustains it means reckoning with the larger, finally incalculable debts of colonialism and apartheid.

Coda:
The Dream of the Postcolonial Future

This book has charted how African literature of US empire confronts the stubbornness of postcolonial optimism. The case studies of Nigerian and South African writing from the 1960s to the 2010s demonstrate how postcolonial optimism has renewed itself across national and continental imaginaries that have been shaped by the developmentalist ideologies of US empire. Within Nigeria and South Africa writing, educational and lending institutions central to visions of national development at the respective onset of postcolonial and postapartheid nationhood have retained a hopeful charge, despite their roles in the expansion and maintenance of US empire. The potential case for the abandonment of optimistic attachments to universities, banks, and the postcolonial nation itself is strong, insofar as imperialism and the nationalisms that support it require these attachments for their continuance. In the Nigerian and South African literature studied here, however, postcolonial optimism is neither naively complicit with nor fastidiously opposed to a global imperial order. It is an ambivalent structure of feeling that transforms the status quo it also extends.

This reading of contemporary African cultural production aligns with Lindsey Green-Simms's recent analysis of African queer cinema, which complicates "any simple binary between subversive and oppressive" in its evaluation of art's political effects.[1] Green-Simms's articulation of "Afri-queer fugitivity" emphasizes that queer African films resist "the limitations of the present by searching for something that can surpass it," while simultaneously marking "the way that constraints of the past and the present continue to hold sway even as one escapes them."[2] Green-Simms identifies an anti-progressivist form of resistance that both sustains "anticipatory hope" and acknowledges the persistence of systemic injustices and embodied pain.[3] Literature of postcolonial optimism similarly articulates what Green-Simms describes as "looping time."[4] Rather than reclaiming defeat for resistance, however, or centering the persistence of suffering through hope,⁵ it foregrounds how ongoing optimism, especially after decades of disappointed hopes invested in the nation, can itself become a source of defeat, injustice, and pain. Yet, literature of postcolonial optimism does not seek to relinquish the optimistic attachments that also nurture survival, aspiration, and pan-African solidarities oriented toward dreams of the postcolonial nation that have yet to be realized. Across the chapters in this book, historical fiction and episodic narratives explore the pan-African dreams of national becoming that inhere even to an exhausted national optimism, or to cycles of national euphoria and despair. Literature of postcolonial optimism registers the inextricability of feeling stuck and unstuck in the world of empire.

The unsettling affective impasse that characterizes these recursive works produces a sense of both recurrent nightmare and persistent vision. The affect of postcolonial optimism, in other words, can be compared to that of a disturbing dream, and it is with a meditation on dreams and the dream-work of literature that I would like to close. This is not least because literal dreams proliferate across the works studied here. Clark-Bekederemo's "live" nightmare, for example, binds his Nigerian brother's life in India to James Meredith's life in Mississippi; the dream registers a profound sense of shared pan-African struggle (chapter 1).⁶ Tlali's narrative likewise offers a crucial account of dreaming, namely Muriel's reverie in what was Sophiatown, in which past resistance overlays present devastation and intimates the protagonist's future commitment to an international antiapartheid movement (chapter 4). In Emecheta's and Abani's novels (chapter 2), the protagonists experience elemental visions, of drowning and burning respectively, that express transatlantic worlds of suffering and care. The many dreams of Mda's fiction similarly signal forms of sociality shaped by violent histories of empire yet resistant to empire's developmentalist scripts (chapter 5). In Iguine and Adichie, protagonists relay visceral experiences of contingent proximity to those currently living in madness and poverty (chapter 3), while Duker's novel closes with nightmarish neon lights that signal the ongoingness of violent and hopeful relations of credit and debt (chapter 6). These dreams and visions, edged with nightmare, remain personal; they do not directly coalesce into political action and aesthetic movement. They do not clearly fall into the Black radical, utopic tradition described by Robin D.G. Kelley as "freedom dreams."⁷

Yet, as these dreams loop time and disquiet the dreamers, they are perhaps not totally apart from that tradition. Intimate as they are, these dreams signal a temporal and affective receptivity that is a possible condition for the imaginative articulation and continuance of freedom dreams. It is useful to think here of Fred Moten's meditation on "the spirit of the postcolonial future," which centers on a reading of a dream with such effects.⁸ Moten notes that, in *Remembering the Present* (1996), the artist Tshibumba Kanda Matulu recounts the genesis of a painting in a dream to the ethnographer Johannes Fabian. In his dream, Tshibumba is chased by skeletons.⁹ Tshibumba continues to describe the dream's key question, which evokes the anticolonial figure of Patrice Lumumba: "If you were to meet Lumumba right now, what would you say? All right. I woke up with a start and told my wife about it."¹⁰ Moten argues:

> This is what it is to receive the spirit of the postcolonial future. The recording of Tshibumba's dream, the recording of his passion, is all bound up with Lumumba's passion, where passion is not only suffering but an overwhelming aesthesis, a massive and surprising sensual experience that *happens* to you, an irruption of the outside in its fullness with regard to every sense.¹¹

Moten's connection of dreams and passion provides a promising framework for understanding the recurrence of dreams in literature of postcolonial optimism. Faced with the felt impasses of nation and empire, with ever-attenuated, maddening optimism and the exhausting repetition of euphoria and despair, these works point toward how this nightmare converts into passion that is "not only suffering" but also an overwhelming sense of the self as overwhelmed by others. Contra the individuation required by universities and creditors that is authorized by national development policies, dreams dissolve fantasies of the discrete self that occupies a singular national space.

In its invitation to take seriously the impassioned sociality of dreams, literature of postcolonial optimism stands to one side of what Xine Yao has called the "ongoing antisocial turn in affect theory."¹² This turn arguably includes such criticism as Sianne Ngai's *Ugly Feelings* (2005) and Sara Ahmed's *The Promise of Happiness* (2010). Both landmark studies attend to how "negative affects" can be recuperated for critical practice. Scenes of irritation or envy (Ngai) or unhappiness and alienation (Ahmed) are scenes of knowing.¹³ This antisocial turn also includes Yao's own study of "queer, racialized, and gendered modes of unfeeling" in nineteenth-century US literature.¹⁴ These "modes of affective disobedience," Yao contends, counter a liberal politics of sentiment; they "capture transgressive desires" and "ambivalences about relationality."¹⁵ "Unfeeling," Yao suggests, "is the detachment from attachments to hegemonic structures of feeling and the potential for striving toward a radical politics of liberation."¹⁶ My work on literature of postcolonial optimism shares this turn's emphasis on ambivalent feeling, racialized emotion, and compromised agency. Rather than celebrating the liberatory potential of disaffection, however, it explores the ways attachment and detachment from something like a national culture of feeling is often never complete. The "negative" and "positive" emotions produced by developmentalist imperial discourses are not easily disentangled. Detachment, disaffection, withdrawal, and, indeed, pessimism do not emerge as centers for renewed liberatory hopes. African literature of US empire registers how dreams for liberation are invested in relations of empire in quotidian ways that rule out disinvestment. A strategy of disaffection from the US university becomes less of an option when, first, disillusionment has already been experienced and is reflexively anticipated and, second, when the university remains a place where one can steal away dreams of pan-African nationhood. Disaffection with lending institutions seems similarly limited given its cyclical entwinement with optimistic investment in the same, as well as with pan-African efforts to imagine transformed relations of debt. The alternative to the exhortations to optimism centered on education and credit in visions of postcolonial nationhood is not pessimism but a fuller felt knowledge of how the nightmare of the imperial present continues to be bound to impassioned dreams for something else.

Literature of postcolonial optimism, I suggest, imparts such knowledge. The claim is a strong one that stands in contrast to, say, Ngai's observation, following Adorno, of literature's position "in a highly differentiated and totally commodified society" as "a relatively autonomous, more or less cordoned-off domain."[17] African literature of US empire seems resistant to an understanding of literary culture as a rarified space. It strives to enact the dreaming it represents. If it communicates the transnational or even global impasses of past and present national dreams in ways that can seem nightmarish and overwhelming—well, that is also its promise.

I would like to conclude by looking beyond Nigeria and South Africa to a novel that confirms the urgency of engaging the stubbornness of postcolonial optimism in contemporary literature, while also clarifying the literary dream-work I am trying to describe here. NoViolet Bulawayo's *Glory* (2022) is a devastating fable of postcolonial Zimbabwean history.[18] Populated by animals who live in the nation of Jidada, the novel recounts the fervent renewal of national dreams following the removal of the Robert Mugabe-like Father of the Nation, the Old Horse, from the Seat of Power. The promise of "Free, Fair, and Credible elections" renews hopes for a "New Jidada" of "justice and real freedom" (99). The heroine, a goat named Destiny, sees everywhere "the sense that a corner has been turned already, that the promised land will shortly be arrived at" (185). This postcolonial optimism fills her "with a gnawing unease":

> there are often times she thinks this could very well be the past itself, as if Jidada has somehow careened ten years backward into that time that was full of many things, including a promise so alive Destiny, like many, was completely swept up by it, tholukuthi taken. (185)[19]

Democracy and a just nation have been promised before, that is, and both Destiny and her mother bear literal scars that mark the brutal, violent ways those promises have been betrayed. As in other literature surveyed in this book, however, past disillusionment offers no inoculation from renewed optimism. Destiny, like the rest of the nation, is "swept up" and "taken" once more by the hope that is the more urgently felt because of past betrayals and ongoing immiseration.

In another point of resonance with Nigerian and South African literature of postcolonial optimism, US empire is central to Bulawayo's analysis of how the postcolonial nation becomes a site of renewed and betrayed hopes. The interim president's team coins the phrase "New Dispensation" to "speak to this new chapter of a New Jidada" (109). The interim president (an allegorical figure for Emmerson Mnangagwa, who assumed the presidency following the 2017 coup) is delighted by the phrase, which makes him feel "larger than Jidada's debt to the IMF [International Monetary Fund]" (109). He employs a lecturer in English to teach his pet parrot to repeat the slogan, and the parrot learns to "sing it with an impeccable American accent that put the Father of the Nation's British accent to shame" (110). The parrot teaches all the other birds the song, "so that Jidada's hedges and trees and air and skies and even jungles" are filled with the promise of the "New Dispensation" in the accent of US imperial power (110). The phrase is a guarantee against all promises of newness. The new Minister of Finance, a pig, explains to the interim president-cum-Savior of the nation that, while it is true the US president, or the "tweeting Baboon," tweets while "sitting on a mountain of debt," Jidada's debt means "we can't access credit to jumpstart the economy as needed" (262). The minister recommends a new program of taxation. The resulting suffering dissipates the "enduring optimism about the New Dispensation" (282), as well as the "tremendous optimism that had greeted the appointment of the famous brilliant Minister of Finance" (318). Bulawayo highlights, as in her first novel *We Need New Names* (2013), the global imperial order institutionalized in organizations such as the US-dominated IMF that sustains some countries as "country-countries" and others as bondsmen.[20]

As in other African literature of US empire taken up in this book, the persistent optimism and anticipated despair in *Glory* are imbued with a pan-African dimension that prohibits a reading of hopes for the postcolonial nation as being ever only national. As supporters of the opposition check social media on their phones while they anxiously await election results, a ram "lets out the most anguished roar" (204). Animals assume this means the Party of Power has declared victory. Instead, the ram has seen a video of a "white Defender in blue uniform" aiming a gun "at the back of a feeling, unarmed, Black brother": "We don't need to be told anymore that what we're looking at is America, and we're not even surprised" (205). The animals' grief at the murder becomes enfolded into their grief when reports come through that the election has been lost. When the Party of Power's Defenders attack the subsequent protest, "the air is so hot, so thick with tear gas we cannot see, we cannot breathe" (214). The evocation of the "most desperate of prayers" that became central to the Black Lives Matter movement in the US in the 2010s, "I can't breathe," binds together that movement with Zimbabwean struggles for democracy in 2018 (214).[21] The Jadadans' passion is not only suffering: "We hold our breath, we exhale, we hind. We are fabulous in our fury, we look resplendent in our rage" (213). Postcolonial national dreams are once more pan-African dreams. A cyclical history of optimism and disappointment yields not disaffection but ever-more passionate investment.

The novel ends in a dream-like sequence that is inaugurated by a literary event. Destiny writes a book that, like *Glory*, loops time. *The Red Butterflies of Jidada* sees Destiny write

> from the present into her past, into her mother's and family's pasts, which is also Jidada's past, then back again into the present and beyond into a hoped-for future, yes, tholukuthi the past and present and future unfolding simultaneously on her pages. (351)[22]

As she reads from her book on a day of Remembrance for the Disappeared of Jidada, Defenders murder her:

> The chest area of Destiny's white dress turned crimson-crimson-crimson, but tholukuthi Destiny stood there and read in that voice that was full of the dead, and read in that voice that was full of the dead, and read in that voice that was full of the dead, and read in that voice that was full of the dead. (359)

What follows from this nightmare of past and present suffering is a vision of what could be. The people of Jidada are taken fully out of themselves; they become a "hurricane" (367). They discover "that the true, the proper love for the nation was coming together" (372). They vow "to wage yet another war for Africa's second Liberation from neocolonial oppression," from "the immovable chains of prodigious debts to the very nations who otherwise depended on our wealth for their prosperity" (376). They dream:

> We stayed dreaming on our feet, dreaming with our hearts, with our intestines, with our mouths, with our imaginations; we dreamed until we could in fact see the New Jidada, the New Africa, the New World we very much yearned for, begin to materialize right in front of our eyes. (377)

The Seat of Power Falls, the Father of the Nation dies, and children design a flag to mark the new Independence Day. Bulawayo's incantatory repetitions, her deployment of allegory and construction of a world inhabited by spirits and animals renders this ending self-reflexively part of the dreaming it describes. The novel invites not so much sympathy for Jidadans or disaffection with their nation, as the passionate recognition that "we need a new world order" (376). The "need," in Bulawayo's novel as in other literature of postcolonial optimism, is centered on transnational histories of racialized unfreedom under US empire, and the "we" is as expansive as readers can make it.

Notes

Introduction

1. E.N. Obiechina, "Post-Independence in Three African Novels," *Nsukka Studies in African Literature* 1.1 (1978): 55.
2. Ibid., 54.
3. Obiechina discusses Wole Soyinka's *The Interpreters* (1965), Achebe's *A Man of the People* (1966), and Ayi Kwei Armah's *The Beautyful Ones Are Not Yet Born* (1968) as examples of literary post-independence disillusionment. Obiechina, "Post-Independence," 56. See too Neil Lazarus, "Great Expectations and the Mourning After," in *Resistance in Postcolonial African Fiction* (New Haven: Yale University Press, 1990), 1–26.
4. Wole Soyinka, "The Writer in a Modern African State," in *The Writer in Modern Africa*, ed. Per Wästberg (New York: Scandinavian Institute of African Studies and Africana Publishing Corp., 1969), 17. Quoted in Obiechina, "Post-Independence," 55.
5. Obiechina, "Post-Independence," 54.
6. Frantz Fanon, *The Wretched of the Earth* (New York: Grove Press, 1968 [1961]), 203.
7. Kwame Anthony Appiah, "Is the Post- in Postmodernism the Post- in Postcolonial?" *Critical Inquiry* 17.2 (1991): 353.
8. Jennifer Wenzel, *Bulletproof: Afterlives of Anticolonial Prophecy in South Africa and Beyond* (Chicago: Chicago University Press, 2009), 15.
9. Rita Barnard, "Rewriting the Nation," in *The Cambridge History of South African Literature*, eds. David Attwell and Derek Attridge (Cambridge: Cambridge University Press, 2012), 656, 652.
10. Keguro Macharia, "From Repair to Pessimism," *Brick: A Literary Journal* 106 (2021): n.p, accessed May 2, 2022, https://brickmag.com/from-repair-to-pessimism/. Criticism that takes up disillusionment with the postcolonial nation is not limited to Africa. To note just one example, Yarimar Bonilla offers the concept of "non-sovereign futures" to describe what follows from Guadeloupean disenchantment with the "national liberation" model of anticolonialism. See Yarimar Bonilla, *Non-Sovereign Futures: French Caribbean Politics in the Wake of Disenchantment* (Chicago: University of Chicago Press, 2015), 4.
11. See Susan Z. Andrade, *The Nation Writ Small: African Fictions and Feminisms, 1958–1988* (Durham: Duke University Press, 2011) and Meg Samuelson, *Remembering the Nation, Dismembering Women: Stories of the South African Transition* (Scottsville: University of KwaZulu-Natal Press, 2007).

12. For a discussion of the multiple affiliations signified by the nation in contemporary African literature, see Madhu Krishnan, "*Affiliation, Disavowal, and National Commitment in Third Generation African Literature,*" *ARIEL* 44.1 (2013): 73–97. For a recent overview of literary Afropolitanism, see Carli Coetzee, ed., *Afropolitanism: Reboot* (New York: Routledge, 2019). For a study of vernacular African literature, see Moradewun Adejunmobi, *Vernacular Palaver* (Clevedon: Multilingual Matters Ltd., 2004). For a recent history of the publishing industry, see Sarah Brouillette, *Underdevelopment and African Literature: Emerging Forms of Reading* (Cambridge: Cambridge University Press, 2020).
13. Tejumola Olaniyan, "African Literature in the Post-Global Age: Provocations on Field Commonsense," *Cambridge Journal of Postcolonial Literary Inquiry* 33.3 (2016): 390.
14. Ibid.
15. Ibid., 395.
16. Ato Quayson, *Oxford Street, Accra* (Durham: Duke University Press, 2014), 199.
17. Ibid, 151.
18. Anne-Maria Makhulu, Beth A. Buggenhagen, and Stephen Jackson, "Introduction," in *Hard Work, Hard Times: Global Volatility and African Subjectivities*, eds. Anne-Maria Makhulu, Beth A. Buggenhagen, and Stephen Jackson (Berkeley: University of California Press, 2010), 26.
19. James Ferguson, *Global Shadows: Africa in the Neoliberal World Order* (Durham: Duke University Press, 2006), 190–92.
20. For an analysis of the relation between Nigerian literary culture and an oil industry that long depended on US markets, see Jennifer Wenzel, "Petro-magic-realism: Toward a Political Ecology of Nigerian Literature," *Postcolonial Studies* 9.4 (2006): 449–64. For a consideration of South African literature and its transnational connections to the US, see Ronit Frenkel and Andrea Spain, "South African Representations of 'America,'" *Safundi: The Journal of South African and American Studies* 18.3 (2017): 193–204.
21. Chinua Achebe, *The Trouble with Nigeria* (Oxford: Heinemann, 1984), 2.
22. Andrew Apter, *The Pan-African Nation: Oil and the Spectacle of Culture in Nigeria* (Chicago: Chicago University Press, 2005), 3.
23. Mahmoud Mamdani, *Citizen and Subject* (Princeton: Princeton University Press, 1996), 27.
24. See for example Martin Luther King, Jr., "The Negro and the American Dream," typed draft of address delivered September 25, 1960, accessed June 29, 2018, https://kinginstitute.stanford.edu/king-papers/documents/negro-and-american-dream-excerpt-address-annual-freedom-mass-meeting-north.
25. Raymond Williams coined "structures of feeling" to describe "a social experience that is still *in process*, often indeed not yet recognized as social." Raymond Williams, *Marxism and Literature* (Oxford: Oxford University Press, 1977), 132.

26. Arif Dirlik, *The Postcolonial Aura: Third World Criticism in the Age of Global Capitalism* (Boulder, CO: Westview Press, 1997), 60.
27. Timothy Brennan, "Cosmo-Theory," *South Atlantic Quarterly* 100.3 (2001): 684.
28. Pheng Cheah, *Spectral Nationality: Passages of Freedom from Kant to Postcolonial Literatures of Liberation* (New York: Columbia University Press, 2003).
29. Weihsin Gui, *National Consciousness and Literary Cosmopolitics: Postcolonial Literature in a Global Moment* (Columbus: The Ohio State University Press, 2013).
30. See for example Bhakti Shringarpure, *Cold War Assemblages: Decolonization to Digital* (New York: Routledge, 2019).
31. See for example Peter Kalliney, "Modernism, African Literature, and the Cold War," *MLQ* 76.3 (2015): 333–68. See also Caroline Davis, *African Literature and the CIA: Networks of Authorship and Publishing* (Cambridge: Cambridge University Press, 2021).
32. Monica Popescu, *At Penpoint: African Literatures, Postcolonial Studies, and the Cold War* (Durham: Duke University Press, 2020), 12.
33. Dirlik, *The Postcolonial Aura*, 70.
34. Michael Hardt and Antonio Negri, *Empire* (Cambridge: Harvard University Press, 2001), xii–xiii.
35. Neil Lazarus, *The Postcolonial Unconscious* (Cambridge: Cambridge University Press, 2011), 5.
36. Ibid., 17.
37. Ibid.
38. In Hardt and Negri's reflection on the twentieth anniversary of *Empire*, they reiterate that US power "must be understood not in terms of unipolar hegemony but instead as part of the intense jockeying among nation-states on the rungs of Empire's mixed constitution." Michael Hardt and Antonio Negri, "Empire, Twenty Years On," *New Left Review* 120 (2019): n.p.
39. For an account of how universities were central to visions of decolonization in a newly-independent Nigeria, see Tim Livsey, *Nigeria's University Age* (Cambridge: Cambridge University Press, 2017), 13.
40. Further, market-driven visions of nationhood have been instantiated in South African universities. See for example Anne W. Gulick, "Campus Fiction and Critical University Studies from Below: *Disgrace, Welcome to Our Hillbrow*, and the Postcolonial University at the Millennium," *Cambridge Journal of Postcolonial Literary Inquiry* 9.2 (2022): 177–97.
41. Adom Getachew, *Worldmaking After Empire: The Rise and Fall of Self-Determination* (Princeton: Princeton University Press, 2019), 2–3.
42. Tsitsi Ella Jaji, *Africa in Stereo: Modernism, Music, and Pan-African Solidarity* (Oxford: Oxford University Press, 2014), 3.
43. Ibid.
44. Ibid.
45. Ibid., 18.

46. See for example Frederick Cooper, *Africa in the World* (Cambridge: Harvard University Press, 2014) and Adom Getachew, *Worldmaking After Empire*.
47. Stefano Harney and Fred Moten, *The Undercommons: Fugitive Planning and Black Study* (Wivenhoe: Minor Compositions, 2013), 26.
48. Yogita Goyal, "Introduction: Africa and the Black Atlantic," *Research in African Literatures* 45.3 (2014): v–xxv.
49. See for example G. Oty Agbajoh-Laoye, "Motherline, Intertext, and Mothertext: African Diasporic Linkages in *Beloved* and *The Joys of Motherhood*," *The Literary Griot* 13.1&2 (2001): 128–46.
50. Stéphane Robolin, *Grounds of Engagement: Apartheid-Era African American and South African Writing* (Urbana-Champaign: University of Illinois Press, 2015).
51. For a consideration of the shift from postcolonial to global anglophone literary studies, see Nasia Anam, ed., "Forms of the Global Anglophone," *Post-45*, published February 22, 2019, accessed June 30, 2022, https://post45.org/sections/contemporaries-essays/global-anglophone/.
52. Karen Laura Thornber, "Breaking Discipline, Integrating Literature: Africa-China Relationships Reconsidered," *Comparative Literature Studies* 53.4 (2016): 694.
53. Duncan M. Yoon, "Africa, China, and the Global South Novel: In Koli Jean Bofane's *Congo Inc.*," *Comparative Literature* 72.3 (2020): 321.
54. Ibid.
55. Eve Kosofsky Sedgwick, "Paranoid Reading and Reparative Reading; or, You're So Paranoid, You Probably Think This Introduction is About You," in *Novel Gazing: Queer Readings in Fiction*, ed. Eve Kosofsky Sedgwick (Durham: Duke University Press, 1997), 1–37.
56. Throughout the book, I use feeling and emotion interchangeably with affect, following Sedgwick and Frank's observation that a theory of affect as an "undifferentiated flow of arousal" that registers as feeling or emotion through cognition is "thoroughly imbued with a Cartesian mind/body dualism." Eve Kosofsky Sedgwick and Adam Frank, "Shame in the Cybernetic Fold," in *Shame and Its Sisters*, eds. Eve Kosofsky Sedgwick and Adam Frank (Durham: Duke University Press, 1995), 19.
57. Sara Ahmed, *The Cultural Politics of Emotion* (New York: Routledge, 2004), 12.
58. Ananya Jahanar Kabir, "On Postcolonial Happiness," in *The Postcolonial World*, eds. Jyotsna G. Singh and David D. Kim (New York: Routledge, 2016), 35–52.
59. Sianne Ngai, *Ugly Feelings* (Cambridge: Harvard University Press, 2005), 3.
60. Andrew van der Vlies, *Present Imperfect: Contemporary South African Writing* (Oxford: Oxford University Press, 2017), 13–14.
61. Neetu Khanna, *The Visceral Logics of Decolonization* (Durham: Duke University Press, 2020), 8, 13.
62. Sneja Gunew, "Translating Postcolonial Affect," in *Affect and Literature*, ed. Alex Houen (Cambridge: Cambridge University Press, 2020), 176.

63. Tyrone S. Palmer "'What Feels More Than Feeling?': Theorizing the Unthinkability of Black Affect," *Critical Ethnic Studies* 3.2 (2017): 31–56.
64. Ibid.
65. Lauren Berlant, *Cruel Optimism* (Durham: Duke University Press, 2011), 1.
66. Deborah James, *Money from Nothing: Indebtedness and Aspiration in South Africa* (Stanford: Stanford University Press, 2015), 8.
67. Martjin Konings, *The Emotional Logic of Capitalism* (Stanford: Stanford University Press, 2015), 118.
68. Neocolonialism describes imperial control in former colonies following political independence. See Kwame Nkrumah, *Neo-Colonialism: The Last Stage of Imperialism* (London: Thomas Nelson & Sons, Ltd., 1965).
69. Ground-breaking work in this field includes Huggan, *The Postcolonial Exotic*, Julien, "The Extroverted," and Sarah Brouillette, *Postcolonial Writers in the Global Literary Marketplace* (London: Palgrave, 2007).
70. David Scott, *Omens of Adversity* (Durham: Duke University Press, 2014), 12.
71. Ibid., 6.
72. Ibid.

Chapter 1

1. Chinua Achebe, *Home and Exile* (Oxford: Oxford University Press, 2000), 97.
2. Ibid., 76.
3. Ibid., 97–98.
4. Ibid., 96.
5. Ibid., 97.
6. Kalyan Nadiminti, "The Global Program Era," *Novel: A Forum on Fiction* 51.3 (2018): 377.
7. Ibid., 377, 380.
8. Ibid., 380.
9. See Graham Huggan, *The Postcolonial Exotic* (London: Routledge, 2001) and Eileen Julien, "The Extroverted African Novel," in *The Novel*, ed. Franco Moretti (Princeton: Princeton University Press, 2006), 667–700.
10. Madhu Krishnan, *Contemporary African Literature in English* (Basingstoke: Palgrave Macmillan, 2014).
11. See *Montage of a Dream Deferred* in *Selected Poems of Langston Hughes* (New York: Vintage Classics, 1990), 221–74. Quotation is from "Let America Be America Again," in *The Collected Poems of Langston Hughes* (New York: Vintage Classics, 1994), 191.
12. Part II of this book examines how South African literary dreams of America have been shaped by a distinctive twentieth-century imaginary that associated African Americans with modernity, such that they center on consumer rights, rather than political rights, and financial, rather than educational, institutions.

13. Chinua Achebe, "The Day I Finally Met Baldwin," PEN America, published January 8, 2007, accessed June 29, 2018, https://pen.org/the-day-i-finally-met-baldwin/.
14. Chinua Achebe, *The Education of a British-Protected Child* (Toronto: Bond Street Books, 2009), 29. Getachew notes that Azikiwe's newspapers were modeled on African-American counterparts. Getachew, *Worldmaking After Empire*, 7.
15. Ibid., 30.
16. Jason C. Parker, "'Made-in-America Revolutions'? The 'Black University' and the American Role in the Decolonization of the Black Atlantic," *The Journal of American History* 96.3 (2009): 732. Azikiwe arrived at Storer College in 1925; transferred to Howard in 1926; left Howard for Lincoln because of financial troubles in 1929, completing his studies there in 1931; abandoned doctoral work at Columbia in 1930; and attended the University of Pennsylvania from 1931 to 1933 before leaving the US in 1934.
17. Apollos O. Nwauwa, "The British Establishment of Universities in Tropical Africa, 1920–1948: A Reaction against the Spread of American 'Radical' Influence," *Cahiers d'Études Africaines* 33.130 (1993): 253. The Phelps Stokes Fund also offered significant financial support to African students.
18. Parker, "Made-in-America," 729.
19. Azikiwe eventually endorsed a gradualist approach to achieving this goal that viewed the consolidation of national sovereignty as a precondition to federation. See Emichika A. Ifidon, "Unity without Unification: The Development of Nigeria's 'Inside-Out' Approach to African Political Integration, 1937–1963," *International Social Science Review* 82.1–2 (2007): 45–46.
20. Frederick Cooper, *Africa in the World* (Cambridge: Harvard University Press, 2014), 64–65.
21. Okechukwu Ikejani, "Nigeria's Made-in-America Revolution," *Magazine Digest*, January 10, 1946, quoted in Parker, "Made-in-America," 740.
22. Achebe's trip occurs during a phase in UNESCO's history (the 1960s and 1970s) that Sarah Brouillette argues was "significantly focused on economic development and rectifying inequality in living standards." Sarah Brouillette, *UNESCO and the Fate of the Literary* (Stanford: Stanford University Press, 2019), 10.
23. James Truslow Adams, *The Epic of America* (New York: Blue Ribbon Books, Inc., 1931), 404.
24. Nnamdi Azikiwe, *Renascent Africa* (London: Frank Cass and Co. Ltd., 1968), 176.
25. Ibid., 173. David Kazanjian read letters from colonial Liberia (1822–47) to identify visions of freedom, "in the wake of slavery and in the midst of colonialism," that exceed those of nation and citizenship enshrined in the 1847 constitution. See David Kazanjian, "The Speculative Freedom of Colonial Nigeria," *American Quarterly* 63.4 (2011): 867.
26. Ibid. Azikiwe's later autobiography *My Odyssey: An Autobiography* (New York: Praeger, 1970) is more unstinting in its praise of the US: "the United States of America impressed me as a haven of refuge for the

oppressed sections of humanity in Europe, Africa, Asia, and the rest of the world. It is only in the United States that any human being can live in a free environment which will give that individual full scope to develop his personality to the full, in spite of the vagaries of human life" (196). He is critical of American "racial intolerance, bigotry and lawlessness" but views these as part of a "passing phase" (195).

27. Nnamdi Azikiwe, *My Odyssey: An Autobiography* (New York: Praeger, 1970), 40.
28. Nnamdi Azikiwe, *Zik: A Selection from the Speeches of Nnamdi Azikiwe* (Cambridge: Cambridge University Press, 1961), 17.
29. Martin Luther King, Jr., "The Negro and the American Dream," typed draft of address delivered September 25, 1960, accessed June 29, 2018, https://kinginstitute.stanford.edu/king-papers/documents/negro-and-american-dream-excerpt-address-annual-freedom-mass-meeting-north.
30. Tim Livsey, *Nigeria's University Age*, (Cambridge: Cambridge University Press, 2017), 13.
31. Ibid., 100.
32. Ibid., 101.
33 Azikiwe to Hannay, 17 September 1959, MSUAHC UA 2.9.5.4. box 185 folder 74, quoted in Livsey, *Nigeria's University Age*, 102. University College Ibadan suspended special relations with London in 1962 and became a degree-granting institution in its own right, as it was renamed the University of Ibadan. Alan Pifer, an official working for the Carnegie Corporation, that Nigerians' resistance to collaboration with the US exclusively had to do with skepticism regarding the quality of US universities: "The fact that MSU is not regarded in the US as a top university will soon reach Nigerian ears . . . and its position here will be rapidly destroyed" (Livsey, *Nigeria's University Age*, 104).
34. The Second Morrill Act allowed states to segregate and unequally distribute funds to African-American and predominately white institutions. For an overview of how the US funded land-grant universities with expropriated Indigenous land, see Robert Lee, Tristan Ahtone, Margaret Pearce, Kalen Goodluck, Geoff McGhee, Cody Leff, Katherine Lanpher and Taryn Salinas, "Land-Grab Universities," *High Country News*, published 2020, accessed May 25, 2020, https://www.landgrabu.org/.
35. Achebe, *The Education*, 34.
36. Maik Nwosu, "Children of the Anthill: Nsukka and the Shaping of Nigeria's 1960s Literary Generation," *English in Africa* 32.1 (2005): 40–41.
37. Azikwe's relation to the US university contrasts with that of an earlier West African leader, J.E. Casely Hayford. Casely Hayford's locally-attuned vision for Mfantsipim, the renowned secondary school and alma mater of United Nations Secretary General Kofi Annan, was partly inspired by Booker T. Washington's Tuskeegee Institute, even as Casely Hayford also critiqued the national circumscription of Washington's work. See Jeanne-Marie Jackson and Adwoa A. Opoku-Agyemang, Introduction, *Ethiopia Unbound* by J.E. Casely Hayford (East Lansing: Michigan State University Press, forthcoming).

38. Achebe, "The Day I finally Met." Especially after University College Ibadan became the University of Ibadan in 1962, it became an "appealing target" for US organizations such as the Rockefeller and Ford foundations, which "saw universities as important sites for the advancement of a Cold War-inflected agenda" that explicitly sought to "diminish British influence" in Nigeria (Livsey 108–09). Achebe was awarded a Rockefeller Fellowship in 1960 that funded six months' travel in East Africa. Nathan Suhr-Sytsma argues that "Ibadan modernism" (including the poetry of Clark-Bekederemo) represented significant cultural and aesthetic autonomy, despite the CIA underwriting several of its key institutions. See Nathan Suhr-Sytsma, "Ibadan Modernism: Poetry and the Literary Present in Mid-century Nigeria," *Journal of Commonwealth Literature* 48.1 (2013): 41–59.
39. Achebe, *The Education*, 55.
40. Michael C. Onwuemene's article on the subject provides an excellent overview of the history of English as a literary Nigerian language. See "Limits of Transliteration: Nigerian Writers' Endeavors toward a National Literary Language," *PMLA* 114.5 (1999): 1055–66. For examples of analyses of the politics of English as a language of world literature, see Rebecca Walkowitz's analysis of the uses of English to remediate an uneven global marketplace in *Born Translated* (New York: Columbia University Press, 2015) and Aamir R. Mufti's account of the dominance of globalized English in world literature in *Forget English!* (Cambridge: Harvard University Press, 2016), 13.
41. Mukoma Wa Ngugi, *The Rise of the African Novel* (Ann Arbor: University of Michigan Press, 2018), 45.
42. Ibid., 46.
43. Chinua Achebe, "English and the African Writer," *Transition* 18 (1965): 28.
44. Ibid., 30. For a comparative analysis of Achebe's and Baldwin's writing, see Ernest A. Champion, *Mr. Baldwin, I Presume: James Baldwin-Chinua Achebe, A Meeting of Minds* (Lanham: University Press of America, 1995). For additional scholarship on Achebe's resonance with another African-American writer, see Christopher N. Okonkwo, *Kindred Spirits: Chinua Achebe and Toni Morrison* (Charlottesville: University of Virginia Press, 2022).
45. Bill Ashcroft, Gareth Griffiths, and Helen Tiffin, *The Empire Writes Back: Theory and Practice in Post-Colonial Literatures* (London: Routledge, 1989). For an account of US englishes and anglophone Nigerian fiction, see Katherine Hallemeier, "The Empires Write Back," *Comparative Literature* 71.2. (2019): 123–38.
46. Obiajunwa Wali, "The Dead End of African Literature?" *Transition* 10 (1963): 13–14. J.P. Clark-Bekederemo, notably, agreed with Achebe as to the uses to which English could be put. John Pepper Clark, "Poetry in Africa Today," *Transition* 18 (1965): 18.
47. Una Maclean, "Song of A Goat," *Ibadan*, October 1962, 28, quoted in Wali, "The Dead End," 13.
48. Peter Kalliney, "Modernism, African Literature, and the Cold War," *Modern Language Quarterly* 76.3 (2015): 341–42.

49. Ibid., 362.
50. Ibid., 340.
51. Ibid., 342, 336.
52. Taiwo Adetunji Osinubi, "Cold War Sponsorships: Chinua Achebe and the Dialectics of Collaboration," *Postcolonial Writing* 50 (2014): 410–22.
53. Monica Popescu, *At Penpoint: African Literatures, Postcolonial Studies, and the Cold War* (Durham: Duke University Press, 2020), 12.
54. Gary Wilder, *Freedom Time: Negritude, Decolonization, and the Future of the World* (Durham: Duke University Press, 2015), 4.
55. J.P. Clark, *America, Their America: The Nigerian Poet and Playwright's Criticism of American Society* (London: Heinemann Educational Books Ltd., 1964), 15.
56. Clark-Bekederemo returned to the US after his retirement from the University of Lagos in 1980 to hold visiting appointments at Yale and Wesleyan University.
57. "University News," *Princeton Alumni Weekly*, February 10, 1961, 7. As John Brooks notes, Albert Parvin was the founder of Parvin-Dohrmann, which owned hotels and casinos in Los Vegas. Some of its "major stockholders" had "suspicious credentials." The fact that Supreme Court Justice William O. Douglas was at the head of the Parvin Foundation—indeed, he co-announced the Princeton fellowship program—was cited by the company to bolster its legitimacy. Clark-Bekederemo could be alluding to this history in his suggestion that the UNESCO sponsorship is more "proper." See John Brooks, *The Go-Go Years: The Drama and Crashing Finale of Wall Street's Bullish '60s* (New York: Open Road, 2014), 275.
58. "University News," 7.
59. Ibid.
60. Azikiwe, *Zik*, 17. See also Parker, "Made-in-America," 729.
61. Nadiminti, "Global Program Era," 379–80.
62. Parker, "Made-in-America," 729.
63. James Nabrit, speech, *Howard University Magazine*, November 3, 1960, quoted in Parker, "Made-in-America," 743.
64. Parker, "Made-in-America," 742.
65. Ibid., 745. As Parker notes, while mid-century white institutions "led the way in hosting programs in African studies, black institutions led the way in hosting actual Africans" (739).
66. Ibid.
67. Azikiwe, *Zik*, 21.
68. Levi A. Nwachuku, "The United States and Nigeria—1960 to 1987: Anatomy of a Pragmatic Relationship," *Journal of Black Studies* 28.5 (1998): 576. The Kennedy administration viewed Nigeria as an important regional power. The discovery of oil in the 1950s also hastened US interest and investment. In 1965, the US Embassy identified 1964 as "the benchmark for when Nigeria moved from a marginal producer to a major world oil producer of great promise for the future." See Robert Brand to State Department, "Oil and Gas-Status Report on Exploration and Production," July 2, 1965, Nigeria Folder, box 1397, Economic: Petroleum, 1964–1966

file, General Records of the Department of State (National Archives, College Park, Md.), quoted in Kairn A. Klieman, "US Oil Companies, the Nigerian Civil War, and the Origins of Opacity in the Nigerian Oil Industry," *The Journal of American History* 99.1 (2012): 157.
69. Livsey, *Nigeria's University*, 99.
70. See Andrew Apter, *The Pan-African Nation: Oil and the Spectacle of Culture in Nigeria* (Chicago: Chicago University Press, 2005).
71. Nelson Mandela, "American Imperialism: A New Menace in Africa," *Liberation* 30 (1958): 25.
72. Ibid.
73. Aimé Césaire, *Discourse on Colonialism*, Trans. Joan Pinkham (New York: Monthly Review Press, 1972), 23.
74. Ngũgĩ wa Thiong'o, *Decolonising the Mind: The Politics of Language in African Literature* (London: J. Currey, 1986), 3.
75. James Ferguson showed how the outsized influence of foreign investors in African governments culminated, by the late 1990s, in a geopolitical situation in which cries for "democracy in Africa" by capital-rich organizations ended up "serving a profoundly antidemocratic end—that is, the simulation of popular legitimation for policies that in fact are made in the most undemocratic way imaginable." James Ferguson, *Global Shadows: Africa in the Neoliberal World Order* (Durham: Duke University Press, 2006), 84.
76. Clark-Bekederemo is scathing, by contrast, in his account of the contemporary "Black Bourgeoisie," as well as what he perceives to be a "phony, gushing business" of a "new emotional response to Africa" that tends toward "collecting masks, and imitations at that" (72–78).
77. Stefano Harney and Fred Moten, *The Undercommons: Fugitive Planning and Black Study* (Wivenhoe: Minor Compositions, 2013), 26.
78. Clark-Bekederemo reports that while he was at Princeton, his brother was serving as a diplomat in India (52).
79. Achebe, *The Education*, 24.
80. Moradewun Adejunmobi, "Native Books and the 'English Book,'" *PMLA* 132.1 (2017): 139–40.
81. Pheng Cheah, *Spectral Nationality* (New York: Columbia University Press, 2003), 395.

Chapter 2

1. Olajide Aluko, "Nigeria, the United States and Southern Africa," *African Affairs* 78.310 (1979): 91.
2. Levi A. Nwachuku, "The United States and Nigeria—1960 to 1987: Anatomy of a Pragmatic Relationship," *Journal of Black Studies* 28.5 (1998): 582.
3. Andrew Apter, *The Pan-African Nation: Oil and the Spectacle of Culture in Nigeria* (Chicago: Chicago University Press, 2005).
4. Quoted in Mitchell, *Jimmy Carter*, 3.
5. Nancy Mitchell, *Jimmy Carter in Africa: Race and the Cold War* (Stanford: Stanford University Press, 2016), 2–3.

6. Stokely Carmichael, "Black Power," typed draft of address delivered October 29, 1966, accessed May 28, 2020, https://voicesofdemocracy.umd.edu/carmichael-black-power-speech-text/.
7. Kwame Anthony Appiah, "Is the Post- in Postmodernism the Post- in Postcolonial?" *Critical Inquiry* 17.2 (1991): 353.
8. Ibid.
9. Buchi Emecheta, *The Joys of Motherhood* (New York: George Braziller, Inc., 1979).
10. Chris Abani, *GraceLand* (New York: Farrar, Straus & Giroux, 2004).
11. Katherine Hallemeier, "The Empires Write Back: The Language of Postcolonial Nigerian Literature and the United States of America," *Comparative Literature* 71.2 (2019): 123–38.
12. Nanjala Nyabola, "Eulogy for Pan-Africanism: Long Live Man-Africanism," *The New Inquiry*, published May, 23, 2016, accessed February 24, 2020, https://thenewinquiry.com/eulogy-for-pan-africanism-long-live-man-africanism/.
13. Robin Goodman, "Capitalists in the Myst: The Mystery and the Joys in the Free Market," *Journal of Cultural Studies* 3.2. (2001): 400.
14. Stéphane Robolin, "Gendered Hauntings: *The Joys of Motherhood*, Interpretive Acts, and Postcolonial Theory," *Research in African Literatures* 35.3 (2004): 87–88. Florence Stratton exemplarily reads Nnu Ego as unable to defy patriarchy. Florence Stratton, "The Shallow Grave: Archetypes of Female Experience in African Fiction," *Research in African Literatures* 19.2 (1988): 153.
15. Madhu Krishnan, "Mami Wata and the Occluded Feminine in Anglophone Nigerian-Igbo Literature," *Research in African Literatures* 43.1 (2012): 10.
16. Pheng Cheah, "The Biopolitics of Recognition: Making Female Subjects of Globalization," *boundary2* 40.2 (2013): 96–97.
17. Lauren Berlant, *Cruel Optimism* (Durham: Duke UP, 2011), 20.
18. Ibid., 37–38.
19. Ibid., 196.
20. Buchi Emecheta, *Head Above Water* (Oxford: Heinemann, 1994), 224.
21. Ibid., 223.
22. Ibid., 225.
23. Ibid., 222–23.
24 Sanford J. Ungar, "Dateline West Africa: Great Expectations," *Foreign Policy* 32 (1978): 188.
25 Oye Ogunbadejo, "A New Turn in US-Nigerian Relations," *The World Today* 35.3 (1979): 119.
26. Wendy Griswold, *Bearing Witness: Readers, Writers, and the Novel in Nigeria* (Princeton: Princeton UP, 2000), 256–57.
27. Ogunbadejo, "A New Turn," 118.
28. United Nations Centre Against Apartheid, *World Conference for Action Against Apartheid, Lagos, Nigeria, 22–26 August 1977: Statements-IV* (New York: United Nations, 1977), 16.
29. Jimmy Carter, "Lagos, Nigeria, Remarks at the National Arts Theatre," typed draft of address delivered April 1, 1978, accessed February 26, 2020,

https://www.presidency.ucsb.edu/documents/lagos-nigeria-remarks-the-national-arts-theatre.
30. Ibid.
31. Mitchell shows how the Carter administration repeatedly tried to curry favor with the Congressional Black Caucus by virtue of its policies toward Africa, despite the fact that the CBC was much more concerned with the domestic economy and "the poverty and unemployment confronting African Americans in the late 1970s" (568). When the administration needed to demonstrate widespread public support for its Rhodesia policy, Andrew Young manufactured it by contacting Black churches and civil rights organizations (570). See Nancy Mitchell, *Jimmy Carter in Africa*, 568–70.
32. Jimmy Carter, "Reception for Black Business Executives Remarks at the White House Reception," typed draft of address delivered June 14, 1978, accessed February 26, 2020, https://www.presidency.ucsb.edu/node/248678. Just as "Andy Young" has been "one of the greatest things that's happened to me in foreign affairs," Carter suggested, Black business owners might be good for US economic affairs: "you might use your position as a trader in international affairs to strengthen the ties of friendship and understanding between our country and those countries that encompass your new customers."
33. Jimmy Carter, "Lagos, Nigeria Question-and-Answer Session with Reporters Following Meetings Between the President and General Obasanjo," typed draft of address delivered April 2, 1978, accessed February 26, 2020, https://www.presidency.ucsb.edu/node/244844.
34. Ibid.
35. Richard L. Sklar, "Democracy for the Second Republic," *Issue: A Journal of Opinion* 11.1–2 (1981): 14.
36. Jean Herskovits, "Dateline Nigeria: A Black Power," *Foreign Policy* 29 (1977–78): 185–86.
37. Daniel Immerwahr, "The Politics of Architecture and Urbanism in Postcolonial Lagos, 1960–1986," *Journal of African Cultural Studies* 19.2 (2007): 180.
38. James S. Read, "The New Constitution of Nigeria, 1979: 'The Washington Model?'" *Journal of African Law* 23.2. (1979): 131.
39. Daniel C. Bach, "Nigerian-American Relations: Converging Interests and Power Relations," in *Nigerian Foreign Policy*, eds. Timothy M. Shaw and Olajide Aluko (London: Palgrave Macmillan, 1983), 49.
40. Ibid.
41. Ungar, "Dateline West Africa," 188.
42. Jason C. Parker, "'Made-in-America Revolutions'? The 'Black University' and the American Role in the Decolonization of the Black Atlantic," *The Journal of American History* 96.3 (2009): 728.
43. Carter, "Lagos, Nigeria Question and Answer."
44. Carter, "Lagos, Nigeria Remarks."
45. Daniel C. Bach usefully characterizes US reliance on Nigerian oil during this period as a source of "might but not of power" (44). The Nigerian

state could threaten to withhold oil to enforce its foreign policy in theory but required oil revenue and foreign capital to pursue domestic policies (44–51). See Bach, "Nigerian-American Relations."
46. Berlant, *Cruel Optimism*, 200.
47. Ibid., 5.
48. Ibid., 199.
49. Robolin, "Gendered Hauntings," 88.
50. Kwame Anthony Appiah, "Is the Post- in Postmodernism the Post- in Postcolonial?" *Critical Inquiry* 17.2 (1991): 353.
51. Yambo Ouologuem, *Bound to Violence*, translated by Ralph Manheim (London: Heinemann, 1971), 181–82, quoted in Appiah, "Is the Post-," 353.
52. Appiah, "Is the Post-," 353.
53. Pheng Cheah, *Spectral Nationality: Passages of Freedom from Kant to Postcolonial Literatures of Liberation* (New York: Columbia University Press, 2003), 245.
54. Robolin, "Gendered Hauntings," 88.
55. Berlant, *Cruel Optimism*, 5.
56. Berlant, *Cruel Optimism*, 199.
57. Krishnan, "Mami Wata," 2.
58. Ibid., 20.
59. Ibid., 10.
60. While Abani's novel does not dwell on Nigeria's most lucrative export in the mid-1970s, oil, the effects of American demand for this commodity on the Nigerian economy and political system entailed the comparable production of risk and violence, as well as systemic environmental degradation. See Andrew Apter, *The Pan-African Nation: Oil and the Spectacle of Culture in Nigeria* (Chicago: Chicago University Press, 2005).
61. Mathew Omelsky, "Chris Abani and the Politics of Ambivalence," *Research in African Literatures*, 42.4 (2011): 93.
62. Yogita Goyal, *Runaway Genres: The Global Afterlives of Slavery* (New York: New York University Press, 2019), 192.
63. Chinua Achebe, "The Day I Finally Met Baldwin," PEN America, published January 8, 2007, ccessed June 29, 2018, https://pen.org/the-day-i-finally-met-baldwin/.
64. Ibid.
65. Jared Sexton, "The Social Life of Social Death," *In*Tensions *Journal* 5 (2011): 28–31.
66. Emecheta, *Head Above Water*, 147.
67. Emecheta wrote powerfully about the experience of being a Black Nigerian woman living in London, where she lived for most of her life. See *In the Ditch* (1972) and *Second Class Citizen* (1974).
68. Emecheta, *Head Above Water*, 227.
69. Feroza Jussawalla and Reed Way Dasenbrock, editors, *Interviews with Writers of the Post-Colonial World* (Jackson: UP of Mississippi, 1992), 93.
70. Rob Roensch and Mary B. Gray, "'If I Strip away Everything, What Is Left?': A Conversation with Chris Abani," *World Literature Today* 92.4. (2018): n.p.

71. Tsitsi Ella Jaji, *Africa in Stereo: Modernism, Music, and Pan-African Solidarity* (Oxford: Oxford UP, 2014), 240.
72. Ibid., 8.

Chapter 3

1. See chapter 2. Chris Abani, *GraceLand* (New York: Farrar, Straus & Giroux, 2004).
2. Adélékè Adéèkó, "Power Shift: America in the New Nigerian Imagination," *The Global South* 2.2. (2008): 14. Adéèkó reads Elvis's flight to the US as a move toward relative safety and political stability; this is in tension with my argument in chapter 2, which emphasizes the novel's pan-African identifications and critique of the US nation.
3. Ibid., 23.
4. Ibid., 20.
5. Ibid., 21.
6. Ibid.
7. Ibid., 23.
8. Ibid., 26.
9. Ike Oguine, *A Squatter's Tale* (Oxford: Heinemann, 2000). One source reports the fiction received the 1997 Association of Nigerian Authors prize in fiction. See "Oguine, Novelist, is Nigeria's Top Petroleum Lawyer," *Africa Oil and Gas Report*, published May 13, 2014, accessed June 17, 2020, https://africaoilgasreport.com/2014/05/petroleum-people/oguine-novelist-is-nigerias-top-petroleum-lawyer/.
10. Adéèkó, "Power Shift," 25.
11. Chimamanda Ngozi Adichie, *Americanah* (New York: Anchor Books, 2014).
12. Christopher N. Okonkwo, "Sound Statements and Counterpoints: Ike Oguine's Channeling of Music, Highlife, and Jazz in *A Squatter's Tale*," *College Literature* 46.3 (2019): 634.
13. Ibid. Okonkwo also links Oguine's novel to Dinaw Mengestu's *The Beautiful Things that Heaven Bears* (2007), Teju Cole's *Open City* (2011), and NoViolent Bulawayo's *We Need New Names* (2013).
14. Jean Baudrillard, *America*, trans. Chris Turner (New York: Verso, 1988), 28.
15. Ibid., 107.
16. Ibid., 28.
17. Kwadwo Osei-Nyame, "Toward the Decolonization of African Postcolonial Theory," in *Texts, Tasks, and Theories: Versions and Subversions of African Literatures*, eds. Tobias Robert Klein, Ulrike Auga, and Viola Prüschenk (Amsterdam: Rodopi, 2007), 88.
18. Ibid.
19. Louisa Uchum Egbunike, "One-Way Traffic: Renegotiating the 'Been-To' Narrative in the Nigerian Novel in the Era of Military Rule," in *Tradition and Change in Contemporary West and East African Fiction*, ed. by Ogaga Okuyade (Amsterdam: Rodopi, 2014), 230.

20. Carrie Tirado Bramen, *American Niceness: A Cultural History* (Cambridge: Harvard University Press, 2017), 5.
21. Andrew Apter, *The Pan-African Nation: Oil and the Spectacle of Culture in Nigeria* (Chicago: University of Chicago Press, 2005), 250–52.
22. Imre Szeman, "Entrepreneurship as the New Common Sense," *South Atlantic Quarterly* 114.3 (2015): 479. Entrepreneurialism and optimism is also central to my discussion of South African literature of the 1990s. See chapter 5.
23. Ibid., 475.
24. Ibid., 476.
25. Ibid., 481.
26. Ibid.
27. "Ike Iguine," Advisory Legal Consultants, accessed June 5, 2019, http://www.advisoryng.com/ike-oguine/.
28. Tim Livsey, *Nigeria's University Age* (Cambridge: Cambridge University Press, 2017), 140.
29. George W. Shepherd, Jr., "An Editorial: Transition to Democracy in Nigeria," *Africa Today* 33.4 (1986): 4.
30. Livsey, *Nigeria's University*, 140.
31. The seeming "obsolescence" of pan-African freedom dreams, Yogita Goyal argues, is recurrent in new African immigrant fiction, in part "because US cultural histories have usually treated immigration and slavery as two distinct stories, and their collision here presages a number of conflicts and challenges to expected ways of narrating both America and Africa." Yogita Goyal, *Runaway Genres: The Global Afterlives of Slavery* (New York: New York University Press, 2019), 176.
32. J. Lorand Matory, *Stigma and Culture: Last-Place Anxiety in Black America* (Chicago: Chicago University Press, 2015), 57.
33. Ibid.
34. Ibid.
35. Ibid., 3.
36. Christina Sharpe, *Monstrous Intimacies: Making Post-Slavery Subjects* (Durham: Duke University Press, 2010), 99.
37. Jemima Pierre, "Black Immigrants in the United States and the 'Cultural Narratives' of Ethnicity," *Identities: Global Studies in Culture and Power* 11 (2004): 143.
38. For an extended reading of music in Oguine, see Okonkwo, "Sound Statements." Okonkwo reads music as central to the novel's "expansive, pan-Africanist objectives" (635); Uncle Happiness's dances are part of how the novel "celebrates black world music and its complex interconnections" (638). My interpretation is more ambivalent.
39. Therí Alyce Pickens, *Black Madness :: Mad Blackness* (Durham: Duke University Press, 2019), 4.
40. Adéèkó, "Power Shift," 26.
41. Ibid., 21.
42. This is not to say it became impossible to rehearse the old illusions. In commencement season of May 2019, US president Donald Trump tweeted,

"With the wonderful College, University, and other Graduations taking place all over the USA, there has never been a better time than now to graduate. Best job market ever, great housing and financing" (@realDonald Trump, May 19, 2019). In the same month, a speech delivered on behalf of Nigerian president Muhammadu Buhari to graduates of Nnamdi Azikiwe University was more circumspect and, by comparison, remarkably grounded: "You are cautioned that university degrees do not usher you into an El Dorado. It rather equips you with the competence to grapple with the ever-changing challenges of life of which youth unemployment is a vexatious part." See John Owen Nwachuckwu, "University Degree Not an Assurance for Jobs—Buhari Tells Nigerian Graduates," *Daily Post*, published May 11, 2019, accessed June 29, 2020, https://dailypost.ng/2019/05/11/university-degree-not-assurance-job-buhari-tells-nigerian-graduates/.
43. J.P. Clark, *America, Their America: The Nigerian Poet and Playwright's Criticism of American Society* (London: Heinemann Educational Books Ltd., 1964), 120.
44. James Ferguson, *Global Shadows: Africa in the Neoliberal World Order* (Durham: Duke University Press, 2006), 84.
45. Ibid.
46. "Remarks by the President in Address to Join Assembly, House of Representatives Chamber, National Assembly Building, Abuja, Nigeria," August 26, 2000, Nigeria—Policy Memos, Clinton Presidential Records, William J. Clinton Presidential Library, 6.
47. Aretha Phiri, "Expanding Black Subjectivities in Toni Morrison's *Song of Solomon* and Chimamanda Ngozi Adichie's *Americanah*," *Cultural Studies* 31.1 (2017): 125–26.
48. I argue for the centrality of uncertainty in the novel's depiction of Nigeria in Katherine Hallemeier, "'To Be from the Country of People Who Gave': National Allegory and the United States of Adichie's *Americanah*," *Studies in the Novel* 27.2 (2015): 231–45.
49. Tejumolan Olaniyan, "African Literature in the Post-Global Age: Provocations on Field Commonsense," *Cambridge Journal of Postcolonial Literary Inquiry* 3.3 (2016): 390.
50. Ibid.
51. "Remarks by the President," 8.
52. Ibid.
53. Ibid.
54. Ibid.
55. Olaniyan, "African Literature," 393.
56. Ibid., 391.
57. Ibid.
58. "Remarks by the President," 8.
59. Ibid.
60. Christopher T. Fan, "Battle Hymn of the Afropolitan: Sino-African Futures in *Ghana Must Go* and *Americanah*," *Journal of Asian American Studies* 20.1 (2017): 86.
61. Ibid., 76.

62. Ibid., 86.
63. Ibid., 83.
64. Olaniyan, "African Literature," 392.
65. Fan, "Battle Hymn," 72.
66. Kalyan Nadiminti, "The Global Program Era," *Novel: A Forum on Fiction* 51.3 (2018): 394–95.
67. Ibid.
68. Lily Saint, "The Danger of a Single Author," *Africa Is a Country*, published April 14, 2017, accessed June 29, 2020, https://africasacountry.com/2017/04/the-danger-of-a-single-author.
69. Nadiminti, "The Global Program," 389–90.
70. Camille Isaacs, "Mediating Women's Globalized Existence Through Social Media in the Work of Adichie and Bulawayo," *Safundi* 17.2 (2016): 176.
71. Ibid., 187.
72. Nadiminti, "The Global Program," 395.
73. Goyal, *Runaway Genres*, 177–78.
74. Imre Szeman, "Entrepreneurship as the New Common Sense," *South Atlantic Quarterly* 114.3 (2015): 484.
75. Ibid., 485.
76. Otosirieze Obi-Young, "Chimamanda's Creative Workshop Returns as the Purple Hibiscus Trust Creative Writing Workshop, Sponsored by Trace Nigeria," Brittle Paper, published September 25, 2018, accessed June 29, 2020, https://brittlepaper.com/2018/09/chimamandas-workshop-returns-as-the-purple-hibiscus-trust-creative-writing-workshop-sponsored-by-trace-nigeria-how-to-apply/.
77. Otosirieze Obi-Young, "Why Adichie's Farafina Workshop Will Not Be Held This Year," *Brittle Paper*, published July 5, 2017, accessed June 29, 2020, https://brittlepaper.com/2017/07/adichies-farafina-workshop-hold-year/.
78. Obi-Young, "Chimamanda's Creative Workshop," n.p.
79. "About Us," *Trace*, updated 2020, accessed June 29, 2020, https://trace.company/about-us/.
80. Obi-Young, "Why Adichie's Farafina," n.p.
81. How Adichie's pan-Africanism is delimited by a trans-exclusionary view of womanhood is an important question that exceeds the scope of this chapter. For an analysis of Adichie's feminism that centers trans people from the African continent, see B. Camminga, "Disregard and Danger: Chimamanda Ngozi Adichie and the Voices of Trans (and Cis) African Feminists," *The Sociological Review Monographs* 68.4 (2020): 817–33.

Chapter 4

1. Sampie Terreblanche, "The New South Africa's Original State Capture," *Africa Is A Country*, published January 28, 2018, accessed May 25, 2020, https://africasacountry.com/2018/01/the-new-south-africas-original-state-capture/.

2. In 2017, the World Bank determined that South Africa had the highest Gini coefficient of 154 countries surveyed, meaning it had the worst results for this measure of inequality. See "Blurring the Rainbow," *The Economist*, published May 20, 2017, accessed May 25, 2020, https://www.economist.com/news/middle-east-and-africa/21722155-democracy-has-brought-wealth-only-few.
3. Rita Barnard, "Rewriting the Nation," in *The Cambridge History of South African Literature*, eds. David Attwell and Derek Attridge (Cambridge: Cambridge University Press, 2012), 656, 652.
4. Ibid., 652.
5. "Struggle for South Africa's Soul after Madiba's Death," *Daily Nation*, published March 9, 2014, accessed May 25, 2020, https://www.nation.co.ke/lifestyle/lifestyle/Struggle-for-South-Africa-soul-after-Nelson-Madiba-death/1214-2236812-xbn9iez/index.html_.
6. Anne-Maria Makhulu, "The Search for Economic Sovereignty," in *Hard Work, Hard Times: Global Volatility and African Subjectivities*, eds. Anne-Maria Makhulu, Beth A. Buggenhagen, and Stephen Jackson (Berkeley: University of California Press, 2010), 34.
7. Ibid.
8. Ibid., 34–35.
9. For a discussion of how the rights guaranteed in the South African constitution are in tension with embodied lived experience, see Rosemary Jolly, *Cultured Violence* (Liverpool: Liverpool University Press, 2010).
10. Deborah James, *Money from Nothing: Indebtedness and Aspiration in South Africa* (Stanford: Stanford University Press, 2015), 8.
11. Ibid., 8.
12. Hylton White, "A Post-Fordist Ethnicity: Insecurity, Authority, and Identity in South Africa," *Anthropological Quarterly* 85.2 (2012): 406.
13. Ibid., 424.
14. James, *Money from Nothing*, 2.
15. Miriam Tlali, *Between Two Worlds* (Toronto: Broadview Press, 2004).
16. James, *Money from Nothing*, 99.
17. Ibid., 100–01.
18. Ibid., 102.
19. Rita Barnard, *Apartheid and Beyond: South African Writers and the Politics of Place* (Oxford: Oxford University Press, 2007), 132.
20. Key pieces of colonial and apartheid legislation that restricted Black ownership rights in South African cities include the Native (Urban Areas) Act of 1923 and the Group Areas Act of 1950. The Native Resettlement Act of 1954 "licensed" the state to remove Black people from any neighborhood in or near Johannesburg.
21. Herman Tobiansky, who bought the land that he would name for his wife in 1897, was forced to offer plots to Black, Indian, and Coloured residents after construction of a sewage disposal plant nearby made the area undesirable to white residents.
22. Es'kia Mphahlele, in *Sophiatown Speaks*, eds. Pippa Stein and Ruth Jacobson (Johannesburg: Junction Avenue Press, 1986), 55.

23. The multicultural, heterogenous character of Sophiatown was not only shaped by American influences. Also known as the "little Paris of the Transvaal," Sophiatown had a culture that Ulf Hannerz described as that of a "global ecumene" (Barnard, *Apartheid*, 136).
24. Pippa Stein and Ruth Jacobson, "Sophiatown Speaks: Introduction," in *Sophiatown Speaks*, eds. Pippa Stein and Ruth Jacobson (Johannesburg: Junction Avenue Press, 1986), 1.
25. Stéphane Robolin, *Grounds of Engagement: Apartheid-Era African American and South African Writing* (Champaign: University of Illinois Press, 2015), 10.
26. Mphahlele, *Sophiatown Speaks*, 56. The importance of African American urban cultures to black South African cultures in the early- and mid-twentieth century is well-documented. Jaji's analysis, which extends to film as well as magazines, demonstrates how these forms were consumed in ways that "laid bare the many contradictions of aspirational consumption." See Tsitsi Ella Jaji, *Africa in Stereo: Modernism, Music, and Pan-African Solidarity* (Oxford: Oxford University Press, 2014), 111.
27. Don Mattera, "Other Faces of Kofifi," in *Sophiatown: Coming of Age in South Africa* (Boston: Beacon Press, 1987), 75.
28. Jaji, *Africa in Stereo*, 121.
29. Robert Trent Vinson, *The Americans are Coming! Dreams of African American Liberation in Segregationist South Africa* (Athens: Ohio University Press, 2012), 24. As Vinson notes, the AME was established by Black Methodists living in the mid-Atlantic region of the US in 1816; the Ethiopian Church of South Africa become its fourteenth district in 1896, as AME ministers undertook a "civilizing" mission that aimed to grow what they understood to be a divinely ordained "black transnational spiritual collective" (21)
30. Ibid., 32.
31. Ibid., 63, 65.
32. Quoted in Vinson, *The Americans*, 138.
33. Vinson, *The Americans*, 3–5.
34. Miriam Tlali, "Introduction: My Background and How I Began to Write," in *Between Two Worlds* (Toronto: Broadview Press, 2004), 9.
35. The priest was scheduled to attend an annual AME conference in the US. He accepted a few chapters and solicited an author's picture; nothing was ever heard from American church officials or publishers, although another conference delegate reported that the priest kept Tlali's picture in his coat pocket (Tlali, "Introduction," 9).
36. Rob Nixon, *Homelands, Harlem and Hollywood: South African Culture and the World Beyond* (New York: Routledge, 1994), 17.
37. White supremacist dreams of the US and South Africa have long been co-constituted. Natal cited the example of the "great Republic of America" in the late nineteenth century as it disenfranchised "Africans" and restricted immigration (Vinson, *The Americans*, 36). British parliamentarians passed the 1909 South Africa Act, which sanctioned a Union of South Africa that furthered the disenfranchisement of Black people, with an eye to the supposed "failure" of Reconstruction in the US South (Vinson, *The Americans*, 43).

38. Mehrsa Baradaran, *The Color of Money: Black Banks and the Racial Wealth Gap* (Cambridge: The Belknap Press of Harvard University Press, 2017), 137.
39. Ibid., 143.
40. Ibid., 146.
41. Martin Luther King, Jr., "The American Dream," typed draft of address delivered July 4, 1965, accessed May 26, 2020, https://kinginstitute.stanford.edu/king-papers/documents/american-dream-sermon-delivered-ebenezer-baptist-church.
42. Baradaran, *The Color of Money*, 159.
43. Ibid., 158.
44. Ibid., 171.
45. Robert F. Kennedy, "Day of Affirmation Address," typed draft of address delivered June 6, 1966, accessed May 26, 2020, https://www.jfklibrary.org/learn/about-jfk/the-kennedy-family/robert-f-kennedy/robert-f-kennedy-speeches/day-of-affirmation-address-university-of-capetown-capetown-south-africa-june-6-1966.
46. On the Kennedy administration's support for apartheid, see Zoe Hyman, "'To Have Its Cake and Eat It Too': US Policy Toward South Africa During the Kennedy Administration," *The Sixties* 8.2. (2015): 139. On Johnson's, see, Eddie Michel, "'You Haven't Been Too Horrible to Us Recently': Lyndon Johnson and Apartheid in South Africa," *Diplomacy & Statecraft* 32.4 (2021): 759.
47. "Freedom Charter," *The Black Scholar* 24.3 (1994): 44.
48. Ibid., 45–46.
49. Kennedy, "Day of Affirmation Address."
50. Ibid.
51. Ibid.
52. Kennedy, "Day of Affirmation Address."
53. Robolin, *Grounds of Engagement*, 5.
54. Ibid.
55. Ibid.
56. Ibid.
57. Ibid.
58. James Baldwin and William Buckley, "The American Dream and the American Negro," *New York Times*, March 7, 1965.
59. "Our language" seems to refer to Fanagalo, a vernacular based on isiZulu that incorporates English and Afrikaans and is frequently named in the novel.
60. James Ferguson, *Give a Man a Fish: Reflections on the New Politics of Distribution* (Durham: Duke University Press, 2019), 82.
61. Albion Ross for the *New York Times* observes of New Year's Day celebrations in South Africa in 1954 that "the white man looks on, but wants no part of it." In an article rife with anti-Black racism and primitivism, Ross rather astutely suggests that this refusal to participate is bound up with white people's paranoia about and fear of those they oppress: "That 'their day' is the day on which everyone's mind is turned toward the future and new beginnings may trouble the more superstitious whites, but it is an

established institution now, and there is no interference." Muriel is not satisfied with mere toleration. See Albion Ross, "Africans' Carnival Ushers in New Year; Their Rhythmic Fete Shunned by Whites," *New York Times*, January 2, 1954.
62. "Freedom Charter," 46.
63. For a good summary of the compromises that went into the writing of the Public Holidays Act of 1994, see Sabine Marschall, "Public Memories as *Lieux de Mémoire*: Nation-Building and the Politics of Public Memory in South Africa," *Anthropology of Southern Africa* 36.1–2 (2013): 11–21.
64. Njabulo S. Ndebele, "South Africans in Search of Common Values," *Pretexts: Literary and Cultural Studies* 10.1 (2001): 78.
65. Njabulo S. Ndebele, *The Cry of Winnie Mandela* (Banbury: Ayebia Clarke Publishing, 2006).
66. Cecily Lockett, "An Interview with Miriam Tlali," *Southern African Review of Books* June/July (1989): 20.
67. Ibid., 21. In a 1994 interview, Tlali describes *Between Two Worlds* as an activist book intended to "get anybody, any African who read the book, to be conscious of the system." In the same interview, she looks forward to writing "like you people write here in free societies. I'll write about love, about girl loving boy and dreaming, dreams, love, write about the moon and the sky, I'll write about everything that is beautiful and so on. I didn't have time to notice the skies. We were busy fighting." See Rosemary Jolly, "Interview," in *Writing South Africa*, eds. Derek Attridge and Rosemary Jolly (Cambridge: Cambridge University Press, 1998), 144–45.
68. Lockett, "An Interview," 21.
69. Ndebele, "South Africans in Search," 77.
70. Andrew van der Vlies, *Present Imperfect: Contemporary South African Writing* (Oxford: Oxford University Press, 2017), 20.
71. Ibid., 14.
72. Martijn Konings, *The Emotional Logic of Capitalism* (Stanford: Stanford University Press, 2015), 67.
73. Ibid., 74.
74. Ibid., 107.
75. Ibid., 76.
76. Ibid., 76.
77. Zakes Mda, *The Heart of Redness* (New York: Picador, 2000).

Chapter 5

1. Zakes Mda, *Ways of Dying* (New York: Picador, 1995).
2. Zakes Mda, "The Story Behind *Ways of Dying*," YouTube Video, 1:00, posted by Oxford University Press Southern Africa, May 23, 2013, https://www.youtube.com/watch?v=4Pwug1uUlNE.
3. Tweede Nuwe Year is traced back to the nineteenth century. It is celebrated on January 2, the one day a year that enslaved people in Cape Town were not required to work.

4. Jenny Gross, "South African Neighborhood Celebrates New Year by Chucking Furniture from Windows," *Wall Street Journal*, published January 1, 2014, accessed June 2, 2020, https://www.wsj.com/articles/south-african-neighborhood-celebrates-new-year-by-chucking-furniture-from-windows-1388623752.
5. *Oxford English Dictionary*, "Euphoria, n.," accessed June 2, 2020, https://www-oed-com.argo.library.okstate.edu/view/Entry/65048?redirectedFrom=euphoria&.
6. Zakes Mda, *The Whale Caller* (New York: Picador, 2005).
7. Njabulo S. Ndebele, "Game Lodges and Leisure Colonialists," published 1999, accessed June 2, 2020, https://www.njabulondebele.co.za/work/game-lodges-and-leisure-colonialists/.
8. Rita Barnard, *Apartheid and Beyond: South African Writers and the Politics of Place* (Oxford: Oxford University Press, 2007), 142.
9. Ndebele, "Game Lodges," n.p.
10. Zakes Mda, *The Heart of Redness* (New York: Picador, 2000).
11. Camagu, notably, calls himself a "tourist" (61) when he first arrives to Qolorha. That he quickly becomes an entrepreneur speaks to the fetishization of work and marginalization of leisure that becomes central to this chapter's argument.
12. Jennifer Wenzel, *Bulletproof: Afterlives of Anticolonial Prophecy in South Africa and Beyond* (Chicago: Chicago University Press, 2009), 187.
13. Mda has somewhat controversially based his account of these events on J.B. Peires's *The Dead Will Arise* (Bloomington: Indiana University Press, 1989). In "Duplicity and Plagiarism in Zakes Mda's *The Heart of Redness*," Andrew Offenburger finds "an abuse of textual borrowings" in *The Heart of Redness* (164); Mda's response to the article appears in the same issue of *Research in African Literatures* (2008): 164–99 and 200–03. I follow Meg Samuelson in avoiding the oft-used nomenclature of "the Xhosa Cattle Killing Movement." As Samuelson demonstrates, the term minimizes the important role of women's labor at cultivation, as well as the devastating effects of its cessation. See Meg Samuelson, "Nongqawuse, National Time and (Female) Authorship in *The Heart of Redness*," in *Ways of Writing: Critical Essays on Zakes Mda*, eds. David Bell and J.U. Jacobs (Pietermaritzburg: University of KwaZulu-Natal Press, 2009), 229–53.
14. Wenzel, *Bulletproof*, 181.
15. Matthew Eatough, "Planning the Future: Scenario Planning, Infrastructural Time, and South African Fiction," *MFS* 61.4 (2015): 593.
16. Wenzel, *Bulletproof*, 187.
17. Ibid., 185.
18. Barnard, *Apartheid and Beyond*, 174.
19. Wenzel, *Bulletproof*, 187.
20. Dolly Parton, *Dream More: Celebrate the Dreamer in You* (New York: Riverhead, 2012), 14.

21. Brian Hiatt, "Eddie Murphy Speaks," *Rolling Stone*, published November 9, 2014, accessed June 3, 2020, https://www.rollingstone.com/movies/movie-news/eddie-murphy-speaks-the-rolling-stone-interview-111885/. *Trading Places*, directed by John Landis (1983; LA: Paramount, 2017), DVD. *Coming to America*, directed by John Landis (1988; LA: Paramount, 2017), DVD.
22. For a full discussion of infrastructure and neoliberal scenario planning in *The Heart of Redness*, see Matthew Eatough, "Planning the Future." Eatough demonstrates how the ANC's commitment to privatization and market competition following the Mont Fleur meeting had negative consequences. I am interested in how hopeful attachments to these strategies persist in Mda's novel.
23. Camagu has plausibly been read as an authorial stand-in. Mda, too, has lived for many years in the US and is a professor at Ohio University.
24. Donald E. Pease, *The New American Exceptionalism* (Minneapolis: University of Minnesota Press, 2009), 21.
25. Camagu's attitude towards dreams of America aligns with Toloki's in *Cion*, who remarks of the African-American family with whom he stays: "They partake of the American dream through the lives of the celebrities whose wealth, love affairs, divorces and pregnancies are followed faithfully. When they comment on them it is as though they know them personally. In this way they are no different from third world people who have never set foot in American soil yet live on a daily diet of these programs and American food aid." Zakes Mda, *Cion* (New York: Picador, 2007), 146.
26. Tom Waas et. al., "Sustainable Development: A Bird's Eye View," *Sustainability* 3 (2011): 1641.
27. Wenzel offers a full and fascinating account of the "afterlives" of amaXhosa anticolonial millenarian movements in "imagining national communities and transnational networks of affiliation" (3). This history includes a millenarian revival in the 1920s in which residents of the eastern Cape expected "deliverance by African Americans in 'aeroplanes': inspired by deliverance associated with Marcus Garvey, some believers understood African Americans to be not only a 'black race' . . . but also the dominant force in the United States" (21). Wenzel, *Bulletproof*.
28. John Winthrop, "A Modell of Christian Charity," Hanover Historical Texts Collection, scanned by Monica Banas, August 1996, accessed June 3, 2020, https://history.hanover.edu/texts/winthmod.html.
29. For a concise genealogy of the fantasy of American exceptionalism and its grounding in and enforcement of Cold War politics, see Pease, *The New American*, 7–13. For a reading of American prophecy and Winthrop's sermon, see Greil Marcus, *The Shape of Things to Come* (New York: Picador, 2007), 7.
30. Jacqueline Rose, *States of Fantasy* (Oxford: Oxford University Press, 1998), 7.
31. Wenzel, *Bulletproof*, 23.

32. Gareth Cornwell, "South African Literature in English since 1945: Long Walk to Ordinariness," in *The Columbia Guide to South African Literature*, eds. Gareth Cornwell, Dirk Klopper, and Craig Mackenzie (New York: Columbia University Press, 2010), 6–7.
33. Martijn Konings, *The Emotional Logic of Capitalism* (Stanford: Stanford University Press, 2015), 109.
34. Ibid., 66.
35. Ibid., 108.
36. Mehrsa Baradaran, *The Color of Money: Black Banks and the Racial Wealth Gap* (Cambridge: The Belknap Press of Harvard University Press, 2017), 218.
37. Ibid., 227.
38. Sheila Boniface Davies challenges Jeff Pieres' claim, replicated by Mda, that Mhlakaza and Wilhelm Goliath were the same person. See "Raising the Dead: The Xhosa Cattle-Killing and the Mhlakaza-Goliat Delusion," *Journal of Southern African Studies* 33.1 (2007): 19–41.
39. Deborah James, *Money from Nothing: Indebtedness and Aspiration in South Africa* (Stanford: Stanford University Press, 2015), 2.
40. Ibid., 4.
41. Ibid.
42. Konings, *The Emotional Logic*, 122.
43. Ibid., 76.
44. Ibid., 118.
45. Ibid., 121.
46. Eric Cazdyn, *The Already Dead* (Durham: Duke University Press, 2012), 5.
47. Njabulo S. Ndebele, "South Africans in Search of Common Values," *Pretexts: Literary and Cultural Studies* 10.1 (2001): 75–81.
48. Ibid., 77.
49. Ibid., 75–76.
50. Ibid., 77.
51. Ibid., 76.
52. Timothy Brennan, "Cosmo-Theory," *South Atlantic Quarterly* 100.3 (2001): 685.
53. Ibid., 683.
54. Ibid.
55. Katherine Hallemeier, "An Art of Hunger: Gender and the Politics of Food Distribution in Zakes Mda's South Africa," *Journal of Commonwealth Literature* 53.3 (2018): 386.
56. Fredric Jameson, "No Magic, No Metaphor," *London Review of Books*, published June 15, 2017, accessed June 4, 2020, https://www.lrb.co.uk/the-paper/v39/n12/fredric-jameson/no-magic-no-metaphor.
57. David Marriott, "On Decadence: *Bling Bling*," *e-flux journal* 79 (2017): n.p., accessed July 27, 2022, https://www.e-flux.com/journal/79/94430/on-decadence-bling-bling/.
58. Sharon Sliwinski, *Mandela's Dark Years: A Political Theory of Dreaming* (Minneapolis: University of Minnesota Press, 2016), n.p.
59. Ibid.

60. Zakes Mda, *Black Diamond* (London: Seagull Books, 2014).
61. Sue Cullinan and Sello Mabotja, "South Africa: Sexwale, the Apprentice," *The Africa Report*, published March 22, 2010, accessed June 23, 2020, http://www.theafricareport.com/News-Analysis/south-africa-sexwale-the-apprentice.html.
62. Ibid.
63. Marc Gunther, "Meet the Trump of South Africa," *Fortune*, published July 25. 2005, accessed June 23, 2020, http://archive.fortune.com/magazines/fortune/fortune_archive/2005/07/25/8266624/index.htm.
64. Cullinan and Mabotia, "South Africa," n.p.
65. For a full comparison of Zuma and Trump, and broader reflections on comparing the US and South Africa in the contemporary moment, see the special issue edited by Rita Barnard, "Trump, Zuma, and the Grounds of US-South African Comparison," *Safundi* 21.4 (2020).
66. Gunther, "Meet the Trump," n.p.
67. Ibid.

Chapter 6

1. Martijn Konings, *The Emotional Logic of Capitalism* (Stanford: Stanford University Press, 2015), 107.
2. Deborah James, *Money from Nothing: Indebtedness and Aspiration in South Africa* (Stanford: Stanford University Press, 2015), 2.
3. Walter Benn Michaels, *The Beauty of a Social Problem* (Chicago: Chicago University Press, 2015), 26–27.
4. Mehrsa Baradaran, *The Color of Money: Black Banks and the Racial Wealth Gap* (Cambridge: The Belknap Press of Harvard University Press, 2017), 150.
5. Ibid.
6. Jackie Wang, *Carceral Capitalism* (South Pasadena, CA: Semiotext(e), 2018), 69.
7. Achille Mbembe, "Africa in Theory," in *African Futures: Essays on Crisis, Emergence, and Possibility*, eds. Brian Goldstone and Juan Obarrio (Chicago: University of Chicago Press, 2016), 224–25.
8. Ibid., 225.
9. Ibid., 227.
10. Anne-Maria Makhulu, "The Search for Economic Sovereignty," in *Hard Work, Hard Times: Global Volatility and African Subjectivities*, eds. Anne-Maria Makhulu, Beth A. Buggenhagen, and Stephen Jackson (Berkeley: University of California Press, 2010), 47.
11. Ibid., 37.
12. Ibid.
13. James, *Money from Nothing*, 8.
14. Anne-Maria Makhulu, "The Conditions for after Work: Financialization and Informalization in Posttransition South Africa," *PMLA* 127.4 (2012): 783.
15. Mbembe, "Africa in Theory," 222.

16. Ibid., 223.
17. Makhulu, "The Conditions," 787.
18. For an analysis of contemporary scholarship on nostalgia for an imagined postwar US, see Laura Renata Martin, "Historicizing White Nostalgia: Race and American Fordism," *Blind Field: A Journal of Cultural Inquiry*, published August 3, 2017, accessed January 11, 2023, https://blindfieldjournal.com/2017/08/03/historicizing-white-nostalgia-race-and-american-fordism/.
19. Ekow Duker, *White Wahala* (Johannesburg: Picador Africa, 2014).
20. Duker had self-published *White Wahalla* [sic] and *Dying in New York* before signing with Picador. See Qama Qukula, "Novelist Ekow Duker Relives His Dynamic Storytelling Journey," CapeTalk, published October 10, 2016, accessed September 14, 2020, http://www.capetalk.co.za/articles/191709/novelist-ekow-duker-relives-his-dynamic-storytelling-journey.
21. Ekow Duker, "A little about me . . .," Ekow Duker, accessed September 14, 2020, http://www.ekowduker.com/a-little-more-about-me.html.
22. Ekow Duker, "Q & A with Author," interview by Lerato Motsoaledi, The Writers College Times, published June 22, 2017, accessed September 15, 2020, https://www.writerscollegeblog.com/q-a-with-author-ekow-duker/.
23. Karina M. Szczurek, review of *Dying in New York* and *White Wahala*, by Ekow Duker, *Sunday Times Books Live*, November 21, 2014, https://www.timeslive.co.za/sunday-times/books/.
24. Relebone Rirhandzu Myambo, review of *White Wahala*, by Ekow Duker, *The Con*, December 5, 2015, http://www.theconmag.co.za/2014/12/05/white-wahala-and-the-king-of-cliches/.
25. James, *Money from Nothing*, 5.
26. T.O. Molefe, "South Africa's Subprime Crisis," *New York Times*, August 24, 2014, https://www.nytimes.com/2014/08/27/opinion/molefe-south-africas-subprime-crisis.html.
27. Ibid., 68.
28. Ibid.
29. Molefe, "South Africa's Subprime."
30. Ibid.
31. Konings, *The Emotional Logic*, 108.
32. James, *Money from Nothing*, 6–7.
33. Names are overdetermined in *White Wahala*, which is highlighted in a scene between Alasdair and his drug dealer, Lerato. Alasdair asks whether Lerato "means love," to which she responds: "And yours?" (23). The rich and corrupt Nicholsons all have self-aggrandizing, anachronistic, pan-European names that are manifestly ironic: Alasdair (defender of men); his father Thor (Norse god of thunder); his mother Agatha ("good woman"); and his sister Ghislaine (from the German *gisil*, meaning a pledge or mutual obligation).
34. James notes that there is something of an "anthropological cottage industry in studying rotating credit and funeral associations" (33); her work in *Money from Nothing* explores how these associations bring together conceptions of the modern and customary (118–46).
35. James, *Money from Nothing*, 6.

36. Makhulu, "The Search," 35.
37. James, *Money from Nothing*, 31.
38. Konings, *The Emotional Logic*, 75.
39. Barack Obama, "Acceptance Speech," typed draft of address delivered August 28, 2008, accessed September 17, 2020, https://www.nytimes.com/2008/08/28/us/politics/28text-obama.html.
40. Abraham Lincoln, "Second Annual Message," typed draft of address delivered December 1, 1862, accessed September 17, 2020, https://millercenter.org/the-presidency/presidential-speeches/december-1-1862-second-annual-message. Although it goes unnoted in the novel, Lincoln in turn alludes to Thomas Jefferson's 1801 first inaugural address, which styles a US government that has "kept us free" as the "world's best hope." Jefferson defends the greatness of a settler colonial government that constitutionally supported chattel slavery. The "us" is white male property owners. See Thomas Jefferson, "First Inaugural Address," typed draft of address delivered March 4, 1801, accessed September 17, 2020, https://jeffersonpapers.princeton.edu/selected-documents/first-inaugural-address.
41. Lincoln, "Second Annual Message."
42. Ibid.
43. Ibid.
44. Ibid.
45. Obama, "Acceptance Speech."
46. Ibid.
47. Ibid.
48. Ibid.
49. Martin Luther King, Jr., "I Have a Dream," typed draft of address delivered August 28, 1963, accessed September 17, 2020, https://kinginstitute.stanford.edu/king-papers/documents/i-have-dream-address-delivered-march-washington-jobs-and-freedom.
50. Ibid.
51. Baradaran, *The Color of Money*, 249.
52. Ibid., 263.
53. A similar tragic dynamic adheres to the idea of America in Duker's *Dying in New York*: Lorato seems to escape horrific abuse and poverty and make it to the Central Park of her dreams. The novel's final chapter (spoiler alert) reveals that this journey has been nothing but a dream, as she has been lying semi-catatonic in a dilapidated asylum, incorporating versions of her care-takers into her fantasy. "New York" is the locus of ongoing hope and the sign of ongoing dispossession. See Ekow Duker, *Dying in New York* (Johannesburg: Picador Africa, 2014).
54. F. Scott Fitzgerald, *The Great Gatsby* (New York: Scribner, 2004): 180.
55. USAID, "South Africa: Economic Growth and Trade," published June 2012 to September 2017, accessed September 17, 2020, https://2012-2017.usaid.gov/south-africa/economic-growth-and-trade.
56. Stacey Balkan, "Rogues in the Postcolony: Chris Abani's *GraceLand* and the Petro-Picaresque," *The Global South* 9.2 (2015): 21.

57. Jens Elze, *Postcolonial Modernism and the Picaresque Novel: Literatures of Precarity* (Basingstoke: Palgrave MacMillan, 2017), 14.
58. Ibid., 17.
59. Ibid., 8.
60. Toni Morrison, "Unspeakable Things Unspoken: The Afro-American Presence in American Literature," typed draft of address delivered October 7, 1988, accessed September 17, 2020, https://tannerlectures.utah.edu/_documents/a-to-z/m/morrison90.pdf, 143.
61. Herman Melville, *Moby-Dick, or The Whale* (London: Collector's Library, 2004), 243. Gladys suggests the tracks Cash follows have been laid by others, but this is perhaps least the case when he invades the book club (91).

Coda

1. Lindsey B. Green-Simms, *Queer African Cinemas* (Durham: Duke University Press, 2022), 25.
2. Ibid., 27.
3. Ibid., 189.
4. Ibid., 183.
5. Ibid., 198.
6. J.P. Clark, *America, Their America: The Nigerian Poet and Playwright's Criticism of American Society* (London: Heinemann Educational Books Ltd., 1964), 64.
7. Robin D.G. Kelley, *Freedom Dreams: The Black Radical Imagination* (Boston: Beacon Press, 2003).
8. Fred Moten, "Not In Between," in *Black and Blur* (Durham: Duke University Press, 2017), 1–27.
9. Ibid., 25.
10. Ibid.
11. Ibid.
12. Xine Yao, *Disaffected: The Cultural Politics of Unfeeling in Nineteenth-Century America* (Durham: Duke University Press, 2021), 10.
13. Sianne Ngai, *Ugly Feelings* (Cambridge: Harvard University Press, 2005). Sara Ahmed, *The Promise of Happiness* (Durham: Duke University Press, 2010).
14. Yao, *Disaffected*, 6.
15. Ibid.
16. Ibid., 17.
17. Ngai, *Ugly Feelings*, 2.
18. NoViolet Bulawayo, *Glory* (New York: Viking, 2022).
19. Lizzy Attree translates the oft-repeated phrase "tholukuthi" as "a Ndebele colloquialism meaning 'I find that.'" Other early reviews of the novel register how the phrase accrues a range of meanings. Lizzy Attree, "Voices of Zimbabwe: On NoViolet Bulawayo's *Glory*," *Los Angeles Review of Books*, published Aug. 22, 2022, accessed Mar. 6 2023, https://lareviewofbooks.org/article/voices-of-zimbabwe-on-noviolet-bulawayos-glory/.

20. NoViolet Bulawayo, *We Need New Names* (New York: Back Bay Books, 2013). For a discussion of the dominant role of the US in the International Monetary Fund and World Bank, see for example Ngaire Woods, "The United States and International Financial Institutions: Power and Influence Within the World Bank and the IMF," in *US Hegemony and International Organizations: The United States and Multilateral Institutions*, eds. Rosemary Foot et. al. (Oxford: Oxford University Press, 2003), 92–114.
21. For an extended consideration the ways novels enable analysis of the global politics of Black Lives Matter, see Justin Mitchell and John Marx, eds., "The Novel and the Global Reach of Black Lives Matter," special issue, *NOVEL: A Forum on Fiction* 55.1 (2022).
22. Attree notes that Bulawayo's fiction writes back to a literary past that includes Yvonne Vera's *Butterfly Burning* (1998) and *Nehanda* (1993). Attree, "Voices of Zimbabwe."

Works Cited

Abani, Chris. *GraceLand*. New York: Farrar, Straus & Giroux, 2004.
"About Us." Trace. Updated 2020. Accessed June 29, 2020. https://trace.company/about-us/.
Achebe, Chinua. "English and the African Writer," *Transition* 18 (1965): 27–30.
——. *Home and Exile*. Oxford: Oxford University Press, 2000.
——. "The Day I Finally Met Baldwin." PEN America. Published January 8, 2007. Accessed June 29, 2018. https://pen.org/the-day-i-finally-met-baldwin/.
——. *The Education of a British-Protected Child*. Toronto: Bond Street Books, 2009.
——. *The Trouble with Nigeria*. Oxford: Heinemann, 1984.
Adams, James Truslow. *The Epic of America*. New York: Blue Ribbon Books, Inc., 1931.
Adéèkó, Adélékè. "Power Shift: America in the New Nigerian Imagination." *The Global South* 2.2. (2008): 10–30.
Adejunmobi, Moradewun. "Native Books and the 'English Book.'" *PMLA* 132.1 (2017): 135–41.
——. *Vernacular Palaver*. Clevedon: Multilingual Matters Ltd., 2004.
Adichie, Chimamanda Ngozi. *Americanah*. New York: Anchor Books, 2014.
Agbajoh-Laoye, G. Oty. "Motherline, Intertext, and Mothertext: African Diasporic Linkages in *Beloved* and *The Joys of Motherhood*." *The Literary Griot* 13.1&2 (2001): 128–46.
Ahmed, Sara. *The Cultural Politics of Emotion*. New York: Routledge, 2004.
——. *The Promise of Happiness*. Durham: Duke University Press, 2010.
Aluko, Olajide. "Nigeria, the United States and Southern Africa," *African Affairs* 78.310 (1979): 91–102.
Anam, Nasia, ed. "Forms of the Global Anglophone." *Post-45*. Published February 22, 2019. Accessed June 30, 2022. https://post45.org/sections/contemporaries-essays/global-anglophone/.
Andrade, Susan Z. *The Nation Writ Small: African Fictions and Feminisms, 1958–1988*. Durham: Duke University Press, 2011.
Appiah, Kwame Anthony. "Is the Post- in Postmodernism the Post- in Postcolonial?" *Critical Inquiry* 17.2 (1991): 336–57.
Apter, Andrew. *The Pan-African Nation: Oil and the Spectacle of Culture in Nigeria*. Chicago: Chicago University Press, 2005.
Ashcroft, Bill, Gareth Griffiths, and Helen Tiffin. *The Empire Writes Back: Theory and Practice in Post-Colonial Literatures*. London: Routledge, 1989.

Attree, Lizzy. "Voices of Zimbabe: On NoViolet Bulawayo's *Glory*." *Los Angeles Review of Books*. Published Aug. 22, 2022. Accessed Mar. 6 2023. https://lareviewofbooks.org/article/voices-of-zimbabwe-on-noviolet-bulawayos-glory/.
Azikiwe, Nnamdi. *My Odyssey: An Autobiography*. New York: Praeger, 1970.
———. *Renascent Africa*. London: Frank Cass & Co. Ltd., 1968.
———. *Zik: A Selection from the Speeches of Nnamdi Azikiwe, Governor-General of the Federation of Nigeria formerly President of the Nigerian Senate formerly Premier of the Eastern Region of Nigeria*. Cambridge: Cambridge University Press, 1961.
Bach, Daniel C. "Nigerian-American Relations: Converging Interests and Power Relations." In *Nigerian Foreign Policy*, edited by Timothy M. Shaw and Olajide Aluko, 35–55. London: Palgrave Macmillan, 1983.
Baldwin, James and William Buckley. "The American Dream and the American Negro." *New York Times*, March 7, 1965.
Balkan, Stacey. "Rogues in the Postcolony: Chris Abani's *GraceLand* and the Petro-Picaresque." *The Global South* 9.2 (2015): 18–37.
Baradaran, Mehrsa. *The Color of Money: Black Banks and the Racial Wealth Gap*. Cambridge: The Belknap Press of Harvard University Press, 2017.
Barnard, Rita. *Apartheid and Beyond: South African Writers and the Politics of Place*. Oxford: Oxford University Press, 2007.
———. "Rewriting the Nation." In *The Cambridge History of South African Literature*, edited by David Attwell and Derek Attridge, 652–75. Cambridge: Cambridge University Press, 2012.
Barnard, Rita, ed. "Trump, Zuma, and the Grounds of US-South African Comparison." Special issue, *Safundi* 21.4 (2020).
Baudrillard, Jean. *America*. Translated by Chris Turner. New York: Verso, 1988.
Benn Michaels, Walter. *The Beauty of a Social Problem*. Chicago: Chicago University Press, 2015.
Berlant, Lauren. *Cruel Optimism*. Durham: Duke University Press, 2011.
"Blurring the Rainbow." *The Economist*. Published, May 20, 2017. Accessed May 25, 2020. https://www.economist.com/news/middle-east-and-africa/21722155-democracy-has-brought-wealth-only-few.
Bonilla, Yarimar. *Non-Sovereign Futures: French Caribbean Politics in the Wake of Disenchantment*. Chicago: University of Chicago Press, 2015.
Bramen, Carrie Tirado. *American Niceness: A Cultural History*. Cambridge: Harvard University Press, 2017.
Brennan, Timothy. "Cosmo-Theory." *South Atlantic Quarterly* 100.3 (2001): 659–91.
Brooks, John. *The Go-Go Years: The Drama and Crashing Finale of Wall Street's Bullish '60s*. New York: Open Road, 2014.
Brouillette, Sarah. *Postcolonial Writers in the Global Literary Marketplace*. London: Palgrave, 2007.
———. *Underdevelopment and African Literature: Emerging Forms of Reading*. Cambridge: Cambridge University Press, 2020.

———. *UNESCO and the Fate of the Literary*. Stanford: Stanford University Press, 2019.
Bulawayo, NoViolet. *Glory*. New York: Viking, 2022.
———. *We Need New Names*. New York: Back Bay Books, 2013.
Camminga, B. "Disregard and Danger: Chimamanda Ngozi Adichie and the Voices of Trans (and Cis) African Feminists." *The Sociological Review Monographs* 68.4 (2020): 817–33.
Carmichael, Stokely. "Black Power." Typed draft of address delivered October 29, 1966. Accessed May 28, 2020. https://voicesofdemocracy.umd.edu/carmichael-black-power-speech-text/.
Carter, Jimmy. "Lagos, Nigeria Question-and-Answer Session with Reporters Following Meetings Between the President and General Obasanjo." Typed draft of address delivered April 2, 1978. Accessed February 26, 2020. https://www.presidency.ucsb.edu/node/244844.
———. "Lagos, Nigeria, Remarks at the National Arts Theatre." Typed draft of address delivered April 1, 1978. Accessed February 26, 2020. https://www.presidency.ucsb.edu/documents/lagos-nigeria-remarks-the-national-arts-theatre.
———. "Reception for Black Business Executives Remarks at the White House Reception." Typed draft of address delivered June 14, 1978. Accessed February 26, 2020. https://www.presidency.ucsb.edu/node/248678.
Cazdyn, Eric. *The Already Dead*. Durham: Duke University Press, 2012.
Césaire, Aimé. *Discourse on Colonialism*. Trans. Joan Pinkham. New York: Monthly Review Press, 1972.
Champion, Ernest A. *Mr. Baldwin, I Presume: James Baldwin-Chinua Achebe, A Meeting of Minds*. Lanham: University Press of America, 1995.
Cheah, Pheng. *Spectral Nationality: Passages of Freedom from Kant to Postcolonial Literatures of Liberation*. New York: Columbia University Press, 2003.
———. "The Biopolitics of Recognition: Making Female Subjects of Globalization." *boundary2* 40.2 (2013): 81–112.
Clark[-Bekederemo], J.P. *America, Their America: The Nigerian Poet and Playwright's Criticism of American Society*. London: Heinemann Educational Books Ltd., 1964.
———. "Poetry in Africa Today," *Transition* 18 (1965): 18.
Coetzee, Carli, ed. *Afropolitanism: Reboot*. New York: Routledge, 2019.
Cooper, Frederick. *Africa in the World: Capitalism, Empire, Nation-State*. Cambridge: Harvard University Press, 2014.
Cornwell, Gareth. "South African Literature in English since 1945: Long Walk to Ordinariness." In *The Columbia Guide to South African Literature*, edited by Gareth Cornwell, Dirk Klopper, and Craig Mackenzie, 1–42. New York: Columbia University Press, 2010.
Cullinan, Sue and Sello Mabotja. "South Africa: Sexwale, the Apprentice." *The Africa Report*. Published March 22, 2010. Accessed June 23, 2020.

http://www.theafricareport.com/News-Analysis/south-africa-sexwale-the-apprentice.html.
Davies, Sheila Boniface. "Raising the Dead: The Xhosa Cattle-Killing and the Mhlakaza-Goliat Delusion." *Journal of Southern African Studies* 33.1 (2007): 19–41.
Davis, Caroline. *African Literature and the CIA: Networks of Authorship and Publishing*. Cambridge: Cambridge University Press, 2021.
Dirlik, Arif. *The Postcolonial Aura: Third World Criticism in the Age of Global Capitalism*. Boulder, CO: Westview Press, 1997.
Duker, Ekow. "A little about me . . ." Ekow Duker. Accessed September 14, 2020. http://www.ekowduker.com/a-little-more-about-me.html.
———. *Dying in New York*. Johannesburg: Picador Africa, 2014.
———. "Q & A with Author." By Lerato Motsoaledi, The Writers College Times, published June 22, 2017, accessed September 15, 2020, https://www.writerscollegeblog.com/q-a-with-author-ekow-duker/.
———. *White Wahala*. Johannesburg: Picador Africa, 2014.
Eatough, Matthew. "Planning the Future: Scenario Planning, Infrastructural Time, and South African Fiction." *Modern Fiction Studies* 61.4 (2015): 587–611.
Egbunike, Louisa Uchum. "One-Way Traffic: Renegotiating the 'Been-To' Narrative in the Nigerian Novel in the Era of Military Rule." In *Tradition and Change in Contemporary West and East African Fiction*, edited by Ogaga Okuyade, 217–32. Amsterdam: Rodopi, 2014.
Elze, Jens. *Postcolonial Modernism and the Picaresque Novel: Literatures of Precarity*. Basingstoke: Palgrave MacMillan, 2017.
Emecheta, Buchi. *Head Above Water*. Oxford: Heinemann, 1994.
———. *The Joys of Motherhood*. New York: George Braziller, Inc., 1979.
Fan, Christopher T. "Battle Hymn of the Afropolitan: Sino-African Futures in *Ghana Must Go* and *Americanah*." *Journal of Asian American Studies* 20.1 (2017): 69–93.
Fanon, Frantz. *The Wretched of the Earth*. New York: Grove Press, 1968 [1961].
Ferguson, James. *Give a Man a Fish: Reflections on the New Politics of Distribution*. Durham: Duke University Press, 2019.
———. *Global Shadows: Africa in the Neoliberal World Order*. Durham: Duke University Press, 2006.
Fitzgerald, F. Scott. *The Great Gatsby*. New York: Scribner, 2004.
"Freedom Charter." *The Black Scholar* 24.3 (1994): 45–46.
Frenkel, Ronit and Andrea Spain. "South African Representations of 'America.'" *Safundi: The Journal of South African and American Studies* 18.3 (2017): 193–204.
Getachew, Adom. *Worldmaking After Empire: The Rise and Fall of Self-Determination*. Princeton: Princeton University Press, 2019.
Goodman, Robin. "Capitalists in the Myst: The Mystery and the Joys in the Free Market," *Journal of Cultural Studies* 3.2. (2001): 385–411.

Goyal, Yogita, "Introduction: Africa and the Black Atlantic." *Research in African Literatures* 45.3 (2014): v-xxv.

———. *Runaway Genres: The Global Afterlives of Slavery*. New York: New York University Press, 2019.

Green-Simms, Lindsey B. *Queer African Cinemas*. Durham: Duke University Press, 2022.

Griswold, Wendy. *Bearing Witness: Readers, Writers, and the Novel in Nigeria*. Princeton: Princeton University Press, 2000.

Gross, Jenny. "South African Neighborhood Celebrates New Year by Chucking Furniture From Windows." *Wall Street Journal*. Published January 1, 2014. Accessed June 2, 2020. https://www.wsj.com/articles/south-african-neighborhood-celebrates-new-year-by-chucking-furniture-from-windows-1388623752.

Gui, Weihsin. *National Consciousness and Literary Cosmopolitics: Postcolonial Literature in a Global Moment*. Columbus: The Ohio State University Press, 2013.

Gulick, Anne W. "Campus Fiction and Critical University Studies from Below: *Disgrace*, *Welcome to Our Hillbrow*, and the Postcolonial University at the Millennium." *Cambridge Journal of Postcolonial Literary Inquiry* 9.2 (2022): 177–97.

Gunew, Sneja. "Translating Postcolonial Affect." In *Affect and Literature*, ed. Alex Houen, 175–89. Cambridge: Cambridge University Press, 2020.

Gunther, Marc. "Meet the Trump of South Africa." *Fortune*. Published July 25, 2005. Accessed June 23, 2020. http://archive.fortune.com/magazines/fortune/fortune_archive/2005/07/25/8266624/index.htm.

Hallemeier, Katherine. "An Art of Hunger: Gender and the Politics of Food Distribution in Zakes Mda's South Africa." *Journal of Commonwealth Literature* 53.3 (2018): 379–93.

———. "The Empires Write Back: The Language of Postcolonial Nigerian Literature and the United States of America." *Comparative Literature* 71.2 (2019): 123–38.

———. "'To Be from the Country of People Who Gave': National Allegory and the United States of Adichie's *Americanah*." *Studies in the Novel* 27.2 (2015): 231–45.

Hardt, Michael and Antonio Negri. *Empire*. Cambridge: Harvard University Press, 2001.

———. "Empire, Twenty Years On." *New Left Review* 120 (2019): n.p.

Harney, Stefano and Fred Moten. *The Undercommons: Fugitive Planning and Black Study*. Wivenhoe: Minor Compositions, 2013.

Herskovits, Jean. "Dateline Nigeria: A Black Power," *Foreign Policy* 29 (1977–78): 167–88.

Huggan, Graham. *The Postcolonial Exotic*. London: Routledge, 2001.

Hughes, Langston, "Let America Be America Again." *The Collected Poems of Langston Hughes*, 189–91. New York: Vintage Classics, 1994.

———. *Montage of a Dream Deferred.* 1951. *Selected Poems of Langston Hughes*, 221–74. New York: Vintage Classics, 1990.

Hyman, Zoe. "'To Have Its Cake and Eat It Too': US Policy Toward South Africa During the Kennedy Administration." *The Sixties* 8.2 (2015): 138–55.

Ifidon, Emichika A. "Unity without Unification: The Development of Nigeria's 'Inside-Out' Approach to African Political Integration, 1937–1963." *International Social Science Review* 82.1–2 (2007): 39–54.

"Ike Iguine." Advisory Legal Consultants. Accessed June 5, 2019. http://www.advisoryng.com/ike-oguine/.

Immerwahr, Daniel. "The Politics of Architecture and Urbanism in Postcolonial Lagos, 1960–1986." *Journal of African Cultural Studies* 19.2 (2007): 165–86.

Isaacs, Camille. "Mediating Women's Globalized Existence Through Social Media in the Work of Adichie and Bulawayo." *Safundi* 17.2 (2016): 174–88.

Jackson, Jeanne-Marie and Adwoa A. Opoku-Agyemang, Introduction, *Ethiopia Unbound* by J.E. Casely Hayford (East Lansing: Michigan State University Press, forthcoming).

Jaji, Tsitsi Ella. *Africa in Stereo: Modernism, Music, and Pan-African Solidarity.* Oxford: Oxford University Press, 2014.

James, Deborah. *Money from Nothing: Indebtedness and Aspiration in South Africa.* Stanford: Stanford University Press, 2015.

Jameson, Fredric. "No Magic, No Metaphor." *London Review of Books.* Published June 15, 2017. Accessed June 4, 2020. https://www.lrb.co.uk/the-paper/v39/n12/fredric-jameson/no-magic-no-metaphor.

Jefferson, Thomas. "First Inaugural Address." Typed draft of address delivered March 4, 1801. Accessed September 17, 2020. https://jeffersonpapers.princeton.edu/selected-documents/first-inaugural-address.

Jolly, Rosemary. *Cultured Violence.* Liverpool: Liverpool University Press, 2010.

———. "Interview." In *Writing South Africa*, eds. Derek Attridge and Rosemary Jolly, 141–48. Cambridge: Cambridge University Press, 1998.

Julien, Eileen. "The Extroverted African Novel." In *The Novel*, edited by Franco Moretti, 667–700. Princeton: Princeton University Press, 2006.

Jussawalla, Feroza and Reed Way Dasenbrock, editors. *Interviews with Writers of the Post-Colonial World.* Jackson: University Press of Mississippi, 1992.

Kabir, Ananya Jahanar. "On Postcolonial Happiness." In *The Postcolonial World*, eds. Jyotsna G. Singh and David D. Kim, 35–52. New York: Routledge, 2016.

Kalliney, Peter. "Modernism, African Literature, and the Cold War." *Modern Language Quarterly* 76.3 (2015): 338–68.

Kazanjian, David. "The Speculative Freedom of Colonial Nigeria." *American Quarterly* 63.4 (2011): 863–93.

Kelley, Robin D.G. *Freedom Dreams: The Black Radical Imagination.* Boston: Beacon Press, 2003.

Kennedy, Robert F. "Day of Affirmation Address." Typed draft of address delivered June 6, 1966. Accessed May 26, 2020. https://www.jfklibrary.org/learn/about-jfk/the-kennedy-family/robert-f-kennedy/robert-f-kennedy-speeches/day-of-affirmation-address-university-of-capetown-capetown-south-africa-june-6-1966.

Khanna, Neetu. *The Visceral Logics of Decolonization.* Durham: Duke University Press, 2020.

King, Jr., Martin Luther. "I Have a Dream." Typed draft of address delivered August 28, 1963. Accessed September 17, 2020. https://kinginstitute.stanford.edu/king-papers/documents/i-have-dream-address-delivered-march-washington-jobs-and-freedom.

——. "The American Dream." Typed draft of address delivered July 4, 1965. Accessed May 26, 2020. https://kinginstitute.stanford.edu/king-papers/documents/american-dream-sermon-delivered-ebenezer-baptist-church.

——. "The Negro and the American Dream." Typed draft of address delivered September 25, 1960. Accessed June, 29, 2018. https://kinginstitute.stanford.edu/king-papers/documents/negro-and-american-dream-excerpt-address-annual-freedom-mass-meeting-north.

Klieman, Kairn A. "US Oil Companies, the Nigerian Civil War, and the Origins of Opacity in the Nigerian Oil Industry." *The Journal of American History* 99.1 (2012): 155–65.

Konings, Martijn. *The Emotional Logic of Capitalism.* Stanford: Stanford University Press, 2015.

Krishnan, Madhu. "Affiliation, Disavowal, and National Commitment in Third Generation African Literature," *ARIEL* 44.1 (2013): 73–97.

——. *Contemporary African Literature in English: Global Locations, Postcolonial Identifications.* Basingstoke: Palgrave Macmillan, 2014.

——. "Mami Wata and the Occluded Feminine in Anglophone Nigerian-Igbo Literature." *Research in African Literatures* 43.1 (2012): 1–18.

Landis, John, dir. *Coming to America.* 1988; LA: Paramount, 2017. DVD.

——. *Trading Places.* 1983; LA: Paramount, 2017. DVD.

Lazarus, Neil. "Great Expectations and the Mourning After." In *Resistance in Postcolonial African Fiction*, 1–26. New Haven: Yale University Press, 1990.

——. *The Postcolonial Unconscious.* Cambridge: Cambridge University Press, 2011.

Lee, Robert, Tristan Ahtone, Margaret Pearce, Kalen Goodluck, Geoff McGhee, Cody Leff, Katherine Lanpher and Taryn Salinas. "Land-Grab Universities." High Country News. Published 2020. Accessed May 25, 2020. https://www.landgrabu.org/.

Lincoln, Abraham. "Second Annual Message." Typed draft of address delivered December 1, 1862. Accessed September 17, 2020. https://millercenter.org/the-presidency/presidential-speeches/december-1-1862-second-annual-message.

Livsey, Tim. *Nigeria's University Age.* Cambridge: Cambridge University Press, 2017.
Lockett, Cecily. "An Interview with Miriam Tlali." *Southern African Review of Books* June/July (1989): 20–21.
Macharia, Keguro. "From Repair to Pessimism," *Brick: A Literary Journal* 106 (2021): n.p. Accessed May 2, 2022. https://brickmag.com/from-repair-to-pessimism/.
Makhulu, Anne-Maria. "The Conditions for after Work: Financialization and Informalization in Posttransition South Africa." *PMLA* 127.4 (2012): 782–99.
———. "The Search for Economic Sovereignty." In *Hard Work, Hard Times: Global Volatility and African Subjectivities*, edited by Anne-Maria Makhulu, Beth A. Buggenhagen, and Stephen Jackson, 28–47. Berkeley: University of California Press, 2010.
Makhulu, Anne-Maria, Beth A. Buggenhagen, and Stephen Jackson. "Introduction." In *Hard Work, Hard Times: Global Volatility and African Subjectivities*, eds. Anne-Markia Makhulu, Beth A. Buggenhagen, and Stephen Jackson, 1–27. Berkeley: University of California Press, 2010.
Mamdani, Mahmoud. *Citizen and Subject.* Princeton: Princeton University Press, 1996.
Mandela, Nelson. "American Imperialism: A New Menace in Africa." *Liberation* 30 (1958): 22–26.
Marcus, Greil. *The Shape of Things to Come: Prophecy in the American Voice.* New York: Picador, 2007.
Marriott, David. "On Decadence: *Bling Bling*," *e-flux journal* 79 (2017): n.p. Accessed July 27, 2022. https://www.e-flux.com/journal/79/94430/on-decadence-bling-bling/.
Marschall, Sabine. "Public Memories as *Lieux de Mémoire*: Nation-Building and the Politics of Public Memory in South Africa." *Anthropology of Southern Africa* 36.1–2 (2013): 11–21.
Martin, Laura Renata. "Historicizing White Nostalgia: Race and American Fordism." *Blind Field: A Journal of Cultural Inquiry.* Published August 3, 2017. Accessed January 11, 2023. https://blindfieldjournal.com/2017/08/03/historicizing-white-nostalgia-race-and-american-fordism/.
Matory, J. Lorand. *Stigma and Culture: Last-Place Anxiety in Black America.* Chicago: Chicago University Press, 2015.
Mattera, Don. "Other Faces of Kofifi." In *Sophiatown: Coming of Age in South Africa*, 73–81. Boston: Beacon Press, 1987.
Mbembe, Achille. "Africa in Theory." In *African Futures: Essays on Crisis, Emergence, and Possibility*, edited by Brian Goldstone and Juan Obarrio, 211–30. Chicago: University of Chicago Press, 2016.
Mda, Zakes. "A Response to 'Duplicity and Plagiarism in Zakes Mda's *The Heart of Redness*." *Research in African Literatures* 39.3 (2008): 200–03.
———. *Black Diamond.* London: Seagull Books, 2014.

———. *Cion*. New York: Picador, 2007.
———. *The Heart of Redness*. New York: Picador, 2000.
———. "The Story Behind *Ways of Dying*." YouTube Video, 1:00. Posted by Oxford University Press Southern Africa, May 23, 2013. https://www.youtube.com/watch?v=4Pwug1uUlNE.
———. *The Whale Caller*. New York: Picador, 2005.
———. *Ways of Dying*. New York: Picador, 1995.
Melville, Herman. *Moby-Dick, or The Whale*. London: Collector's Library, 2004.
Michel, Eddie. "'You Haven't Been Too Horrible to Us Recently': Lyndon Johnson and Apartheid in South Africa." *Diplomacy & Statecraft* 32.4 (2021): 743–65.
Mitchell, Justin and John Marx, eds. "The Novel and the Global Reach of Black Lives Matter." Special issue, *NOVEL: A Forum on Fiction* 55.1 (2022).
Mitchell, Nancy. *Jimmy Carter in Africa: Race and the Cold War*. Stanford: Stanford UP, 2016.
Molefe, T.O. "South Africa's Subprime Crisis." *New York Times*. August 24, 2014. https://www.nytimes.com/2014/08/27/opinion/molefe-south-africas-subprime-crisis.html.
Morrison, Toni. "Unspeakable Things Unspoken: The Afro-American Presence in American Literature." Typed draft of address delivered October 7, 1988. Accessed September 17, 2020. https://tannerlectures.utah.edu/_documents/a-to-z/m/morrison90.pdf.
Moten, Fred. "Not In Between." In *Black and Blur*, 1–27. Durham: Duke University Press, 2017.
Mphahlele, Es'kia. In *Sophiatown Speaks*, edited by Pippa Stein and Ruth Jacobson, 55–60. Johannesburg: Junction Avenue Press, 1986.
Mufti, Aamir R. *Forget English!: Orientalisms and World Literatures*. Cambridge: Harvard University Press, 2016.
Myambo, Relebone Rirhandzu. Review of *White Wahala*, by Ekow Duker. *The Con*. December 5, 2015. http://www.theconmag.co.za/2014/12/05/white-wahala-and-the-king-of-cliches/.
Nadiminti, Kalyan. "The Global Program Era: Contemporary International Fiction in the American Creative Economy." *Novel: A Forum on Fiction* 51.3 (2018): 375–98.
Ndebele, Njabulo S. "Game Lodges and Leisure Colonialists." Published 1999. Accessed June 2, 2020, https://www.njabulondebele.co.za/work/game-lodges-and-leisure-colonialists/.
———. "South Africans in Search of Common Values." *Pretexts: Literary and Cultural Studies* 10.1 (2001): 75–81.
———. *The Cry of Winnie Mandela*. Banbury: Ayebia Clarke Publishing, 2006.
Ngai, Sianne. *Ugly Feelings*. Cambridge: Harvard University Press, 2005.
Ngugi, Mukoma Wa. *The Rise of the African Novel: Politics of Language, Identity, and Ownership*. Ann Arbor: University of Michigan Press, 2018.

Nixon, Rob. *Homelands, Harlem and Hollywood: South African Culture and the World Beyond.* New York: Routledge, 1994.

Nkrumah, Kwame. *Neo-Colonialism: The Last Stage of Imperialism.* London: Thomas Nelson & Sons, Ltd., 1965.

Nwachuckwu, John Owen. "University Degree Not an Assurance for Jobs—Buhari Tells Nigerian Graduates." *Daily Post.* Published May 11, 2019. Accessed June 29, 2020. https://dailypost.ng/2019/05/11/university-degree-not-assurance-job-buhari-tells-nigerian-graduates/.

Nwachuku, Levi A. "The United States and Nigeria-1960 to 1987: Anatomy of a Pragmatic Relationship." *Journal of Black Studies* 28.5 (1998): 575–93.

Nwauwa, Apollos O. "The British Establishment of Universities in Tropical Africa, 1920–1948: A Reaction against the Spread of American 'Radical' Influence," *Cahiers d'Études Africaines* 33.130 (1993): 247–74.

Nwosu, Maik. "Children of the Anthill: Nsukka and the Shaping of Nigeria's 1960s Literary Generation." *English in Africa* 32.1 (2005): 37–50.

Nyabola, Nanjala. "Eulogy for Pan-Africanism: Long Live Man-Africanism," *The New Inquiry.* Published May, 23, 2016. Accessed February 24, 2020. https://thenewinquiry.com/eulogy-for-pan-africanism-long-live-man-africanism/.

Obama, Barack. "Acceptance Speech." Typed draft of address delivered August 28, 2008. Accessed September 17, 2020. https://www.nytimes.com/2008/08/28/us/politics/28text-obama.html.

Obiechina, E.N. "Post-Independence in Three African Novels," *Nsukka Studies in African Literature* 1.1 (1978): 54–78.

Obiwu. "The Pan-African Brotherhood of Langston Hughes and Nnamdi Azikiwe." *Dialectical Anthropology* 31.1 (2007). 143 65.

Obi-Young, Otosirieze. "Chimamanda's Creative Workshop Returns as the Purple Hibiscus Trust Creative Writing Workshop, Sponsored by Trace Nigeria." Brittle Paper. Published September 25, 2018. Accessed June 29, 2020. https://brittlepaper.com/2018/09/chimamandas-workshop-returns-as-the-purple-hibiscus-trust-creative-writing-workshop-sponsored-by-trace-nigeria-how-to-apply/.

——. "Why Adichie's Farafina Workshop Will Not Be Held This Year." Brittle Paper. Published July 5, 2017. Accessed June 29, 2020. https://brittlepaper.com/2017/07/adichies-farafina-workshop-hold-year/.

Offenburger, Andrew. "Duplicity and Plagiarism in Zakes Mda's *The Heart of Redness.*" *Research in African Literatures* 39.3 (2008): 164–99.

Oguine, Ike. *A Squatter's Tale.* Oxford: Heinemann, 2000.

"Oguine, Novelist, is Nigeria's Top Petroleum Lawyer." *Africa Oil and Gas Report.* Published May 13, 2014. Accessed June 17, 2020. https://africaoilgasreport.com/2014/05/petroleum-people/oguine-novelist-is-nigerias-top-petroleum-lawyer/.

Ogunbadejo, Oye. "A New Turn in US-Nigerian Relations." *The World Today* 35.3 (1979): 117–26.

Okonkwo, Christopher N. *Kindred Spirits: Chinua Achebe and Toni Morrison* (Charlottesville: University of Virginia Press, 2022).

———. "Sound Statements and Counterpoints: Ike Oguine's Channeling of Music, Highlife, and Jazz in *A Squatter's Tale*." *College Literature* 46.3 (2019): 628–58.

Olaniyan, Tejumolan. "African Literature in the Post-Global Age: Provocations on Field Commonsense." *Cambridge Journal of Postcolonial Literary Inquiry* 3.3 (2016): 387–96.

Omelsky, Mathew. "Chris Abani and the Politics of Ambivalence." *Research in African Literatures*, 42.4 (2011): 84–96.

Onwuemene, Michael C. "Limits of Transliteration: Nigerian Writers' Endeavors toward a National Literary Language." *PMLA* 114.5 (1999): 1055–66.

Osei-Nyame, Kwadwo. "Toward the Decolonization of African Postcolonial Theory." In *Texts, Tasks, and Theories: Versions and Subversions of African Literatures*, edited by Tobias Robert Klein, Ulrike Auga, and Viola Prüschenk, 71–92. Amsterdam: Rodopi, 2007.

Osinubi, Taiwo Adetunji. "Cold War Sponsorships: Chinua Achebe and the Dialectics of Collaboration." *Postcolonial Writing* 50 (2014): 410–22.

Oxford English Dictionary. "Euphoria, *n*." Accessed June 2, 2020. https://www-oed-com.argo.library.okstate.edu/view/Entry/65048?redirectedFrom=euphoria&.

Palmer, Tyrone S. "'What Feels More Than Feeling?': Theorizing the Unthinkability of Black Affect." *Critical Ethnic Studies* 3.2 (2017): 31–56.

Parker, Jason C. "'Made-in-America Revolutions'? The 'Black University' and the American Role in the Decolonization of the Black Atlantic." *The Journal of American History* 96.3 (2009): 727–50.

Parton, Dolly. *Dream More: Celebrate the Dreamer in You*. New York: Riverhead, 2012.

Pease, Donald E. *The New American Exceptionalism*. Minneapolis: University of Minnesota Press, 2009.

Peires, J.B. *The Dead Will Arise: Nongqawuse and the Great Xhosa Cattle-Killing Movement of 1856-7*. Bloomington: Indiana University Press, 1989.

Phiri, Aretha. "Expanding Black Subjectivities in Toni Morrison's *Song of Solomon* and Chimamanda Ngozi Adichie's *Americanah*." *Cultural Studies* 31.1 (2017): 121–42.

Pickens, Therí Alyce. *Black Madness :: Mad Blackness*. Durham: Duke University Press, 2019.

Pierre, Jemima. "Black Immigrants in the United States and the 'Cultural Narratives' of Ethnicity." *Identities: Global Studies in Culture and Power* 11 (2004): 141–70.

Popescu, Monica. *At Penpoint: African Literatures, Postcolonial Studies, and the Cold War*. Durham: Duke University Press, 2020.

Quayson, Ato. *Oxford Street, Accra*. Durham: Duke University Press, 2014.

Qukula, Qama. "Novelist Ekow Duker Relives His Dynamic Storytelling Journey." CapeTalk. Published October 10, 2016. Accessed September 14, 2020. http://www.capetalk.co.za/articles/191709/novelist-ekow-duker-relives-his-dynamic-storytelling-journey.
Read, James S. "The New Constitution of Nigeria, 1979: 'The Washington Model?'" *Journal of African Law* 23.2 (1979): 131–74.
"Remarks by the President in Address to Join Assembly, House of Representatives Chamber, National Assembly Building, Abuja, Nigeria." August 26, 2000. Nigeria—Policy Memos. Clinton Presidential Records. William J. Clinton Presidential Library.
Robolin, Stéphane. "Gendered Hauntings: *The Joys of Motherhood*, Interpretive Acts, and Postcolonial Theory." *Research in African Literatures* 35.3 (2004): 76–92.
———. *Grounds of Engagement: Apartheid-Era African American and South African Writing*. Urbana-Champaign: University of Illinois Press, 2015.
Roensch, Rob and Mary B. Gray, "'If I Strip away Everything, What Is Left?': A Conversation with Chris Abani." *World Literature Today* 92.4. (2018): n.p.
Rose, Jacqueline. *States of Fantasy*. Oxford: Oxford University Press, 1998.
Ross, Albion "Africans' Carnival Ushers in New Year; Their Rhythmic Fete Shunned by Whites." *New York Times*. January 2, 1954.
Saint, Lily. "The Danger of a Single Author." Africa is a Country. Published April 14, 2017. Accessed January 13, 2021. https://africasacountry.com/2017/04/the-danger-of-a-single-author.
Samuelson, Meg. "Nongqawuse, National Time and (Female) Authorship in *The Heart of Redness*." In *Ways of Writing: Critical Essays on Zakes Mda*, edited by David Bell and J.U. Jacobs, 229–53. Pietermaritzburg: University of KwaZulu-Natal Press, 2009.
———. *Remembering the Nation, Dismembering Women: Stories of the South African Transition*. Scottsville: University of KwaZulu-Natal Press, 2007.
Scott, David. *Omens of Adversity*. Durham: Duke University Press, 2014.
Sedgwick, Eve Kosofsky. "Paranoid Reading and Reparative Reading; or, You're So Paranoid, You Probably Think This Introduction is About You." In *Novel Gazing: Queer Readings in Fiction*, ed. Eve Kosofsky Sedgwick, 1–37. Durham: Duke University Press, 1997.
Sedgwick, Eve Kosofsky and Adam Frank, "Shame in the Cybernetic Fold." In *Shame and Its Sisters*, edited by Eve Kosofsky Sedgwick and Adam Frank, 1–28. Durham: Duke University Press, 1995.
Sexton, Jared. "The Social Life of Social Death." *In*Tensions *Journal* 5 (2011): 1–47.
Sharpe, Christina. *Monstrous Intimacies: Making Post-Slavery Subjects*. Durham: Duke University Press, 2010.
Shepherd, Jr., George W. "An Editorial: Transition to Democracy in Nigeria." *Africa Today* 33.4 (1986): 3–5.

Shringarpure, Bhakti. *Cold War Assemblages: Decolonization to Digital.* New York: Routledge, 2019.
Sklar, Richard L. "Democracy for the Second Republic," *Issue: A Journal of Opinion* 11.1–2 (1981): 14–16.
Sliwinski, Sharon. *Mandela's Dark Years: A Political Theory of Dreaming.* Minneapolis: University of Minnesota Press, 2016.
Soyinka, Wole. "The Writer in a Modern African State." In *The Writer in Modern Africa*, edited by Per Wästberg, 14–36. New York: Scandinavian Institute of African Studies and Africana Publishing Corp., 1969.
Stein, Pippa and Ruth Jacobson. "Sophiatown Speaks: Introduction." In *Sophiatown Speaks*, edited by Pippa Stein and Ruth Jacobson, 1–4. Johannesburg: Junction Avenue Press, 1986.
Stratton, Florence. "The Shallow Grave: Archetypes of Female Experience in African Fiction." *Research in African Literatures* 19.2 (1988): 143–69.
"Struggle for South Africa's Soul after Madiba's Death." *Daily Nation.* Published March 9, 2014. Accessed May 25, 2020. https://www.nation.co.ke/lifestyle/lifestyle/Struggle-for-South-Africa-soul-after-Nelson-Madiba-death/1214-2236812-xbn9iez/index.html_.
Suhr-Sytsma, Nathan. "Ibadan Modernism: Poetry and the Literary Present in Mid-century Nigeria." *Journal of Commonwealth Literature* 48.1 (2013): 41–59.
Szczurek, Karina M. Review of *Dying in New York* and *White Wahala*, by Ekow Duker. *Sunday Times Books Live.* Published November 21, 2014. Accessed May 25, 2020, https://www.timeslive.co.za/sunday-times/books/.
Szeman, Imre. "Entrepreneurship as the New Common Sense." *South Atlantic Quarterly* 114.3 (2015): 471–90.
Terreblanche, Sampie. "The New South Africa's Original State Capture." *Africa Is A Country.* Published January 28, 2018. Accessed May 25, 2020. https://africasacountry.com/2018/01/the-new-south-africas-original-state-capture/.
Thornber, Karen Laura. "Breaking Discipline, Integrating Literature: Africa-China Relationships Reconsidered." *Comparative Literature Studies* 53.4 (2016): 694–721.
Tlali, Miriam. *Between Two Worlds.* Toronto: Broadview Press, 2004.
———. "Introduction: My Background and How I Began to Write." In *Between Two Worlds*, 7–10. Toronto: Broadview Press, 2004.
Ungar, Sanford J. "Dateline West Africa: Great Expectations." *Foreign Policy* 32 (1978): 184–94.
United Nations Centre Against Apartheid. *World Conference for Action Against Apartheid, Lagos, Nigeria, 22–26 August 1977: Statements-IV.* New York: United Nations, 1977.
"University News." *Princeton Alumni Weekly*, February 10, 1961, 7.
USAID, "South Africa: Economic Growth and Trade." Published June 2012 to September 2017. Accessed September 17, 2020. https://2012-2017.usaid.gov/south-africa/economic-growth-and-trade.

Van der Vlies, Andrew. *Present Imperfect: Contemporary South African Writing*. Oxford: Oxford University Press, 2017.
Vinson, Robert Trent. *The Americans are Coming! Dreams of African American Liberation in Segregationist South Africa*. Athens: Ohio University Press, 2012.
Waas, Tom, Jean Hugé, Aviel Verbruggen, and Tarah Wright. "Sustainable Development: A Bird's Eye View." *Sustainability* 3 (2011): 1637–61.
Wali, Obiajunwa. "The Dead End of African Literature?" *Transition* 10 (1963): 13–15.
Walkowitz, Rebecca L. *Born Translated: The Contemporary Novel in an Age of World Literature*. New York: Columbia University Press, 2017.
Wang, Jackie. *Carceral Capitalism*. South Pasadena, CA: Semiotext(e), 2018.
Wenzel, Jennifer. *Bulletproof: Afterlives of Anticolonial Prophecy in South Africa and Beyond*. Chicago: Chicago University Press, 2009.
———. "Petro-magic-realism: Toward a Political Ecology of Nigerian Literature." *Postcolonial Studies* 9.4 (2006): 449–64.
White, Hylton. "A Post-Fordist Ethnicity: Insecurity, Authority, and Identity in South Africa." *Anthropological Quarterly* 85.2 (2012): 397–427.
Wilder, Gary. *Freedom Time: Negritude, Decolonization, and the Future of the World*. Durham: Duke UP, 2015.
Williams, Raymond. *Marxism and Literature*. Oxford: Oxford University Press, 1977.
Winthrop, John. "A Modell of Christian Charity." Hanover Historical Texts Collection. Scanned by Monica Banas, August 1996. Accessed June 3, 2020. https://history.hanover.edu/texts/winthmod.html.
Woods, Ngaire. "The United States and International Financial Institutions: Power and Influence Within the World Bank and the IMF." In *US Hegemony and International Organizations: The United States and Multilateral Institutions*, eds. Rosemary Foot et. al., 92–114. Oxford: Oxford University Press, 2003.
Yao, Xine. *Disaffected: The Cultural Politics of Unfeeling in Nineteenth-Century America*. Durham: Duke University Press, 2021.
Yoon, Duncan M. "Africa, China, and the Global South Novel: In Koli Jean Bofane's *Congo Inc*." *Comparative Literature* 72.3 (2020): 316–39.

Index

Abani, Chris, 59; see also *GraceLand* (Abani)
Achebe, Chinua
  on Anglophone African literature, 32
  Azikiwe, 27
  Black solidarity and the American dream, 27, 30, 40
  Clark-Bekederemo's caution to, 34, 35, 37
  defense of English as an African language, 32
  disillusionment with the postcolonial nation, 1
  Home and Exile, 25
  meeting with James Baldwin, 58
  on Nigerian exceptionalism, 4
  Nigerian national becoming through US universities, 25–7, 28–9, 45
  postcolonial optimism, 26–7, 40–1
  on a restorative Nigerian literary culture, 25
  time in US universities, 25, 28, 31–2, 34
Adams, James Truslow, 29
Adéèkó, Adélékè, 61–2, 65, 72
Adejunmobi, Moradewun, 41
Adichie, Chimamanda Ngozi
  as a global professional writer, 10, 79
  Purple Hibiscus, 61
  uncertain futurity, 13
  writing workshops, 9, 80
  see also *Americanah* (Adichie)
affect theory
  affective power of nationalisms, 3
  antisocial turn in, 142
  the assumed universality of the subject, 12
  Black studies and, 12
  credit and debt as affective mechanisms, 14
  cruel optimism and, 13
  literature of postcolonial optimism and, 5, 11
  postcolonial studies and, 12
Aggrey, James, 30
Ahmed, Sara, 11, 142
American dream
  "The American Dream and the American Negro" (Baldwin), 96
  Black solidarity and, 27, 30, 40
  Black sovereignty and, 29–30
  credit and, 101
  globalization of, 3, 27, 29
  as illusory in *Americanah* (Adichie), 73–4, 75
Americanah (Adichie)
  affective workings of nation and empire, 63, 73
  critical reception, 62–3, 79
  the fiction of the American dream, 73–4, 75
  foreign capital investment, 17, 78
  national democracy in, 74–5

Nigerian national belonging, 17, 76–7
performative optimism, 63, 73
the post-global world, 78–80
postoptimistic optimism, 17, 63
precarity of Nigerian nationhood, 17, 63, 73, 77–9
psychic costs of performative optimism, 75
white nationalism and anti-Blackness of America, 75
Anglophone African literary studies
British empire and, 10
the nation as a framework for, 2
postcolonial Cold War studies, 6, 33–4
as post-global, 2
production and reception of, 26
role of English language, 32–3
transnationalism, 5
Appiah, Kwame Anthony, 1, 12, 44, 53
Apter, Andrew, 4, 66
Armah, Ayi Kwei, 1
Azikiwe, Nnamdi
on the American Declaration of Independence, 29
the American dream and Black sovereignty, 29–30
criticism of written style, 28
foundation of the University of Nigeria, Nsukka, 31
NAACP address, 30, 37
role of the university for decolonization, 30–1
ties to Historically Black Colleges and Universities, 14, 27, 28, 33–4
time in US universities, 28
US universities as alternatives to British colonialism, 28–9, 31, 46

Babangida, Ibrahim, 61, 66
Baldwin, James
"The American Dream and the American Negro," 96
Chinua Achebe and, 31, 58
on the English language, 32–3
Going to Meet the Man in *GraceLand*, 57
influence on Chris Abani, 59
influence on Clark-Bekederemo, 39
Balkan, Stacey, 137
Baradaran, Mehrsa, 93, 124, 134
Barnard, Rita, 83, 88, 105, 109
Baudrillard, Jean, 64
Berlant, Lauren, 13, 44, 49, 53, 54, 55, 67
Between Two Worlds (Tlali)
African Methodist Episcopal (AME) church, 90
Black economic rights within white supremacist nations, 18, 86–7, 97–8
Black property ownership, 88–9, 92, 104, 113–14
credit apartheid, 87–8
cycles of hope and disillusionment, 18, 87, 92–4, 95, 100
disillusionment following the US civil rights movement, 86, 93
gendered and classed inequalities of apartheid, 99
hope and despair of Sophiatown, 17–18, 86, 89, 90–1, 94, 99–100
inspiration of Black American mobility and prosperity, 17, 86, 89–90
Kennedy's "Day of Affirmation Address," 86, 94–6
parallel histories of Black struggle in South Africa and the US, 17, 86, 89–90, 92, 95–6
persistent optimism of property and credit, 100–1, 102
publication of, 86, 90, 98
time and Black economic liberation, 97–100, 103, 104–5

Between Two Worlds (*cont.*)
  the US as a site for pan-African solidarity, 86, 87, 89–90, 94
  writing of, 17, 86
Black feminism, 9
Bloch, Ernest, 12
Bofane, Koli Jean, 10
Bramen, Carrie Tirado, 65
Brennan, Timothy, 5, 116
Bulawayo, NoViolet, *Glory*, 143–6

Carmichael, Stokely, 43
Carroll, Vinnette, 39
Carter, Jimmy, 44, 50, 51, 63
Césaire, Aimé, 37–8
Cheah, Pheng, 5, 41, 42, 48, 54
Clark-Bekederemo, J. P.
  America, Their America, 16, 27, 34–5, 40
  on American aid as exploitation, 38–9
  cautionary admonishment to Achebe, 34, 35, 37
  cautious optimism, 13, 39, 40–1
  critiques of Princeton, 36, 39
  literature of postcolonial disillusionment, 35
  optimism regarding US universities, 35–6
  solidarity with African-American artists, 10, 16, 27, 39–40, 45
  as the "Tennessee Williams of the Tropics," 33
  time in US universities, 27, 34–5
  US universities as drivers of imperial oppression, 35, 37–9
Clinton, Bill, 75, 76, 77, 113, 124
Cold War agendas
  postcolonial literary studies and, 6, 33–4
  of US universities, 26, 27, 36–7
Cornwell, Gareth, 111
credit
  as an affective mechanism, 14
  the American dream and, 101
  American racialized, gendered and classed access to, 101–2, 124
  credit apartheid, 87–8, 114
  cycles of hope and disillusionment, 134–5, 136
  democratization of, 84, 101–2, 106, 113–14, 121, 123–4, 126, 128
  equitable access to, postapartheid, 85
  inequalities in America, 93
  moral-economic credit relationships, 18, 112–15
  the neoliberal project and, 9, 14
  the ongoing servicing of debt, 114–15
  persistent optimism of property and credit, 100–1, 102
  racialized inequalities of, 123–4
  satirization of credit apartheid, 19, 125–6, 128–31, 137–8
  South African lending sectors, 128–9
cruel optimism
  affect and, 13
  definition, 13
  the impasse of postcolonial optimism, 45, 52–8
  in *The Joys of Motherhood*, 16, 44, 49, 53–4
  in literature of postcolonial optimism, 13–14
  Nigerian nationhood and cruel optimism, 45–52

Dirlik, Arif, 5
dreams
  affective power of dreams, 141
  cruel optimism of dreams of Nigerian nationhood, 16, 44, 49, 53–4
  dream-like aesthetic of *The Heart of Redness* (Mda), 18, 119–20
  as impasse and despair, 17, 62, 65–8

indebtedness and national dreams, 19, 134–6
literary dream-work and postcolonial optimism, 141–3
of Nigerian national becoming, 26–7, 28–9, 45, 50, 85
of pan-African postcolonial nationhood, 27, 29
see also American dream
DuBois, W. E. B., 29, 39
Duker, Ekow, 21, 127; see also White Wahala (Duker)

Egbunike, Louisa Uchum, 65
Elze, Jens, 137
Emecheta, Buchi
literary tour of the US, 58–9
personal challenges accessing education, 49–50
see also Joys of Motherhood, The (Emecheta)

Fan, Christopher T., 78
Fanon, Frantz, 1
Ferguson, James, 2–3, 74, 75

Garfield, James A., 30
Garvey, Marcus, 29, 30, 36, 39
gender
American racialized, gendered and classed access to credit, 101–2, 124
gendered inequalities of postcolonial Nigeria, 16, 44–5, 46–7, 48–9
Man-Africanism, 47
Getachew, Adom, 8
Ghana, 2
Goodman, Robin, 47
Goyal, Yogita, 57, 79–80
GraceLand (Abani)
the impasse of postcolonial optimism, 45, 56–8
national dreams in, 56
postoptimistic literary pan-Africanism, 58–9, 61

publication of, 59
the Third Republic and, 56, 61
Green-Simms, Lindsey, 140
Griswold, Wendy, 50
Gui, Weihsin, 5
Gunew, Sneja, 12

Habila, Helon, 61
Hardt, Michael, 6
Harney, Stefano, 9, 16, 39–40
Heart of Redness, The (Mda)
credit apartheid, 114
cycles of euphoria and despair, 18, 106, 111–12, 123, 131
democratization of credit, 106, 114, 115, 123
disillusionment with ideals of South African exceptionalism, 106–7, 111–12, 113, 116–17, 123, 131
dream-like aesthetic, 18, 119–20
heterotemporality of, 108, 110–11, 115, 118
idealizations of the US, 106, 109–10
the local and global, 107–11
magic realism, 117–18, 137
markets of US empire, 106, 110, 111
moral-economic credit relationships, 18, 112–15
nation-building under empire, 109, 110, 117–19
the ongoing servicing of debt, 18, 106, 114–15
postcolonial optimism, 106, 110, 111, 123
redemptive work ethic, 18, 106, 112, 131
role of the nation, 116–17
salvific Protestantism, 113
time for Black leisure and creativity, 104–5, 117
visions of the future, 18, 106, 107–8

Huggan, Graham, 26
Hughes, Langston, 16, 27, 31, 32, 39, 83

Ikejani, Okechukwu, 29

Jaji, Tsitsi, 8, 89
James, Deborah, 14, 84, 85, 87, 88, 93, 114, 123, 125, 128, 130
Jameson, Fredric, 118
Joys of Motherhood, The (Emecheta)
  British colonialism as superseded by US neocolonialism, 44, 47, 49
  cruel optimism of Nigerian dreams, 16, 44, 49, 53–4
  gendered inequalities of postcolonial Nigeria, 16, 44–5, 46–7, 48–9
  the impasse of postcolonial optimism, 45, 52–6
  Nigerian dream of full national sovereignty, 45
  optimistic orientation to the US, 45–6, 47–9, 52
  as a postcolonial literature of disillusionment, 16, 46–7, 49, 54
  postoptimism of, 54–5, 58–9
  the Second Republic and, 44, 49–50
  trope of the water goddess Mami Wata, 55–6
  US education and postcolonial nationhood, 44, 46, 52
Julien, Eileen, 26

Kabir, Ananya Jahanar, 11
Kalliney, Peter, 33
Kennedy, John F., 37, 94, 95
Kennedy, Robert F., 18, 86, 94–6
Khanna, Neetu, 12
King Jr., Martin Luther, 30, 40, 93, 133–4

Kissinger, Henry, 41
Konings, Martjin, 13, 14, 101, 113, 114–15, 123–4, 128, 130
Kosofsky Sedgwick, Eve, 11
Krishnan, Madhu, 26, 55

Lazarus, Neil, 6
Liberia, 29–30, 36
Lincoln, Abraham, 132–3
literature of postcolonial optimism
  affect studies and, 5, 11
  ambivalent feeling in, 141–2
  contradictions, 11–12
  cruel optimism and, 13–14
  within the global literary marketplace, 19–20
  Glory (Bulawayo), 143–6
  literary dream-work, 141–3
  national optimism under US empire, 4, 8
  Nigerian literature within, 14, 19–21
  persistence of, 14, 40, 44, 47
  postcolonial futures, 3
  the postcolonial nation and, 3
  South African literature within, 14–15, 19–21
  US empire expansion, 3
  US imperialism and, 10
Livsey, Tim, 30–1

Macharia, Keguro, 1–2
Makhulu, Anne-Maria, 84, 124–5, 129
Malcom X, 40
Mamdani, Mahmoud, 4
Mandela, Nelson, 37–8, 93, 103, 119
Marriott, David, 119
Masekela, Hugh, 9, 99–100
Matory, J. Lorand, 69, 70
Mattera, Don, 89
Mbeki, Thabo, 83, 84
Mbembe, Achille, 124, 125

Mda, Zakes
  Black Diamond, 120–1
  magic realism, 21, 118
  Ways of Dying, 103–4
  The Whale Caller, 105–6
  see also Heart of Redness, The (Mda)
Meredith, James, 40
Michaels, Walter Benn, 124
Mohammed, Murtala, 51
Molefe, T. O., 128
Morrison, Toni, 9, 139
Moten, Fred, 9, 16, 39–40, 141–2
Mphahlele, Es'kia, 89
Myambo, Relebone Rirhandzu, 127

Nadiminti, Kalyan, 26, 36, 79
nation, the
  in Anglophone African literary studies, 2
  individual aspirations over, 2–3
  pan-Africanism and, 4–5
  postcolonial discourse of disillusionment and, 1–2
  US empire and, 4–5, 6
Ndebele, Njabulo S., 98, 99, 105, 116–17
Negri, Antonio, 6
Ngai, Sianne, 12, 142, 143
Ngugi, Mukoma wa, 32
Ngũgĩ wa Thiong'o, 38–9
Nigeria
  national democracy, 74–5, 76
  national optimism under US empire, 4, 8
  Nigerian national becoming and US universities, 26–7, 28–9, 45, 50
  Nigerian nationhood and cruel optimism, 45–52
  oil exports to the US, 50, 63
  pan-African postcolonial nationhood, 3, 4, 27, 29
  renewed optimism over US investment in, 51–2
  resilience of postcolonial optimism under US empire, 61–2
  Second World Black and African Festival of Arts and Culture (FESTAC '77), 50
  structural adjustment of the 1990s, 61, 66, 69
  University College, Ibadan, 31
  University of Nigeria, Nsukka, 31
  US influence on Nigerian education, 3, 7–8, 9
  US investment in during the Carter administration, 51–2
  US investment in during the Kennedy administration, 37
  US-Nigeria relations, 3, 16, 43, 44, 50–1, 63
Nigerian literature
  Farafina Trust Creative Writing Workshop, 80
  historical fiction, 20
  turn to the US in the 1990s, 61–2
Nkosi, Lewis, 91
Nwosu, Maik, 31
Nyabola, Nanjala, 47

Obama, Barack, 7, 19, 74, 75, 132, 133–4
Obasanjo, Olusegun, 51, 74
Obiechina, E. N., 1
Oguine, Ike, 68; see also *Squatter's Tale, A* (Oguine)
Ogunbadejo, Oye, 50
Okonkwo, Christopher N., 63
Olaniyan, Tejumola, 2, 3, 76
o'Matigere, Nduko, 47
Omelsky, Matthew, 57
Orizu, Nwafor, 28
Osei-Nyame, Kwadwo, 65
Osinubi, Taiwo Adetunji, 33
Ouologuem, Yambo, 53

Palmer, Tyrone S., 12
pan-Africanism
  and African-American artists, 9, 16, 27, 39–40, 45
  the American dream and Black sovereignty, 29–30
  anticolonial Black solidarity, 12, 13
  literary and cultural connections, 9–10
  Nigerian postcolonial nationhood and, 3, 4, 27, 29
  postcolonial optimism and, 4–5, 8, 16, 27, 39–40, 140–1
  postoptimistic literary pan-Africanism, 45, 52–60, 61
  resistance to US hegemony, 27
  role of English language, 32–3
  role of US universities, 9, 27
  term, 8
  transnational visions, 8
  US universities and, 9, 27
Pan-Africanism
  term, 8
  politics of, 28–9
Parker, Jason C., 28, 36
Pease, Donald, 110
Phiri, Aretha, 71
Pickens, Therí Alyce, 72
Popescu, Monica, 6, 33–4
postcolonial disillusionment
  in *America, Their America*, 35
  credit's cycles of hope and disillusionment in *White Wahala* (Duker), 131–2, 134–5, 136
  cycles of hope and disillusionment in *Between Two Worlds* (Tlali), 18, 87, 92–4, 95, 100
  disillusionment following the US civil rights movement, 86, 93
  in Nigeria's second republic, 43
  progressive disillusionment narratives, 1–2, 35

postcolonial happiness, definition, 11
postcolonial nationhood
  challenges of self-actualization, 41–2, 61
  China's investment in Africa, 10
  MFA/MBA programs and Nigerian nationhood, 7, 17, 62, 65, 68–9, 70, 72–3, 79
  Nigerian nationhood and cruel optimism, 45–52
  nonprogressive temporalizations, 2–3
  postcolonial optimism and, 21
  progressive disillusionment narrative, 1–2, 35
postcolonial optimism
  affective power of dreams, 141
  alongside disillusionment, 104
  and the dream of decolonized nationhood, 41–2
  the impasse of postcolonial optimism, 45, 52–8
  in Nigeria and South Africa literature, 140
  within pan-African exchange, 4–5, 8, 16, 27, 39–40, 140–1
  as postoptimism, 44, 53
  see also literature of postcolonial optimism
postoptimism
  of *Joys of Motherhood, The* (Emecheta), 54–5, 58–9
  postcolonial optimism as, 44, 53
  postoptimistic literary pan-Africanism, 45, 52–60, 61
  term, 12, 14
postoptimistic optimism
  concept, 14
  in *A Squatter's Tale* (Oguine), 17, 62, 65, 67, 70–2

Quayson, Ato, 2
queer African film, 140

Ramaphosa, Cyril, 83
Robolin, Stéphane, 9, 48, 53, 54, 95
Rose, Jacqueline, 111

Saint, Lily, 79
Scott, David, 21
Sexton, Jared, 58
Sexwale, Tokyo, 121–2
Sharpe, Christina, 70
Sliwinski, Sharon, 119
South Africa
  ANC's economic policies, 83, 84, 113
  The Apprentice South Africa, 121–2
  Black elites, 120–1
  Black workers' rights, 98
  Carter policy, 50
  credit and the neoliberal project, 9, 14
  democratic elections, 103
  democratization of credit, 113–14, 121, 123
  entrepreneurship, 121–2
  as the exceptionalist postcolonial state, 1, 4
  financialization, 84, 85
  hopes for redistribution and justice, 84–5, 125
  housing market contraction, 18–19
  Kennedy's "Day of Affirmation Address," 86, 94–6
  labor insecurities, 124–5
  leisure time, 98–9, 105–6
  National Credit Act, 19, 125, 127–8
  national optimism under US empire, 4, 8
  national trajectory from elation to disillusionment, 83–4, 86
  New Year's traditions, 103–4
  the new/rainbow nation, 3, 103, 105
  redistributive neoliberalism, 84
  repression of anti-apartheid movements, 93
  state welfare policies, 84
  US influence on economic policy, 3, 4, 7–8
  US-led neoliberal economics, 83–4
  US-South Africa relations, 3
South African literature
  boom-and-bust cycles of capitalism, 85–6
  episodic narratives, 20–1
  gendered and classed inequalities of access to, 99
  national becoming shaped by US empire, 104
  optimism to disillusionment trajectories, 83, 86
  periodization, 83
  postcolonial optimism, 136
Soyinka, Wole, 1
Squatter's Tale, A (Oguine)
  affective workings of nation and empire, 63
  critical reception, 62, 63
  dreams as impasse and despair, 17, 62, 65–8
  the entrepreneurial subject, 66–8
  the Nigerian turn to the US in the 1990s, 62
  performative optimism of "America," 17, 62, 63–5
  postoptimistic optimism, 17, 62, 65, 67, 70–2
  precarity of immigrant life, 65, 71
  psychic costs of performative optimism, 71, 72
  structural adjustment of the 1990s, 66, 69
  US consumer culture, 63–4, 68
  US universities and Nigerian nationhood, 17, 62, 65, 68–9, 73

Szczurek, Karina M., 127
Szeman, Imre, 67, 80

Terreblanche, Sampie, 83
Tlali, Miriam
  first nationally published Black South African woman, 86, 98
  interlinked, realist scenes, 20
  retrospective hopefulness, 13
  see also Between Two Worlds (Tlali)
Tshibumba Kanda Matulu, 142

United States of America (USA)
  African American economic mobilities, 90
  African-American artists and Black solidarity, 9–10, 16, 27, 39–40, 45
  "America" as the "last, best hope" for freedom, 19, 126, 132–4
  democratization of credit, 101–2, 123–4
  disillusionment following the US civil rights movement, 86, 93
  dreams of national redemption, 125
  financial crisis, 125, 127, 134
  investment in Nigeria duirng the Kennedy administration, 37
  investment in Nigeria during the Carter administration, 51–2
  labor insecurities, 125
  1964 Civil Rights Act, 86, 93
  racialized, gendered and classed access to credit, 101–2, 124
  reliance on Nigerian oil, 50, 63
  revolving debt, 128
  US-Nigeria relations, 16, 43, 44, 50–1, 63
  US-South Africa relations, 3
  see also American dream

US empire
  Africa's dilemma over American investment in Africa, 37–8
  capitalist imperialism, 6–7
  Cold War agendas, 6
  educational aid to Nigeria, 7–8
  in *Glory* (Bulawayo), 144–5, 146
  neoliberal ideologies in South Africa, 7–8
  the postcolonial nation and, 4–5, 6
  postcolonial optimism and, 13, 104
  postcolonial optimism under, 3, 4
  within the US, 43
  US-led neoliberal economics in South Africa, 83–4

US universities
  Anglophone literature circulation, 45
  as anticolonial alternatives to British institutions, 28–9, 31, 46
  Azikiwe's connections with HBCUs, 14, 27, 28, 33–4
  Cold War agendas, 26, 27, 36–7
  critiques of by postcolonial writers, 26
  as drivers of US imperialism, 35, 37–9
  internationalization of, 36–7
  as the means to challenge US empire, 9, 14, 16, 40–1, 45
  MFA/MBA programs and Nigerian nationhood, 7, 17, 62, 65, 68–9, 70, 72–3, 79
  Nigerian democratic belonging and, 7, 9, 14
  Nigerian national becoming and, 26–7, 28–9, 45, 50, 85
  pan-African exchange and, 9, 27
  and the production of Nigerian literature, 20

Van der Vlies, Andrew, 12, 100
Vinson, Robert Trent, 90

Wali, Obiajunwa, 33
Wang, Jackie, 124
Washington, Booker T., 90
Wenzel, Jennifer, 1, 108–9, 111
White, Hylton, 84
White Wahala (Duker)
   credit's cycles of hope and disillusionment, 131–2, 134–5, 136
   critical reception, 127
   democratization of credit, 126, 128
   exhaustion within a financialized economy, 19, 126, 136–7
   indebtedness and national dreams, 19, 134–6
   "Last Best Hope Financial Service" kiosk, 19, 126, 131–5
   networks of indebtedness, 129–30
   as picaresque fiction, 18, 125, 137
   the in-principle agreement, 137–9
   publication of, 127
   satirization of credit apartheid, 19, 125–6, 128–31, 137–8
   South Africa under conditions of US empire, 125, 126
Wilder, Gary, 34
Winthrop, John, 110

Xuma, Alfred B., 90

Yao, Xine, 142
Yoon, Duncan M., 10
Young, Andrew, 16, 50–1

Zuma, Jacob, 84, 85

EU representative:
Easy Access System Europe
Mustamäe tee 50, 10621 Tallinn, Estonia
Gpsr.requests@easproject.com

www.ingramcontent.com/pod-product-compliance
Lightning Source LLC
Chambersburg PA
CBHW051125160426
43195CB00014B/2351